Boston's
South End

Also by Russ López

Urban Health: Readings in the Built, Social and Physical Environment. (With Patricia Hynes)

The Built Environment and Public Health.

Building American Public Health: Urban Planning, Architecture, and the Quest for Public Health

Boston 1945 – 2015: The Decline and Rise of a Great World City

The Hub of the Gay Universe: An LGBTQ History of Boston, Provincetown, and Beyond.

BOSTON'S SOUTH END

THE CLASH OF IDEAS IN A HISTORIC NEIGHBORHOOD

Russ López

Shawmut Peninsula Press
Boston, Massachusetts

© 2015, 2024 Russ Lopez

First edition, 2015
Second edition, 2024

ISBN 978-0-578-41088-3

Library of Congress Control Number 2016901124

Photo Credits

Unless noted othewise, photography by Russ Lóez

Photographs on pages 3, 28, 31, 36, 53, 56, 70, 75, 109, 141, 187, coutesy of the Library of Congress

Photographs on pages 46, 65, 94, 135, 141 couttesy of the South End Historical Society

Photograph on page 177 courtesy of the Boston Redevelopment Authority

Photograph on page 236 by Nancy Pullen

To the greatest generation of South End activists, those who fought for their vision of the neighborhood in the years between 1960 and 1990.

With a special appreciation for Mel King, 1928-2023.

Table of Contents

Preface to the Second Edition

The South End has continued to change in the ten years since the first edition was written, though in many parts of the neighborhood, this is not apparent. While trees may have matured, a few street amenities have been added or fallen into disrepair, and businesses have closed or opened, outwardly at least, the solid brick facades of the rowhouses look the same. But three major changes have come to the community.

Most important has been the relentless increase in housing prices making the South End one of the most expensive places to live in the United States. With prices blowing past a thousand dollars per square foot, most people cannot afford to buy in the neighborhood. Fortunately, the South End's large stock of assisted housing remains in place. But middle-class people and many families with significant incomes have been priced out. Consequently, the South End has lost a lot of its lovable quirkiness.

A second change has been the loss of the great generation of activists, those who fought for justice and equality in the 1960s and 70s. The many people who made the South End a beacon of enlightenment and a hotbed of social change during urban renewal and the decade afterwards are in their eighties and nineties. Some had passed on. Others have retired out of the neighborhood as stairs and declining health have made South End living difficult. While there are still many people devoted to progressive issues and promoting social change, the golden age of South End activism is in the past.

The third change has been the construction of thousands of housing units in the southern half of the neighborhood. Much of the land to the south of Shawmut Avenue had been cleared for urban renewal or abandoned by industry. These vacant lots have been replaced by stylish condo and rental buildings adding thousands of new residents. These new complexes include two luxuries undreamed of in the older rowhouse blocks: underground parking spaces and elevators. Despite some fears before they were built, the new residents have nicely integrated into the spirit of the community.

The South End continues to thrive and is a great place to live, work, and visit. It has never been perfect and its flaws, particularly its overwhelming affordability problem, lack of open space, and problematic traffic, are as irksome as ever. Yet it is still one of the best communities around and people still love to live here.

Introduction

My **first foray** into the South End ce ntered around a Saturday night party. I was an innocent from California, newly arrived to study at Harvard with Boston a big unknown. Wide-eyed as my cab drove up Tremont Street, I was terrified by the many blocks of burned out rowhouses and abandoned tenements. At the time, I had no knowledge of the economic forces and policy decisions that had caused this Hollywood movie landscape of destruction. Arriving at the party at a lone occupied row house in a sea of abandonment, I was impressed by the chic apartment occupied by beautiful people of all races. In my brief time in Boston, no place had been so racially integrated.

A few weeks later, I came across a report on the Latino population of Massachusetts prepared by the Hispanic Office of Planning and Evaluation, Inc. (HOPE), headquartered on Tremont Street at Villa Victoria. As I had been awarded a fellowship that required I volunteer ten hours a week for a non-profit organization, I offered my services to HOPE, beginning my life-long association with the South End. I was hired full time after graduating and then moved to the neighborhood four years later. I live there still.

This is not a book of colorful anecdotes and eccentric characters. There are others who have much better skills at capturing the special personalities of the community. Instead, this book relies on public records, newspaper articles, older books, published reports, and the personal papers of past and current residents to document the neighborhood's economic, physical, and social history. These forces shaped the landscape that has supported the people of the South End and enabled them to become the interesting, creative folks that we find so entertaining.

Today, there is an abundant vibrancy and prosperity that was impossible to predict on the night of my first visit, but there are other aspects of the neighborhood that have been constant. There is still a diversity of races and ethnic groups that is all too rare in this world, and the rowhouses, now renovated several times over, are as beautiful as ever. A South End party or restaurant is as chic as it always has been, and the way people dress, even while standing in line for an hour to vote, makes the wealthy and the poor, the young and the old, express a sophistication that most other places lack. Despite its many changes, I still love the South End. This book is a thank you to all the people who contributed to making this a great neighborhood, special in its diversity and streetscapes.

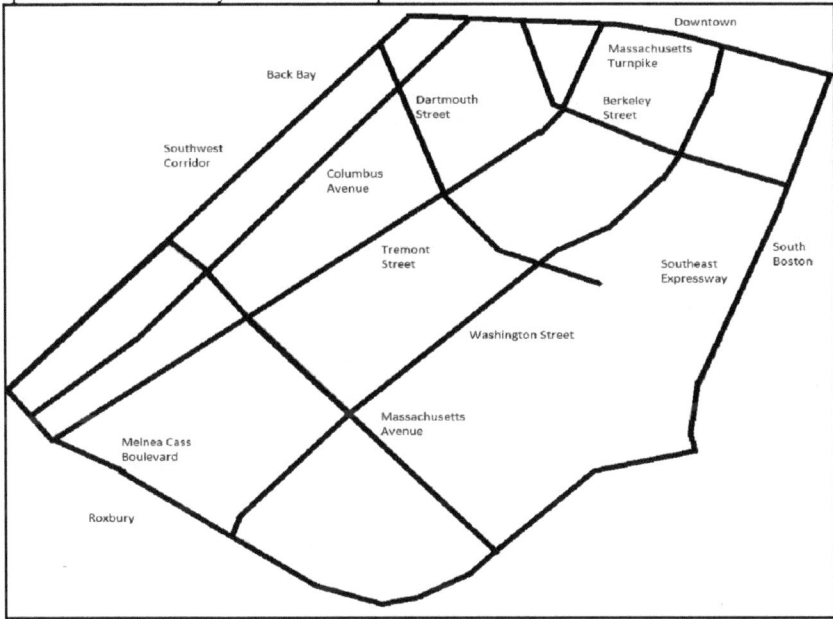

THE SOUTH END

This book seeks to increase our understanding of the South End. Much of its history is unknown or misunderstood, even by its residents. There is a standard historical narrative about the South End, repeated in guidebooks, retold by neighbors to newcomers, related in background information in newspaper stories, and sometimes even recited by scholars and officials.

The usual story describes a neighborhood built on filled land in the years before the Civil War. It was originally a fashionable part of Boston, but Back Bay's emergence and the Financial Panic of 1873 caused a flight of the wealthy out of the South End. For nearly one hundred years, it was a slum, a dirty community of bars and rooming houses unsafe at night. Then, beginning in the 1960s and accelerating in the decades following, new residents—an urban gentry—bought up the abandoned row houses, restored them into single-family homes and condominiums, and saved the neighborhood by creating a new community that is white, wealthy, and trendy.

Each part of this narrative contains some truth, and a superficial review of the South End would support this broad outline. This quick summary, however, masks a much more nuanced history. In the thousands of years between the retreat of the icesheets and the arrival of Europeans, the neck of land that would become the South End was an important bridge between the mainland and the ocean for the people who lived around what would be called Massachusetts Bay. For the first two hundred years after the arrival of English colonists, the mostly undeveloped South End neck was just beyond the limits of one of the most important towns in North America. The City of Boston and a small number of publicly chartered companies eventually built the South End, beginning with the filling of a few areas along the Boston Neck in the early nineteenth century and ending with the final creation of land at South Bay in the 1960s. But these developments often struggled financially, and it sometimes took a decade or more for a given block to be developed. Despite the grand townhouses on some of the major squares, developers constructed other, more modest row houses designed to serve as tenements and lodging houses that never had their nineteenth-century moment of glory. Furthermore, the South End did not attract more than a handful of Boston's famous Brahmins. Instead, it was mostly a neighborhood of business owners, merchants, shop clerks, bookkeepers, house servants, and laborers that toiled in the factories that lined the southern edge of the neighborhood or worked downtown. While many think the Back Bay supplanted the established South End, the two neighborhoods were actually developed almost simultaneously. Construction began in the South End in 1851 and in the Back Bay in 1855.

It is true that the Financial Crisis of 1873 had a devastating impact on the neighborhood, but one of the causes of that economic crunch was the Great Boston Fire of 1872. Occurring only a few months before what would become a global crash, the fire devastated the finances of many South End residents who lost jobs and businesses in the wake of the conflagration that destroyed more than one thousand buildings in central Boston. But contrary to popular history, the neighborhood was already in decline before the crisis, and at least one source suggests the fall of the real estate market began in the 1860s. In any event, the crash did not create an immediate overwhelming decline in the neighborhood. The downscaling took place over several decades; the decay did not reach the western half of the neighborhood until after 1900.

Most importantly, the one hundred years after the Financial Crisis of 1873 were not dark ages of unremitting poverty and degradation that many think it was. During this period, the South End was a community that welcomed newcomers: young people from rural New England, Syrians, Greeks, Jews, Italians, Germans, and Irish. From the 1890s on, when even Northern-born Blacks shunned them, Southern Blacks found homes here, first along the streets between Columbus Avenue and the railroad tracks and then deeper into the South End from the New York Streets to Lower Roxbury. At the same time, Caribbean Blacks built churches and enjoyed the social programs encouraged by Marcus Garvey and the United Negro Improvement Association. Then beginning in the 1950s, the South End became the city's center for Latino immigrants.

Throughout these decades the people of the South End enjoyed advantages not available elsewhere. The neighborhood was a place where people chose to live, not a slum that housed Boston's undesirables. The neighborhood empowered women at a time when most options were closed to them, fostered Black unions during an era of systemic racism, and promoted freedom and equality for gay men and lesbians long before other places moved toward acceptance. It was a neighborhood with a rich network of medical and social services that demonstrated the willingness of the comfortable to assist those less fortunate. The South End had institutions for children, immigrants, and the destitute. Furthermore, the community was culturally wealthy. For most of its history, it was crowded with theaters, nightclubs, and other forms of popular entertainment.

The standard history also fails to mention that the worst deterioration did not begin until the 1950s, after the city earmarked most of the neighborhood for destruction. City and state agencies condemned thousands of units, many just as rehabable as their uncondemned neighbors, and when owners and tenants fled the disinvestment and chaos caused by renewal and highway construction, planners and city officials justified their actions by citing the population decline they had provoked. Renewal didn't save the neighborhood from devastation; it caused it.

It is true that gentrification transformed the neighborhood, but it did not save it because it never needed saving. In addition, the process of neighborhood change had a tremendous cost, displacing thousands of residents— mostly the poor and the elderly, who were unable to afford the twin pressures of rising property values and government programming. These often-fragile people paid a terrible social, physical, and financial price for this neighborhood change. Furthermore, they were only the first to be pushed out of the South End. Later waves of gentrification made the neighborhood unaffordable for middle-income renters, and then it placed it beyond the reach of more affluent middle-class people. The most recent wave may make it a place for only the wealthiest as its relentless price increases continue. The price of gentrification involves more than just real estate costs.

The South End's story is not just one of change, but one of resilience. It demonstrates the possibilities of what can happen when neighborhood residents work together to resist displacement and build, own, and manage their housing. Today, the South End has thousands of assisted units created by tenant action and the efforts of community organizers and enlightened funders. It is important to remember that though the South End is a place where it takes a minimum-wage worker ten hours to pay for a meal at its most expensive restaurants, it is also a neighborhood with more than five thousand units for low-income households, numerous halfway houses, abundant community gardens, and the state's largest provider of medical care for the poor.

While gentrification displaced thousands, the people who moved into this community were hardly all rich, uncaring souls. On the contrary, many of the newcomers to the South End after 1960 brought their energy and talents to the neighborhood and worked in diverse partnerships to make it a beautiful place to live. Without the passion of new residents volunteering their energy for groups such as the South End Committee on Transportation, South End/ Lower Roxbury Land Trust, Four Corners Development, and the South End Historical Society, the neighborhood would not be as nice as it is today.

Lurking just below the surface of the South End is an intriguing story of how ideas shape urban form. The neighborhood's initial design came from English ideals regarding genteel middle class urban living. But when tastes changed, the South End lost out first to other core neighborhoods and then to the suburbs. The belief that the community was an urban wilderness shaped how many perceived the South End, and its residents, for most of the twentieth century from the settlement house workers laboring to save immigrants around 1900 to the "urban pioneers" gentrifying its housing in the 1970s and 80s. Midcentury urban renewal was based on the idea that urban neighborhood

s like the South End were unhealthy: these ideas almost resulted in the bulldozing of the entire community. But it was saved by new theories regarding the desirability of density and walkable streets. Now codified into a planning movement called New Urbanism, these ideas have shaped new development in the neighborhood since the 1900s.

Buildings, streets, and parks are mute, but their construction, perseverance, and demolition tell us much about the people who built, occupied, and destroyed them. In that sense, the row houses, squares, and modern housing complexes of the South End have much to say to us, if only we take the time to listen to their stories and understand their pasts. Their important history tells us how our counterparts lived decades and centuries ago and enables us to comprehend how the neighborhood contributes to our own way of living today. The stories locked in the bricks and mortar of the South End contain more than enough information to fill a host of books. Along with the great volume of papers, reports, correspondence, and other materials donated by hundreds of residents, here is some of what the neighborhood's built environment has to say.

CHAPTER 1

Before It Was the South End: 10,000 BC – 1850 AD

The South End's story begins at the end of the Ice Age as the glaciers that created its flat features began to melt. Glaciation's final advance began about twelve thousand years ago, when at least three pulses of ice moved through the area. The spine of the central South End along Washington Street is referred to as "the Neck." This stretch is a section of the Back Bay Moraine, a long, low ridge of dirt and debris that goes all the way to Fresh Pond in Cambridge. It was formed by ice that moved in from the northeast.

After the glaciers melted, extensive peat bogs formed in what would eventually become the Back Bay. When sea levels rose and inundated the area, clay covered these bogs.[1] For a brief time, crustal rebound (rising land caused by the removal of the great weight of the ice sheet) outpaced sea-level rise (a result of the melting glaciers), and the area was dry. Then, about 8,500 years ago, the area flooded again. This was followed by another land rise, creating dry terrain, with another high-water period around 4000 BC that submerged the Neck again. Since the Neck reappeared above the tides around 2000 BC, sea level has been fairly constant, remaining at a level near where it is today. However, this recent stasis is threatened by global warming. The repeated submergence of the area resulted in the buildup of hydrogen sulfide (the gas that gives rotten eggs their odor) in the soil. When the city drained the marshes on either side of the Neck in the nineteenth century, it released this gas into the air, much to the distress of South End residents.[2]

The Boston Basin was a major outlet for glacial outwash which deposited enormous amounts of sediments that range in size from fine clay to coarse sand and gravel.[3] The thickness of these sediments also varies. A boring at Brookline and Washington Streets found bedrock eighty-three feet below the surface; one at Tremont and Northampton Streets reached bedrock at 170 feet.[4] The modern South End is mostly unconsolidated sediment covered by fill of varying quality that is saturated and highly unstable. These poor soil conditions set the stage for issues that will recur many times over the South

End's history because loose, waterlogged soils require piles for buildings. With salt marshes at sea level, filling in the areas adjacent to the Neck was easy, but subsurface conditions were difficult to address, and drainage was costly.

The result of these sea level fluctuations was a small, hilly peninsula of about eight hundred acres, now downtown Boston, connected to the mainland by the Neck.[5] There were two large embayments on either side that would be eventually filled in, much of which became the South End. Along some stretches, the Neck was barely a half block wide, and it was hardly dry land. It would often flood during exceptionally high tides while the water-covered tidal flats were exposed during astronomical low tides.[6]

A tundra-like environment enveloped Eastern Massachusetts until well after 10,000 BC, though there may have been isolated woodland areas. Reconstruction of the paleo-environment suggests the region was not hospitable for human occupation until 6000 BC, when the area developed a pine-deciduous forest. Up to that point, the coastal environment was harsh, with oysters the only easily available food source. However, interior valleys and uplands were already attracting large scale human occupation.

The first signs of human activity near the South End are a series of wooden stakes and fish traps along the Charles River between Berkeley and Clarendon Streets, the Boylston Fishweir, that date between 2900 and 2500 BC.[6] From 2000 to 1000 BC, climate and sea level changes promoted the establishment of large expanses of marshes that were highly supportive of food sources. By 1000 AD, the numbers and prosperity of coastal habitants greatly increased. At the same time, the changing climate caused inland productivity to decline, and the population shifted to the coast.[7]

The South End had such little dry land that it could not have supported major settlements, but it was part of a large regional economy and the route between the mainland and the harbor, providing access to nearby marshes and islands. It was an important contributor to the region, as the people in the area created a highly modified environment that allowed for the sustainable exploitation of the vast amounts of foodstuffs available in the fields, woodlands, and marshes surrounding the Neck.[8] Residents carefully shaped the New England environment by burning forests to increase open space for agriculture and creating trails to link villages and important sites.[9] Local groups were nomadic but territorial, moving their settlements along rivers and the coastal plain and planting corn, beans, and other crops with sophisticated adaptations to local conditions.[10]

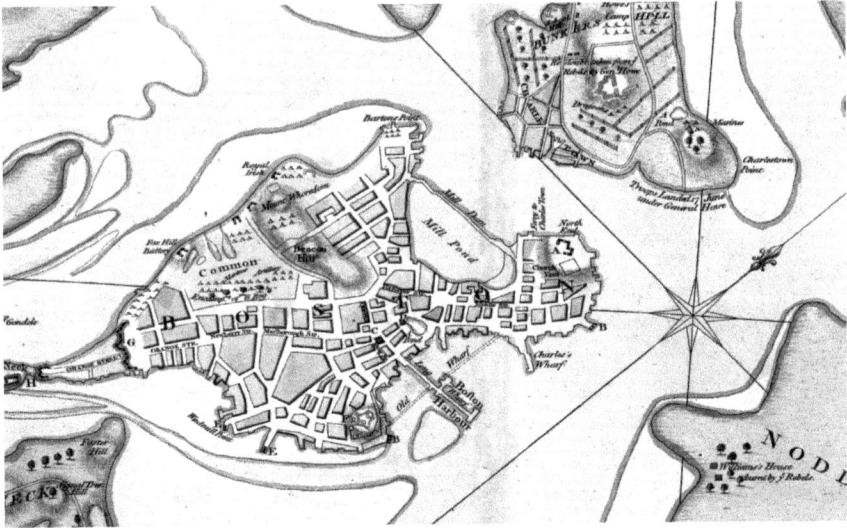

1.1 BOSTON'S ORIGINAL SHORLINE

For the several thousand years before the epidemic of 1618, there was a prosperous group of people living around the South End, which was part of a regional population of 70,000 to 144,000. Stretching from southeastern New Hampshire to eastern Connecticut and central Massachusetts, these interrelated tribes spoke a variety of Eastern Algonquian dialects. These were linguistically similar to those of the natives on Long Island but very distinct from their Iroquois neighbors to the west. Each group, including those in the Boston area, was composed of small villages linked by roads and extensive kinship networks. They dispersed in late fall to hunt and reconvened for the winter. Every few years, settlements relocated because of declining fertility in surrounding fields.[9] It was a stable, prosperous, and dynamic society that collapsed when the English came to dominate the area.

There was extensive contact between Natives and Europeans well before the founding of the Plymouth Colony in 1620 and the Massachusetts Bay Colony in 1623. The organizers of the second colony intended to focus their settlement at Salem, but that location proved inadequate for the large number of settlers arriving from England. In 1629, a group went to modern-day Charlestown and then moved across the harbor to William Blackstone's land on the tip of the Shawmut Peninsula the following year. The colonists quickly spread, and by the next year, there were English settlements at seven points around Boston Harbor. One such settlement, Boston, had a safe anchorage, an adequate water supply, and an easily defensible position; it quickly became the most popular site. Boston began to grow and dominate both the Plymouth and Massachusetts Bay colonies. From these first coastal settlements, Europeans spread across the region.[13]

Epidemics brought by the Europeans caused large scale mortality in the Native population after 1614. When a survey party from Plymouth traveled through the area a few years afterwards, they found it sparsely occupied.[11] Survivors tried accommodation, confrontation, and negotiated alliances but were ultimately overwhelmed by the invaders. Several important incidents facilitated English dominance: a second smallpox epidemic in 1618, another outbreak in 1633, the Pequot War in 1637, and King Philip's War in 1675. Just as devastating were the economic changes that disrupted traditional trade patterns and forced the abandonment of long held agricultural and hunting practices. As Native Americans became more dependent on trading furs for personal goods, growing foodstuffs for Europeans, and working for wages, their traditional way of life collapsed.[9] As Native society declined, so did its numbers; warfare was responsible for about a quarter of the deaths, and disease and the destruction of local economies were responsible for the remainder.[14] On the eve of King Phillip's War, the 1675-78 conflict between Natives and Europeans that resulted in the destruction of several colonial settlements and the obliteration of most of the remaining Native villages in southern New England, the New England Native American population had been reduced to about 18,000.[12]

The destruction caused by disease and the growing English presence drove many surviving Native Americans to convert to Christianity and yield to efforts by the Reverend John Elliot and others to relocate them to the Praying Towns, settlements specifically founded to provide permanent homes for Natives apart from Europeans.[15] After 1650, many of the remaining Natives in the Boston area moved to Natick, one of the earliest Praying Towns. But though they went there for protection from the abuses of the Europeans, these Christianized Natives found little safe shelter. At the outbreak of King Phillip's War, Natick's fragile population was forced to move to Deer Island in Boston Harbor, where many perished from starvation and exposure.[9]

While the Natives were dying by the thousands, the numbers of English colonists increased. The total European population of Massachusetts was 15,500 in 1650, 56,000 in 1700, and 188,000 in 1750. Two of the major roadblocks to more rapid population growth were the lack of a base economy and insufficient crops to feed the region's people. Food supply issues were not just caused by rocky soils and harsh climates; they were also the result of poor agricultural practices brought from England along with a fungal blight that substantially reduced wheat harvests. Many farmers had switched to planting orchards and raising livestock by the beginning of the eighteenth century. Grain was imported from the mid-Atlantic region, increasing the importance of Boston as a trading port but also making the city's population dependent on the limited amount of incoming supplies while straining the population's wealth.[13] The result of this dependence was that the region's population, while not poor, had little wealth.[16]

As the town became the major warehousing, wholesaling, and trading center for the region, Boston had two thousand to three thousand residents in 1650, seven thousand in 1700, and sixteen thousand in 1775. Its small population size meant that the acreage on the end of the peninsula could easily accommodate settlers with the Neck serving as its connection to the mainland. Though the eighteenth century saw little development activity in what would become the South End, the area gradually degraded.[17] The Neck was so narrow for much of its length that there was little dry land on either side of its road, and people would sometimes find themselves sliding into the muck. To address the dangers of the unlighted path and the treacherous marshes nearby, the town granted land along the road in exchange for the construction of barriers. In 1758, the town paved the road with rock using a combination of public and private funding. On the Back Bay side there was a picket fence and on the South Bay side, also called Roxbury or Gallows Bay, a stone fence served to protect against tidal overwash.[18] The marshes were a great place for hunting game, much to the displeasure of officials in the neighboring town of Roxbury, who claimed jurisdiction over the Back Bay, and the town posted sentinels to prevent hunting on the Sabbath.[19]

For many decades, the Neck was a place for noxious land uses that were best kept out of the town proper. One of these was distilling molasses into rum, which required burning copious amounts of firewood that created pollution. Merchants used this rum in the notorious triangle trade, which exchanged rum for slaves and then sold these people for the molasses they shipped up to Boston. Thus, the South End was part of a global economy that brought kidnapped men, women, and children from Africa to the New World.[13]

Fearful of Native American attacks, the colonists constructed a fort across the Neck consisting of earthen barricades. It was manned by order of the town, but as threats subsided, the fortification was allowed to decay. In 1710, new walls of brick and stone were built just to the west of present-day East Berkeley Street. There were substantial gates, one for carriages and one for pedestrians.[18] But again, these fortifications were allowed to fall into disuse.

Deteriorating relations between the colonists and the British government caused a gradual tightening of political and economic control over Boston and the region. Eventually, the Crown disbanded the colonial legislature, revoked the royal charter, and imposed new taxes and economic sanctions. The colonists responded with an escalating series of actions, which prompted more troops, tighter security, and increased legal strictures. To punish the town for dumping tea into the harbor, the British closed the port, further alienating the population by putting many out of work. The action also meant that all goods, including food, had to enter the town via the Neck. Then, in 1774, a British customs official was chased by a group of colonists up the Neck back to the safety of the town. This prompted General Gage, the commander of British troops, to rebuild the Neck's fortifications as the region was on the brink of rebellion.[20]

The Neck played a key role on the night of April 18, 1775, when Paul Revere and William Dawes rode to Lexington and Concord to warn the colonists about British plans to confiscate military supplies and arrest John Hancock and Samuel Adams. The "one if by land" path would have meant the British soldiers intended to march down the Neck, but they chose the "two if by sea" route instead, rowing across the Charles River. Revere crossed over to Charlestown to begin his ride, while Dawes rode down the Neck and met up with Revere in Lexington, arriving about a half hour later.

In the days after Lexington and Concord, Boston was surrounded by hostile troops with the Neck strategically situated between British forces occupying the town and colonial militias besieging it. A stalemate occurred; the British lacked sufficient manpower and confidence to attack the besieging militias, and the rebel forces were too disorganized and insufficiently armed to force the British out. Gage had four thousand troops against fifteen thousand rebel volunteers who slowly tightened the cordon around the town and cut off supplies.[20] The British constructed a fort about where Canton Street is now. The area presently occupied by Blackstone Park/Franklin Square was heavily armed with artillery, while the American fortifications were closer to the Roxbury line. Caught in between, the buildings on the Neck were burned.[19] Gage's inaction prompted his recall in October 1775, and he was replaced by General William Howe, who continued the strategy of inertia. As the British called for reinforcements and settled in for winter, food was monotonous, but the town did not starve.

Meanwhile, cannons seized by Benedict Arnold's forces at Ticonderoga were transported to Boston, and George Washington, who had assumed command of the army surrounding the town, was ready to move against the British by placing the artillery on Dorchester Heights (in what is now South

Boston). To divert their attention, Washington ordered his batteries to shell the town on March 2, 1776. The bombing covered Washington's advance, and on the morning of March 5, he fortified the Heights. A surprised Howe planned an attack on the new positions with an advance down the Neck that would serve as a diversion. But a strong storm blew in, delaying his offensive and giving the rebels time to strengthen their position. With Boston no longer defensible, Howe had no choice but to evacuate.[20]

The siege and occupation reduced Boston's population to less than three thousand in 1776, but after the war, the population began to rapidly increase. For the first fifty years after independence, the area that would become the South End was mostly unchanged; it continued to serve as the land conduit between the growing town of Boston and the rest of the state, but little development occurred. Newly independent Massachusetts briefly authorized a mint at what is now Rollins Square, but once the Constitution reserved coinage to the federal government, it ceased operation. The Neck was also used for brickyards.[19] Reflecting revived commerce, King's Roxbury Omnibuses ran once an hour up and down the Neck with a four-horse coach, and every half hour there was a two-horse coach. The fare was nine pence (12.5 cents).[21]

A serene, if mostly inaccessible, spot to this day, the South End burial ground was opened in 1810. Many of the people hanged at the nearby gallows, popular events that drew crowds, were buried in this quiet spot on Washington Street, though the vast majority of the eleven thousand people interred here were simply poor, not criminals. Because they lacked resources, it was never a prosperous cemetery. Though the city built 146 tombs around the periphery for private owners, the cemetery had few gravestones. One problem was that the boggy soil made burying people difficult until additional soil was brought in to raise the ground level in 1837. The cemetery did not receive the same respect paid to other town burial grounds, and some bodies were moved to Deer Island when James Street was built in 1856. Other graves were destroyed in 1859 for the construction of a tunnel for the Hallet and Davis piano factory, and the graveyard ceased operations in 1866. After the factory burned in 1867, the Franklin Hotel was built at that corner, eliminating additional gravesites, but there was no reburial of bodies; bones were discarded by workers as they were discovered.[18] Altogether, abutters have encroached on nearly half the original burial ground.

1.2 THE SOUTH END BURIAL GROUND

When the New England Conservatory of Music moved into the Franklin Hotel in 1882 and tried to buy more of the burial ground for an expansion, the city refused. By this point, the cemetery was in great disrepair and described as being desolate and an eyesore. The neglect continued for a century. In 1984, a city inventory of the site found trash, many tombs structurally failing, graffiti, and the wall along Washington Street in need of major repairs.[22] Following a restoration program in the 1990s, the burial ground was clean but isolated, and its gates were opened once or twice a year at most.

As time passed, the city slowly made efforts to expand its land area by filling in the marshlands along the Neck, creating the neighborhood of the South End. Boston's prosperity, rising economic activity across New England, and the town's links to Europe boosted its population, creating strong incentives for expansion. In 1790, Boston had 18,320 inhabitants, by 1840, its population was 93,383. At first, the tip of the peninsula could accommodate growth, but eventually the city reached physical limits to expansion.[6]

Even though he died in 1844, before the development of the South End began in earnest, Charles Bulfinch profoundly influenced the urban form of the neighborhood. One of the most important architects of the early re-

$56,000, and opened in October 1805. It became known for its views of the city, leisurely strolls, and as a place for lovers to meet, giving it the nickname "Bridge of Sighs."

The twenty-nine property owners along the south side of Washington Street, acting in concert as the Front Street Corporation, built a parallel new street, now called Harrison Avenue. Each owner filled in the marshland between their existing property and the new street with a total of nine acres of new land created by October 1805 at the cost of $65,000.[26]

During the first half of the nineteenth century, the South End was mostly undeveloped with marshlands lining Washington Street. In 1814, proposed cross streets were named after Massachusetts towns: Brookline, Newton, Concord, Springfield, Northampton, and Lenox, but these mostly existed on paper. The outbound streets were limited with only Washington Street, renamed from Orange Street in 1788, connecting Boston with Roxbury. There was a planned set of streets parallel to Washington Street to be named after Massachusetts counties: Berkshire, Hampshire, Worcester, Middlesex, Suffolk, Norfolk, and Plymouth, but only Suffolk, now Shawmut Avenue, was ever constructed as planned.[18] Meanwhile, the Boston Water Power Company (BWPC) constructed a series of dams across Back Bay that caused a great deterioration of environmental conditions in the marshes north of Washington Street. In the 1830s, the BWPC assumed control over most of the tidelands along the Back Bay side of the South End (mostly north of Tremont Street) and would eventually be a major developer of both neighborhoods.[26]

After decades of inactivity, S. P. Fuller developed a new plan for the South End in 1828. He doubled the number of cross streets and shifted the building plan from single family homes to row houses, honoring Bulfinch's preferred residential style and reflecting the influence of Beacon Hill's architecture. The Fuller plan also failed to stimulate development but influenced the final form of the neighborhood.[24]

The city found that infrastructure improvements could easily overwhelm revenues from land sales. In 1846, for example, the city purchased nearly six acres of marshland along South Bay and built a new sea wall to promote development. But the project cost almost one million dollars and resulted in a loss of several hundred dollars by the time the finished lands were sold to developers. The city spent another $600,000 on land improvements along the Neck, but this infrastructure again failed to stimulate land sales. Because selling unimproved land in the Neck wasn't working, in 1847, Mayor Josiah Quincy III proposed that the city auction off finished building lots.[28] But that strategy fell short as well. As the desire to develop the South End grew, the city was having a challenging time launching the neighborhood.

One factor that contributed to the northern expansion of the South End was the construction of railroads across the Back Bay. In 1829, Mayor Harrison Gray Otis called for a program of capital improvements, including building railroads to western Massachusetts and beyond to maintain the economic competitiveness of the city. In response, the Boston and Worcester and the Boston and Providence railroads were chartered in 1831. The Worcester railroad crossed the Back Bay from the tip of Gravelly Point (approximately at the intersection of Massachusetts and Commonwealth Avenues) to the current route of tracks along Herald Street and the Massachusetts Turnpike, while the Providence alignment is where the Amtrak route is today. The two lines crossed at the present day Back Bay Station.[6]

Because they were built over the Charles River Estuary, the causeways disrupted the tides and made the nearby shore areas brackish and polluted. Since many believed that foul odors caused disease, eliminating them was a major public health priority.[29] Along with a series of midcentury epidemics, the miasmas from the festering wetlands increased public support for the filling in of the Back Bay. The railroads also fostered the development of the port of Boston and helped make the city a regional financial center, further fueling growth in the city and creating the demand for more housing, commerce, and industry.

Despite their advantages, railroads and their support yards consumed large amounts of land. Their terminals at the southern and western edges of the city created the need for more land while penning in the city. At the same time, the railroads enabled higher-income families to relocate to the towns surrounding Boston, contributing to the flight of native, white Protestants to the suburbs. By the 1840s, the number of people commuting into the city was large enough to change the structure of the metropolitan area.[30] Caught between the growing population of these towns and the increasing congestion of the city center, the South End was an appealing place to build a new neighborhood.

The city had not been happy with the location of the Dover Street Bridge, and critics pointed out that Bostonians needed a central, more direct connection to South Boston. After much give and take between the city, state, and property owners, the city authorized a new bridge at Federal Street in 1826. As a result, the value of the Dover Street Bridge plummeted, and it was sold to the city for just $3,500 in 1832.[26]

The opening of the Free Bridge in 1828 prevented ocean-bound ships from reaching the South Cove docks, but smaller lumber and coal barges were able to reach the wharfs along Albany Street well into the twentieth century. Given that their deep-water piers were no longer usable, property owners decided there was more money to be made by filling in the area. In 1833, they created the South Cove Corporation with part of this newly made land to go to the Worcester and Providence Railroad for its terminal.[31] The company bought seventy-three submerged acres for the construction of tracks and yards on land that would be filled in the far southeast corner of the South End.[19]

One result of the South Cove and Front Street projects was the creation of Fort Point Channel to connect South Bay and the wharfs along Albany Street to the Harbor.[6] The South Cove Corporation filled in its land in 1843 to create a tight grid with streets named for railroad stops in the state of New York. This gave the area its name: the New York Streets neighborhood. Its streets were lined with tenements occupied first by native-born whites followed by Irish immigrants in the late 1850s when the city leveled the Fort Hill slum district to make way for an expanded downtown.

Though the area to the west of Savoy Street and south of Washington Street was technically land, it was marshy and needed to be protected by a dike. The South Bay Lands Project filled in the area from Albany Street to what is now the Expressway from Malden to East Brookline Streets beginning in 1845. Also in 1845, the city stables were relocated to the land at the intersection of Harrison Avenue and East Brookline/East Canton Street. The area to the south of Harrison Avenue was to be sold off as house lots, but after decades-long problems with contractors, the easternmost section became primarily industrial while the western portion became reserved for institutional uses. Mayor Josiah Quincy Jr's administration filled in the remainder of South Cove in 1847.[32] Slowly, other streets were extended through the South End to better connect the growing city with the mainland. Tremont Street was built when the Mill Dam was constructed across the Back Bay.[26] Albany Street was built between 1834 and 1868, after the first major cross arterial, Dover Street, was constructed from 1804 to 1834.[19] Expansion was slow and many of the cross streets were barely a block long, but despite this arduous process, the stage was now set for the creation of the South End.

It would have been difficult, if not impossible, for the city to develop the South End without a sufficient water source to serve the new neighborhood. Given that it was built on filled land, occupants would not have been able to use ground water wells for drinking. The entire city needed a safe water supply. Jamaica Pond had been tapped for water in 1785, and 1840s Boston relied on wells, springs, rainwater, and private water suppliers. But many sources were polluted or dysfunctional.[33] In addition to the business interests pushing the city to secure a water source to promote growth, Boston's medical community advocated for clean water for health reasons. Prominent physicians such as Walter Channing and John Ware joined forces with moral reformers who saw clean water to be a substitute for alcohol and thus a way to advance the city's strong temperance movement.[34]

The eventual solution to the water supply issue was to dam the Sudbury River in Natick. The completion of the aqueduct from the Cochichuate Reservoir, about fifteen miles away, was cause for major celebration. On October 26, 1848, the "tumult of one hundred guns and the ringing of church bells greeted the rising of the sun on the day of the opening of the supply." [35] By 1851, almost 80 percent of the city's population was using Cochichuate water.[36] The health and safety of the residents immediately improved as fresh, reliable water systems reduced illnesses and enabled the beginnings of effective fire suppression. The new, abundant water supply also made it possible for the city to develop the South End.

As in other cities, the introduction of secure, low-priced, plentiful water encouraged a rapid increase in usage, which overwhelmed existing infrastructure.[37] By 1851, the city was consuming twice as much water as predicted, causing wastewater to flood its surface drainage, cesspools, and privies. To address these problems in the southern section of the city, it was necessary to establish a new system of storm and sewer drains.[38] In general, this infrastructure moved waste and storm water from north of the Neck to the South Bay, but these drains were poorly engineered with insufficient pitch to ensure adequate flow. Drainage problems would persist for the next 150 years.

Despite the abundance of resources, the real estate market was not quite ready for a new neighborhood. Efforts to promote free-standing estates mostly failed—except for a mansion on Washington Street called Deacon House, built by Harrison Grey Otis's next-door neighbor on Beacon Hill for his daughter and son-in-law. Edward Preble Deacon had married Sarah Annabella Parker in 1841. Their house achieved fame largely due to Jean Lemoulnier and Gridley J. F. Bryant's French design. It had one of the city's first mansard roofs and was considered extravagant in a city where tastes were generally bland.[39] Completed in 1848, the house was candlelit, men in French attire waited on the visitors, and there was a reputed "Marie Antoinette" boudoir, said to be a room taken from France. Unfortunately, Edward Preble Deacon died of consumption in 1851.[26] His widow moved to France, where the family became internationally prominent. One granddaughter, Gladys, was the Duchess of Marlborough; another, Dorothy, was Princess Radziwill.[40]

Though long demolished, the Deacon House remains famous to this day because of a mystery regarding lost artwork. The highlight of the house was a series of four paintings by Jean Honoré Fragonard entitled "The History of Love." When the contents of the house were auctioned off in 1871, the paintings were purchased by the prominent Bostonian Henry Lee for $1,200. While other items from the auction are now at the Museum of Fine Arts, the whereabouts of the Fragonards are unknown. If found, the paintings would be worth millions.[41]

One person with ties to the neighborhood in this era was Louisa May Alcott, the author of Little Women and other novels. Her father was Amos Branson Alcott, a well-known member of the Transcendentalist movement who had strong ideas regarding education and social welfare. He had organized several failed communal farms and periodically moved his family to the South End whenever he suffered one of his many financial reversals. In November 1847, the Alcotts lived in a basement apartment on West Dedham Street in a unit Louisa May thought dark and dingy. But it was close enough to the city's tenement district that her father could put into practice his ideas on how to assist the poor.[42] In 1849, the Alcotts lived on Groton Street, where Peters Park is now. Louisa May kept house for her family and helped her sister, who taught school on West Canton Street.[43] Though she eventually moved elsewhere, she would frequently return to the neighborhood.

As late as 1850, the core of the South End row house district was unbuilt and remained mostly degraded marshland. In the 1840s, a hunter could shoot "plover, peep, and yellow legs" near present-day Copley Square. There were black ducks and wild geese, and boys would ice skate in the area during the winter.[21]

In the midst of this wilderness, the first efforts to expand the city into what is now the South End produced tenement districts, industrial areas, and infrastructure for railroads, but overall, growth was limited. However, the South End was strategically located between the growing communities of Boston and Roxbury. Though development had yet to reach the neighborhood, the city now had a shared vision of what it wanted to see in new urban residential areas and had gained experience with the development and promoting of capital improvements.[26] It also had new reasons for creating an upscale neighborhood on its periphery.

1. Shimer HW. Post-glacial history of Boston. *Proceedings of the American Academy of Arts and Sciences* 1916; 53:441-63.

2. Kaye CA, Barghoorn ES. Late Quaternary Sea-Level Change and Crustal Rise at Boston, Massachusetts, with Notes on the Autocompaction of Peat. *The Geological Society of America Bulletin* 1964; 75:63-80.

3. Kaye CA. Bedrock and Quaternary geology of the Boston area, Massachusetts. In: Legget RF, ed. *Geology Under Cities*. Boulder, Colorado: The Geological Society of America; 1982.

4. Clapp FG. Geological History of the Charles Rive. *Technology Quarterly* 1901; 14:171-201.

5. Bunting B. The plan of the Back Bay area in Boston. *The Journal of the Society of Architectural Historians 1954*;13:19-24.

6. Seasholes NS. *Gaining Ground: A History of Landmaking in Boston*. Cambridge, Massachusetts: The MIT Press; 2003.

7. Lavin L. Coastal adaptation in Southern New England and Southern New York. *Archeology of Eastern North America* 1988; 16:191-20.

8. Denevan WM. The pristine myth: The landscape of the Americas in 1492. *Annals of the Association of American Geographers* 1992;82:369-85.

9. O'Brien JM. *Dispossession by Degrees: Indian land and identity in Natick, Massachusetts, 1650-1790*. New York: Cambridge University Press; 1997.

10. Cave AA. The Pequot invasion of southern New England: A reassessment of the evidence. *The New England Quarterly* 1989; 62:27-44.

11. Russell HS. *Indian New England Before the Mayflower*. Hanover, New Hampshire: University Press of New England; 1980.

12. Drake JD. King Philip's War: *Civil War in New England, 1675-1676*. Amherst, Massachusetts: University of Massachusetts Press; 1999.

13. McManus DR. *Colonial New England: A Historical Geography*. New York: Oxford University Press; 1975.

14. Cook SF. Interracial Warfare and Population Decline among the New England Indians. *Ethnohistory* 1973; 20:1-24.

15. Elliot J, Morrison KM. "That art of coyning Christians": John Elliot and the Praying Indians of Massachusetts. *Ethnohistory* 1974; 21:77-92.

16. Durst C. *Daily Life in Colonial New England*. Westport, Connecticut: Greenwood Press; 2002.

17. South End Historical Society. *Down Washington Street: Visions of Past, Present, and Future*. 1994.

18.Shurtleff NB. *A Topographical and Historical Description of Boston. Boston*: City of Boston; 1871.

19. Woods RA. *The City Wilderness: A Settlement Study*. Boston: Houghton, Mifflin and Company; 1898.

20. French A. *The Siege of Boston*. Boston: The Macmillan Company; 1911.

21. Jones WP. Notes Of the Old South End - Breweries And Distilleries. *Boston Globe* 1900 August 23.

22. Historic Burial Grounds Inventory Project. *South Burial Ground*. 1984.

23. Wickersham J. The Financial Misadventures of Charles Bulfinch. *The New England Quarterly* 2010; 83:413-81.

24. Smith MS. *Between City and Suburb: Architecture and Planning in Boston's South End Providence*, Rhode Island: Brown University; 1977.

25. Goodman PS. *The Garden Squares of Boston*. Lebanon, New Hampshire: University Press of New England; 2003.

26. Whitehill WM, Kennedy LW. *Boston: A Topographical History*. Cambridge, MA: Belnap Press of Harvard University Press; 2000.

27. Peacock VT. *Famous American Belles of the Nineteenth Century Philadelphia*. J.B. Lippincott Company; 1901.

28. Huse CP. *The Financial History of Boston from May 1, 1822, to January 31, 1909*. Cambridge, Massachusetts: Harvard University Press; 1916.

29. Lopez R. *Building American Public Health: Urban Planning, Architecture, and the Quest for Better Health in the United States*. New York: Palgrave Macmillan; 2012.

30. O'Connell JC. *The Hub's Metropolis*. Cambridge, MA: The MIT Press; 2013.

31. Kennedy CJ. The Early Business History of Four Massachusetts Railroads. *Bulletin of the Business Historical Society* 1951; 25:52-72.

32. State Street Trust Company. *Boston's Growth: A Bird's-Eye View of Boston's Increase in Territory and Population from its Beginning to the Present* Boston. 1901.

33. Mason CY. Municipal Water Supplies in New England. *Economic Geography* 1937; 13:347-64.

34. Rawson M. The Nature of Water: Reform and the Antebellum Crusade for Municipal Water in Boston. *Environmental History* 2004; 9:411-35. 35. Fahey JJ. Boston's 45 Mayors. Boston: The City Record; 1875.

36. Meckel RA. Immigration, Mortality, and Population Growth in Boston, 1840-1880. *The Journal of Interdisciplinary History* 1985; 15:393-417.

37. Cosgrove J. *A History of Sanitation*. Pittsburg, PA: Standard Sanitary Manufacturing Company; 1909.

38. Peterson JA. The Impact of Sanitary Reform Upon American Urban Planning, 1840-1890. *Journal of Social History* 1979;13:83-103.

39. Shand-Tucci D. *Built in Boston: City and Suburb 1800-1950.* Amherst, Massachusetts: The University of Massachusetts Press; 1978.

40. Shannon HJ. *Legendary Locals of Boston's South End.* Charleston, South Carolina: Arcadia Publishing; 2014.

41. Neale J. *The Mystery of the Missing Fragonards.* South End Historical Society. Undated:2.

42. Matteson J. *Eden's Outcasts: The Story of Louisa May Alcott and Her Father.* New York: W. W. Norton; 2007.
43. Card RO. *Boston's South End: An Urban Walker's Handbook.* South End Historical Society; 1992.

CHAPTER 2

A Neighborhood Emerges: 1850-1873

There were two key issues that led to the decades-long effort to create the South End. One was immigration. In 1840, a decade before the beginning of the neighborhood's development, the city covered about six square miles and had a population of 84,401.[1] Thirty percent were foreign born or the children of immigrants. By the time the South End's development was complete in 1880, the city's population was 362,849. Sixty-four percent were immigrants or their children; they were part of a metropolitan area that covered thirty-six square miles.[2]

Boston reeled from this wave of newcomers. Even though the city's 1845 demographer declared that no more people could be accommodated in Boston, the population grew by fifty thousand over the next decade. For many poor residents, conditions were appalling; four percent of the city's population lived in cellars.[3] Many units had dirt floors, periodic floods, and lacked windows. Others lived in tenements with entire extended families crammed into a single room. Many dwellings were unsafe and unsanitary.

Boston's Protestants reacted to this influx with bigotry, fear, and political and social agitation. Fleeing disorder, squalor, and immigrants, native whites left Boston. New railroads made commuting easier and allowed families to access better quality housing in the ring of towns surrounding the city. Options for keeping Boston from becoming dominated by Irish immigrants—who were poor, Catholic, and inassimilable—were bleak, and many saw them as a threat to the established order. The city's establishment renewed its efforts to develop the South End to create a bastion for the Boston's Protestants.[4]

Native-born whites in the South End shared this anti-Irish prejudice. In 1855, for example, residents around Blackstone Square were so angered by a proposal to convert the Chickering Warehouse into housing for Irish immigrants that some advertised their houses for sale in protest. One source of information on this era is a series of letters written by Elizabeth and Otis Everett to their son, Otis Blake Everett, who was living in India. The Everetts were an upper-middle-class, well-connected family; their cousin was Edward Everett Hale, the famous churchman. The family first lived on Washington Street near Union Park Street, then in a row house on Shawmut Avenue near

Concord Street. When writing to their son about the plan to house the Irish, the Everetts expressed their belief that such an outrage would never be allowed to happen.[5] The South End was intended for upper-class native whites.

The second incentive to create the neighborhood was the odors rising from the stagnant Back Bay. The mill dams and railroads had created acres of putrid water and dying salt marshes; by the 1840s, the stench was unbearable.[6] The public demanded a solution, so the state, city, and BWPC decided to fill the basin. Eventually, this project led to the creation of almost all the land from the Neck to Storrow Drive and from the Public Garden to the Back Bay Fens, including land for most of the South End's row house district north of Washington Street.[7]

As part of the preparation for renewed city efforts to sell building lots, two city engineers—Ellis S. Chesbrough and William P. Parrott— laid out the core of the South End. Neither had any experience with urban planning; they mainly updated Bulfinch's and Fuller's plans.[4] Born in Maryland in 1813, Chesbrough went to work for a railroad when he was nine, then took a surveying job where his employers were mostly West Point-trained engineers who helped expand his technical knowledge. In 1846, Chesbrough became Chief Engineer of the Boston Water Works, then Commissioner, and eventually the city's first Chief Engineer. Soon after completing his work on the South End, Chesbrough was hired away by Chicago to solve that city's tremendous water, waste, and drainage issues.[8]

A particularly important contribution of Chesbrough and Parrott's plan was the Bulfinch-inspired squares inserted into Fuller's modified grid. Two of these, Union Park and Chester Square, were about equidistant from the now refurbished Blackstone Park/Franklin Square. Worcester Square was the third major square, and two interior parks, Montgomery and Leighton, were created out of land left over from fitting the various grids of the South End together. Leighton Square did not last, and Montgomery Park is private while another square, Ashland Park, disappeared within two decades as new development pressures emerged. In addition, BWPC built a series of modest squares on the land it owned on side streets along Columbus Avenue, similarly hoping that the small open spaces would promote lot sales.

Albert T. Minot designed the three key squares.[9] His inspiration was the English architect and philosopher John Ruskin, who sought to create harmony between humanity and nature, leading some to credit him with contributing to the beginning of the environmental movement. Ruskin's writings and examples encouraged followers to adopt simple ideas to convey complex meaning.[10] In this aesthetic, placing a square where people could observe nature was a method of promoting a moral way of life. Similarly, Ruskin's ideas led to lining the new neighborhood's streets with trees and the construction of broad arterials. The open spaces and small natural areas were thought to promote better health by providing sunlight and ventilation and connecting people to nature.[4]

Since these expensive squares could have been otherwise sold to developers and thus were costly to the city via lost revenues, their main purpose was to attract high-income residents. These squares also committed the city to their landscaping and maintenance, but this was considered a necessary expense if the wealthy were going to buy in the neighborhood. Ironically, these beautiful squares did not represent forward thinking on the part of the city or its engineers to meet the open needs of the impoverished. In fact, they represented a longstanding tradition in the United States of creating open spaces for the wealthy, insulating them from the poor. In a sense, South End squares were the "degraded Victorian descendants of the elegant eighteenth-century crescents and parks of London and Bath."[4]

Regardless of the city's social aims, it was with great optimism for the South End's future that the first house lots on Chester Square were put to auction on October 30, 1850. Platted by Ezra Lincoln, Chester Square's lots contained deed restrictions that permitted only residential uses for the first twenty years. Buyers were required to put down a 10 percent deposit by January 1851 and pay the rest in installments of nine annual payments. Belying the city's confidence, it would take years for buyers to move into the neighborhood, and the city would end up relaxing the terms as development lagged. As late as 1860, a photograph showed substantial numbers of vacant lots.[11] Yet when it was finished, the Chester Square was a beautiful mix of stately mansions and more modest townhouses, and it set the standard for the neighborhood's Victorian architectural style.

Lots on Union Park went to auction in November 1851. At the time, it was a block from the stagnant waters of Back Bay, and Washington Street was a dusty, gravel-covered thoroughfare. The city had started paving the street, but the project had barely reached beyond Dover Street.[12] Not surprisingly, there was limited demand and the auction saw only twenty-four out of 108 lots sold the first day. However, the city continued to work on the landscaping and amenities of the area. Development was slow, and construction was not yet complete by 1859.

Worcester Square went to auction in May 1859. Lots went for higher sums than those on Union Park or Chester Square, and this time, the city put a contractual obligation on deeds that construction had to begin within two years. But again, there were problems finding buyers; half the lots sold in 1859 and it took until 1861 for the remainder to sell.[13]

The city graded streets but required developers to fill in the building lots. The interim condition was a streetscape of completed row houses interspersed with vacant lots surrounded by fencing to keep passersby from falling into the holes between buildings.[13] By only filling in the land under the streets, the city saved on development costs, but the result was that many alleys are eight to ten feet lower than street level. This difference in depth enabled basement kitchens to have windows on the back sides of row houses, but created an issue that would plague the South End for the next 150 years: flooding. The alleys were low, marshy, and unpaved, and drainage would frequently fail.

2.1 WORCESTER SQUARE 2014

To increase sales in 1852, the city reduced down payments to one percent.[14] Then, in 1855, Mayor Jerome Smith called for selling South End lots to "mechanics of limited means," because marketing to the wealthy and middle class had failed.[13] Thus, attempts to make the South End an exclusive neighborhood for the rich barely lasted five years. In addition, many lots were purchased and developed using highly leveraged mortgages, a problem that would haunt the neighborhood after the Great Boston Fire of 1872 and the Financial Panic of 1873. By 1859, it became clear to the city that the market for the highest quality townhouses had failed to materialize, and municipal finances made it impossible to build any more squares on city-owned land still being developed. However, the BWPC laid out Concord Square (1866 to 1868), Rutland Square (1866 to 1867), and Braddock Park (1869). These squares differed from the older ones in that they were inserted into streets that had already been created and they were smaller and less ornamented.[13] They succeeded in attracting middle-class buyers but not the wealthy.

Many later buildings and streets in the South End are much less grand than the signature blocks around its squares. Another change was a shift away from row houses—a residential form rapidly falling out of style— to apartment houses. The final east-west arterial, Columbus Avenue, had a different purpose from earlier ones; the originally wood-planked street was meant to be a promenade and had a focal point on the Common as it moved out diagonally. Though the BWPC tried to increase its return on investment through building chic apartments, the blocks along this street failed as quickly as they were built.[15]

Several areas were very modest; Gray and Lawrence Streets were built on land intended to be the backyards of other buildings.[16] A pattern emerged: upscale residents, mostly merchants, lived on the main squares. Nearby, middle-class residents—such as grocers, jewelers, and other small business owners—were prone to rent out to lodgers even in the 1860s. Further out, there were the even more downscale residents— mostly renters in buildings that were lodging houses or tenements from the beginning.[13]

Retaining the few wealthy residents was a struggle. Illustrative of the pattern of their tepid movements in and quick move outs, the history of the Allen House mirrors that of the South End. Aaron H. Allen, a furniture dealer specializing in combined Italianate and Second Empire styles, built the Allen House at the corner of Worcester Square and Washington Street in 1859. But Allen left for the Back Bay in 1871; it was becoming clear the South End was in decline.[17] In the years afterward, the Allen House was a private men's club, a home for the Catholic Union, an offsite facility for Boston College, and the site of the Lebanese-American Club before it was abandoned in 1953. The city took it over in 1958, and the vacant shell was sold to a developer for high-end condominiums in 1999.[18]

Developing the South End was not profitable for the city. Looking back at the period from 1822 to 1894, Mayor Nathan Matthews reported that Boston spent $4,619,000 on land and improvements for various South End projects while only bringing in $4,839,000 in revenue.[19]

The development of Boston's Back Bay would have long-term implications for the South End, as the Back Bay proved to be more attractive to upper-income residents. Even in 2014, when the South End was one of the priciest neighborhoods in Boston (the median price per square foot was $710), the Back Bay was still be more expensive (with an incredible $795 per square foot median price).[20] Contrary to later beliefs, however, the two neighborhoods were developed almost simultaneously as blocks were filled westward of the Public Garden beginning in 1855.[7] The South End suffered from competition with the Back Bay from the start.

The Back Bay had many advantages over the South End, such as better connections to Beacon Hill and the Public Garden and architectural guidelines that allowed more innovation. Reflecting changing tastes, the Back Bay was designed in the more fashionable French style rather than fading English ideals.[21] The South End appeared increasingly dated as it came into being, frozen into an outmoded design.

BWPC's South End efforts fared worse than the city's. Even as early as 1855, it fell behind in capital needed for the project, and to raise funds it auctioned off seventeen acres of land—including the area between Arlington, Clarendon, Tremont, and Chandler Streets. Unfortunately for the company, the auctions only brought in about 37 cents per square foot, barely half of what had been anticipated, and not all the lots sold.[22] BWPC often cut corners to reduce costs, and many of its blocks were constructed over muck dredged from nearby tidal flats despite odors and instability.[7] This approach had repercussions well into the twenty-first century.

There was little coordination between the South End and Back Bay since few streets crossed the railroad tracks and the two grids had an ungainly 45-degree meet up point. There were attempts to reconcile the grids of the two neighborhoods in 1853, but these were abandoned because of the need to accommodate the railroads, constraints imposed by the shoreline, and a city council decision to develop municipal land holdings in a temporal and physical manner that was incompatible with the plan for Back Bay streets.[6] Travel between the two neighborhoods would never progress smoothly.

BWPC frequently angered its customers. John L. Gardner, father-in-law to the famous Isabella Stewart Gardner, bought lots in 1851 where the Boston Center for the Arts (BCA) is now, but he grew frustrated when, in 1861, he was still waiting for his land to be filled in. Around the same time, residents along Appleton and Clarendon Streets wrote a letter to the BWPC complaining about the mosquitos coming from the stagnant waters in the area. Pressing on despite complaints, the BWPC sold lots along Columbus Avenue in 1866. In 1869, the streets in the area were deeded to the city, though their grading and filling was not yet complete. In 1870, Holyoke Street had only six owner-occupied houses, another unoccupied nine, and the remainder of the block was vacant.[14] In 1871, the president of the BWPC tried to buy all the shares of the company at below market prices, severely straining the company's finances. This stress prompted the BWPC to make deals to fill in land for larger purchasers and sell off individual lots at cut rate prices, further imperiling the economy just as the market was about to collapse.[7]

The older part of the South End was in poor shape. By 1868, the area east of Dover Street was already becoming a well-known tenement district, while many owners of row houses in the rest of the South End were taking in lodgers. As time passed, the number of rooms rented out increased and the neighborhood's real estate market was already showing signs of cracking prior to the twin crises of the Great Boston Fire of 1872 and the Financial Panic of 1873. [22]

The city also filled in land south of Washington Street during this period. Manufacturing companies such as furniture and woodworking factories and businesses that were dependent on barge deliveries of coal and other raw materials became predominant in the area east of Brookline Street. A variety of city departments—such as paving, health, sewer, and water—used the land west of Brookline Street.[23]

Three major factors shaped the architectural unity of the neighborhood. First, almost the entire South End was laid out on land owned by just two entities, the City of Boston and BWPC, and neither altered their basic design requirements even as sales faltered. Second, lots were sold with very detailed restrictions regarding setbacks, heights, building materials, and other parameters; developers had limited options for innovation. Finally, most row houses were designed by builders with few identifiable architects involved. Instead, developers used pattern books to guide their construction, sometimes purchasing pre-built elements to incorporate into façades. This homogenous approach reduced construction costs and contributed to uniformity.[4] As a result, South End row houses tend to be variations on a few styles.

Lots vary from fifteen by forty feet to twenty-five by one hundred feet in size with buildings often covering 50 percent or more of the lot area. The city passed an ordinance in 1803 requiring all buildings taller than ten feet to be built of brick or stone. As a result, South End buildings are uniform in materials and color. The most popular style of row house in the South End is the bow front. But there are also flat front rowhouses that range from ornate to Spartan and square front rowhouses, most common in the later period of development along Columbus Avenue and Warren Street. Altogether, "six distinct architectural styles can be seen: Greek Revival, Italianate, Renaissance

Revival, Victorian Gothic, Flemish Revival, and Neo-Greek." The most popular style was the Italianate with a bow front, a hood over the front door, a high stoop, and often with a mansard roof. Another common building type, especially in prominent locations, was large townhouses with flat façades, pediments, and that were mostly either built of brownstone or brick with brownstone accents.[24] Many buildings had small but interesting details. The even side of Tremont between Concord and Rutland Streets, for example, was called "Poets' Row" because each building had a carved figurehead of a poet on its façade.[11] These are long gone. Today, there are high stoops and buildings with entries barely above the sidewalk. Some have elaborate iron work, others are plain, and many row houses were constructed in sets of two, producing mirror image buildings. The variations are almost infinite.

The interiors of many of the original single-family townhouses were built with a grand parlor on the first floor, which was entered from the street by a substantial set of front stairs with the kitchen sitting below street grade with access under the stairs or through the back alley. Parlor-level condominiums, with their lofty ceilings and intricate detailing, command a premium price today. Bedrooms tended to occupy the second and third floors with small rooms on the side for each main bedroom. The bathroom—it was rare to have more than one—was generally on the fourth floor and was fed from city pipes to a holding tank on the top floor to provide even water pressure. Originally, coal fireplaces were used for heating.[14] Reminders of this era are the small, round holes in many sidewalks that served as coal chutes for deliveries—often now covered by metal plates or cemented over—and coal cinders in the alleys and open spaces of the neighborhood.

Middle-class families lavishly decorated their row houses. The Everett family's Shawmut Avenue townhouse had "one long large parlour opening with glass folding doors into a large library, which has a bay window for our elegant flower-pots, with flowers, of course. These rooms are finished with tinted fresco ceilings and are sunny and pleasant." There was only one bathroom, but water was available to both of the floors that had bedrooms.[25] Some of the neighborhood's rowhouses were built with state-of-the-art amenities; many Union Park buildings had every luxury at the time of their construction with water delivered through lead pipes, heat from hot air furnaces, and lighting by city gas.[26] Other buildings were more modest and had as few comforts as the law would allow.

Nathanial J. Bradlee (1829-1888) was the architect of many prominent houses, churches, and apartment buildings in the neighborhood. He lived at 660 Tremont Street and designed over 500 buildings in his career, including the South Congregational Church on Union Park Street.[27] His Hotel St. Cloud, built from 1869 to 1870, was a luxury apartment building with "parlors, chambers, dining room, kitchen and bath room, furnished in black walnut, heated by steam, grates in all principal rooms, and sun on three sides."[26] Though this building is still standing today, many others he designed have been demolished.

One of the largest buildings in the neighborhood was the Franklin Hotel, fronting on Franklin Square. It attracted many famous guests, including President Grant (1869) and Johan Strauss (1872). The hotel's architecture was influenced by the French Second Empire style of Old City Hall and was designed by Gridley J. F. Bryant and Arthur Gilman.[28] In the 1980s, the building's façade would be used as the exterior of the fictional hospital in the television series, St. Elsewhere.

Not everyone appreciated the South End's architecture. In 1913, one resident of South End House complained, "The first impression is one of insufferable monotony. The architects of fifty years ago seemed to have lacked creative imagination."[15] In the same vein was a lament in a 1968 poem sponsored by the South End Historical Society: "So much alike that children in their doubt must count, poor things, to know which house is home."[29] A particularly damning assessment is through omission by one of the South End's greatest residents, the architect Louis Sullivan, who lived here as a child. He spent many of his young years roaming around the city and his autobiography praises several buildings in Boston. But of the South End's architecture, he says nothing except for expressing an admiration for the Rice School, which he attended.[30]

There are physical issues. The Bay Village and Castle Square areas had been filled in the 1820s and 1830s at five feet above the low tide level. At first, this low elevation wasn't an issue, but with the advent of piped-in water and indoor toilets, the drainage problem grew acute, and sewage began to back up into basements.[7] New development made it worse, and the city had to revisit the elevation of the area. Between 1870 and 1872, as part of sanitary engineering improvements in the northeastern corner of the South End, new fill was brought in to raise Bay Village's streets. About 150 buildings were demolished and another two hundred were raised to fourteen feet above sea level. The project served to better connect Tremont Street and Shawmut Avenue to downtown, but it also resulted in an influx of slum dwellers into the eastern portion of the South End along Dover Street.[22] There were similar drainage problems at the opposite end of the neighborhood and in 1873 landowners outbound from Northampton Street were required to raise their lots to twelve feet above sea level.[23]

2.2 BOSTON IN 1856

There were also complaints about the neighborhood's street layout. In his monumental 1954 book on the houses of the Back Bay, Bainbridge Bunting complains there is no dominant sense of direction in the South End and its parks are haphazardly located. He charged that a pedestrian does not know where he or she may be and the neighborhood's individual blocks sit isolated from each other.[6] This was also the criticism of pioneering urban designer Kevin Lynch, whose 1960 book on how people perceive the built environment, Image of the City, was to influence generations of architects and planners. Lynch saw the South End as formless with no center and no landmarks to guide visitors.[31] The South End's overall design and architecture was widely unloved until the 1960s.

Despite real estate issues, residents found the new neighborhood an entertaining place to live. In 1855, for example, the city held an agricultural fair on fifty acres of newly filled land between Northampton and East Brookline Streets. "In the middle of the ground is a racecourse, where each afternoon during the week the speed of horses can be tried."[5] Other pastimes included going to concerts, operas, and theatrical performances, entertaining family and friends, and attending church services. Families visited each other, celebrated weddings, and in the winter, flooded the open fields for skating. In 1856, Mr. Lang of Chester Square hosted an elaborate masquerade ball where guests dressed as Little Red Riding Hood, Summer, a harlequin, and Turks, Greeks, and Arabs.[32]

Altogether, the South End was a mixture of sublime prosperous living, middle- and working-class propriety, and grinding poverty. Representative of life for working-class residents were the experiences of one of the most prominent South End residents of all time, the famous boxer John L. Sullivan. John's father, Michael, was from County Kerry. He settled in the South End, married Catherine Kelly of County Roscommon in 1856 at St. Patrick's Church on Northampton Street,[33] and welcomed the birth of John in 1858. Though the Sullivan family residence was on East Concord Street, many reports have John born in Roxbury.

Michael Sullivan supported his family by working as a mason and day laborer for about fifteen dollars a week, a good income for a man of his skills and education. John stressed the normalcy of his childhood and recalled he "played ball, marbles, spun tops, and did everything of the kind that boys do." He would go to South Boston to swim at the waterfront and walk over to the South End Grounds to loudly cheer for the Boston Red Stockings. He first went to a school on Concord Street, then the Dwight School on Springfield Street. His teachers were kind but strict and he bragged he was only caned once, but by thirteen he was done with school.[33]

Earning four dollars a week, Sullivan spent six months as an apprentice plumber, then eighteen months working for a tin smith.[34] He didn't like either job and turned to boxing where he quickly rose through the ranks of prize fighters. As his career ebbed and alcohol and hard living ruined his health, Sullivan returned to the South End as a bar owner and promoter. Sober, he died in 1918 in his suburban home.

Many of the row houses of the South End have a grandeur that suggests a golden age, but a closer look at the neighborhood quickly reveals that the mansions of Union Park are around the corner from flat-faced tenements on Bradford Street. On some blocks, rows of high-stooped residences abut more modest houses. Though these contrasts add to the architectural variety of the neighborhood, they reflect the ups and downs of trends in this first era of development. Overall, the South End was an unsuccessful real estate venture, as many historians have noted. Walter Muir Whitehill, the author of one of the best histories of the city, Boston: A Topographical History, bluntly stated, "this seemingly attractive new South End never fulfilled its promise."[22] Analyzing city directories, Whitehill found that just three of the five hundred Boston residents worth more than $100,000 in 1851 lived in the South End and only seventeen moved into the neighborhood over the next two decades. Just two of these were worth more than $200,000 and none were millionaires.[22]

There were some notable residents, however. Anna Cabot Lowell Quincy Waterston, the daughter of Mayor Josiah Quincy III and sister of Mayor Josiah Quincy, Jr., lived at 71 Chester Square from 1860 until her death in 1899. Alexander Rice, a resident of 34 Union Park, was mayor of Boston from 1856 to 1857 and governor of Massachusetts from 1875 to 1879. Ambrose Raney was born in Vermont and lived at 26 Chester Square from the late 1850s until his death in 1899. He was the owner of the Chester Hotel at Shawmut Avenue and Northampton Street, a representative in the Massachusetts House, and a three-term congressman. Louise Chandler Moulton, the author of This, That, and the Other, lived at 28 Rutland Street with her husband William for more than forty years beginning in 1860. Their home was the site of a popular literary salon which attracted Ralph Waldo Emerson, Bronson Alcott, Henry Wadsworth Longfellow, Julia Ward Howe, and others.[27] For the most part, however, the city's elite avoided the neighborhood.

The neighborhood was important for those of limited means. City Hospital, now part of Boston University Medical Center (BUMC), a major South End institution, was established in the neighborhood in this era. A series of epidemics, including outbreaks of cholera in 1849 and 1854, provided the incentive to build a hospital.[3] Also in 1849, Elisha Goodnow bequeathed $21,000 to the city to help build a hospital; one half of the funds were to be used to provide free beds.[39]

The city set aside land for the hospital in 1860 and began construction of the first buildings in 1861.[19] The site was considered undesirable, but "not even the malodorous breezes from the putrid South Bay disconcerted the City Fathers at that time." Much of the surrounding land was still mudflats, and the southern boundary of the site was the Roxbury Canal, an open sewer drain. But the city already owned the land and other sites were either too expensive or too distant; this far corner of the South End was selected by default even though it still flooded from time to time.[40] The hospital grew to 208 beds in 1864; by 1905 there were 619 beds in the main facility and 264 in the area west of Massachusetts Avenue.[40] The other half of this major medical institution, the former Boston University Hospital, also dates to this time. Samuel Gregory, its founder, had tried his hand at mesmerism and phrenology. Turning to medicine, he attracted publicity by denouncing the evils of male physicians attending women during childbirth. To solve this moral crisis, he founded the New England Female Medical College in 1848.

2.3 BOSTON CITY HOSPITAL, 1903

A medical college for women brought forth many issues including which subjects and methods were proper for female students, the role of women in society and the work force, and whether to allow non-doctors to teach medicine. There were concerns regarding whether women should be allowed to treat men or should be limited to ministering to the needs of women and children. Others questioned if women had the physical stamina to be doctors and if they should be allowed to work outside the home or alone in a room with strangers. Forging ahead in the face of these sexist barriers, twelve brave women were in the first class of the college, part of a national movement to train female physicians. But the school struggled as it was challenged by the unwillingness of men to join as faculty. Despite many obstacles, by the time the first class graduated in 1854, some of the opposition had abated, and Mayor Jerome Van Crowninshield Smith gave the commencement address.

In 1859, the school purchased the building that had housed the Boston Lying-In Hospital, one of the predecessors of the world-famous Brigham and Women's Hospital, on East Springfield Street for $50,000. The building had a lecture hall, library, meeting space, faculty offices, and beds for six paying patients and six charity patients, making it the largest hospital for women in the United States at the time. But operating the school and hospital was challenging, and the administration had serious disagreements on how to spend money. One dispute, for example, centered on whether medicine was a science or an art. This was not just a philosophical debate; it shaped discussions regarding whether the school ought to buy a thermometer and microscope or if a good doctor should be able to diagnose a patient without the need of such equipment, allowing the school's limited dollars to be spent elsewhere.

The school was unable to meet the payments on its building and was forced to move to East Canton Street in 1862 as its hospital closed, enrollment declined, and professors left. Despite these troubles, however, there were notable successes, including graduating its first Black physician, Rebecca Lee Crumpler, in 1864. Upon finishing school, she moved back to her native Richmond and cared for former slaves until returning to Boston several decades later.

In the late 1860s, the school began negotiating with the city to purchase a lot to build a new facility. The contract obligated the school's trustees to raise $100,000, but accusations of mismanagement and personality conflicts set back fundraising. The school also continued to face sexism, as City Hospital refused to let female medical students enter its wards. Without hands-on experience, learning was difficult. In 1870, the school moved into a new building a block closer to City Hospital, designed by Nathanial J. Bradlee and fronting on East Concord Street. The building was demolished in 1968 as part of the expansion of the BUMC. Despite its new quarters, the school continued to struggle, and when Gregory died of tuberculosis in 1872, the school faced the possibility of closing.

A merger with the nearby Massachusetts Homeopathic Hospital rescued the women's medical school. This was an era when mainstream medicine sought to professionalize itself and eliminate other healing professions. Homeopathy was a dangerous rival that had to be defeated as it was a seemingly rational construct based on the principle of "like cures like." Under this theory, a very small dose of a chemical known to cause symptoms similar to the patient's disease was administered as a cure. Today, we know this has limited scientific validity, but in the nineteenth century homeopathic physicians were renowned for their diagnostic abilities and knowledge of pharmacology. This made them popular threats to mainstream medicine.[41]

A homeopathic hospital was proposed by Israel Tisdale Talbot, an 1853 graduate of the Homeopathic Medical College in Philadelphia and editor of the New England Medical Gazette, a prominent homeopathic journal. Talbot raised money for the hospital, which opened with forty beds in what is now the Talbot Building, home to the Boston University School of Public Health. Reaction to the proposed hospital was sharp, and the Massachusetts Medical Society expelled eight homeopathic doctors, signaling an escalation in the conflict between the competing theories of medicine. This expulsion backfired when it stimulated the construction of a companion medical school devoted to homeopathy.

Meanwhile, desperate to save their school, the trustees of the Female Medical College approached Reverend Edward Everett Hale, a member of the Harvard Board of Overseers, regarding a merger. Harvard was agreeable and talks proceeded, leading to terms that included the trustees' raising $50,000. The Board also dictated that the female school be a separate entity from Harvard Medical School. But the Great Fire of 1872 ruined any chance of raising money when thirteen of sixteen trustees lost their businesses to the flames. Because Boston University was taking over Talbot's homeopathic medical college, the trustees solicited that school about a merger. This represented a significant shift in teaching from medicine to homeopathy, and some of the trustees and faculty balked. But the school was failing. The merger proceeded, and the combined school opened on November 5, 1874. The Massachusetts Memorial Hospital, eventually called University Hospital, would be merged with City Hospital and renamed Boston University Medical Center in 1995.

These were not the only medical institutions in the neighborhood. Children's Hospital was founded in 1869 at 9 Rutland Square with room for twenty patients at a time. Its founder was Dr. Francis Henry Brown, who had traveled to Europe and was so influenced by practices there that he became one of the United States' first advocates of pediatrics as a special medical discipline. The hospital, which primarily focused on broken bones, moved down the street to the corner of Washington Street and then to Huntington Avenue in 1871.[42]

It was commonplace for physicians and others involved in ministering to the public's physical needs to have their offices in the South End. This included Alexander Graham Bell, who opened his school for deaf students on West Newton Street at Blackstone Square in 1872. Reflecting his economic status and the way many physicians lived at the time, Bell both saw patients and slept in his small suite of rooms.

In 1870, on the eve of the South End housing market's collapse, the city had been grappling with its tenement problem for decades with little positive movement; many of the poor lived in absolute squalor.[3] Influenced by English efforts to create better housing for the poor, one of the earliest experiments in the United States to build low-income housing was launched in the neighborhood, a development that continues to provide quality affordable housing to this day. The initiative was led by Henry I. Bowditch, whose interest in helping the poor dates to at least the 1840s when he had been an ardent and active abolitionist. During a trip to London, he visited efforts to build model tenements and met Octavia Hill, the famous social worker and housing advocate. She had used money from John Ruskin and others to buy and renovate buildings for workers' families with methods involving "firmness and kindness". [43]

Upon returning to Boston, Bowditch organized the Boston Cooperative Building Company, whose directors included Phillips Brooks, the pastor of Trinity Church, and Robert Treat Paine, Jr., the director of Associated Charities of Massachusetts. It was funded by a $50,000 donation from the estate of Abbott Lawrence, one of the founders of the textile city that bears his name. Lawrence was a congressman and the ambassador to England, where he took interest in a group advocating for the poor and built a two-story, four-unit model tenement building in Hyde Park.[43] At first, Bowditch tried operating a model tenement downtown by taking over an existing building that was a notorious center of crime and vice,[44] but it was a failure.

In 1872, the company built ten small houses on East Canton Street that were easily rented. This time, the group was able to prohibit boarders and lodgers and screen potential tenants who had to supply references and agree to a set of rules including weekly rents paid in advance.[3] In addition, tenants could be evicted for intemperance or if sickness or job loss made it impossible for a family to continue to pay rent.[45] There was a limit to charity.

At first, the East Canton Street project consisted of thirty-nine houses spanning several blocks which contained 450 rooms rented to 150 families.[46] Eventually, four large apartment buildings were built on the street; Charles Kirby designed the first three and William Goodwin the last. The foundation operated the buildings until they were sold to a private owner in 1940. They severely deteriorated and were acquired by the city for nonpayment of taxes in 1979. They have since been rehabilitated into affordable housing and a plaque marks their historic importance.[43]

Even with incoming residents and institutions, the South End's fortunes dropped in the early 1870s. Robert Woods, the founder of South End House, blamed the development of industry south of Washington Street for the decay as much as the development of Back Bay.[47] Albert Benedict Wolfe, another South End House resident, believed that the slide of the neighborhood was imminent and noted "it is said that the first faint whisperings of impending change were first heard after the civil war."[15] Wolfe was one of the earliest to credit the Financial Panic of 1873 for the demise of the South End, noting that the financial crash caused banks to call mortgages on buildings along Columbus Avenue. Wolfe thought that these foreclosures caused defaults across the South End.

A major—if less appreciated—cause of the decline of the neighborhood may have been the Great Boston Fire of 1872, which occurred just a few months before the 1873 financial crunch. The effect on the city was calamitous, and the insurance and banking losses may have contributed to the global crisis as bankruptcies caused by the fire destabilized the country's financial system. For the South End, the fire may have been even more important because it was the home of the city's merchant class and their workers, two groups greatly harmed by the fire.

The conflagration started small but expanded rapidly, which was not surprising given the clutter of combustibles in downtown buildings. The structure where the inferno began, located at the corner of Kingston and Summer Streets, contained a dry goods store, a purveyor of hats, scarves, and other accessories, and a manufacturer of women's hoops skirts, all likely employers of South End residents. By the time it was over, more than eight hundred buildings were destroyed, and downtown Boston was devastated. The destruction stretched from Faneuil Hall to what is now South Station. "Those who had been most familiar with this section before the fire were utterly unable to find their way, and groped about, or clambered over the obstructing rock, brick, iron, and still hot rubbish, dazed and bewildered."[48]

The loss of jobs and places of employment had a tremendous impact on the working men and women of Boston. "Starvation and cold and their pathways, and bitter poverty compelled them to ask for food and work." One analysis suggested that thirty thousand women and girls were put out of work by the fire, including those employed in the needle trades, waitresses, saleswomen, and toy and doll manufacturers. Because of the fire, "an army of shop-girls was disbanded."[49] As the neighborhood of choice for these workers, the South End teetered into despair.

Many of the businessmen and merchants of the South End were ruined as well; more than 450 shoe and leather businesses, many owned by South Enders, were burned out by the fire.[50] A later analysis estimated the total value of lost buildings, businesses, and goods to be about $70 million (about $7 billion in 2010 dollars), roughly ten percent of the city's assessed value.[51] The city as a whole was substantially impoverished and the calamity reached far across the economy.[48] Within six months, the global slowdown took hold and the United States would be in recession for the next several years. The South End would not recover for a century.

2.4 BOSTON AFTER THE GREAT FIRE , 1872

The decay was relentless, stalking the neighborhood until urban renewal and gentrification changed the South End beginning around 1960.[52] For almost one hundred years, the South End would be synonymous with hardship for most other Bostonians, who would warn their children to behave lest they end up on Dover Street. It would be home to some of the country's most prominent Black leaders and a striving Black middle class, as well as a place where parents would be afraid to send their children to school. The neighborhood would attract the efforts of those concerned with the spiritual and moral condition of its residents as well as reformers who sought to create better physical conditions for tenement dwellers and lodging house residents. For the next century, the South End would stand apart: nurturing, feared, misunderstood, and despised.

1. Bond M. *A Centennial Pageant 1850-1950*. 1950.

2. Meckel RA. *Mortality, and Population Growth in Boston, 1840-1880*. The Journal of Interdisciplinary History 1985; 15:393-417.

3. Culver D. *Tenement house reform in Boston, 1846-1898*: Boston University; 1972.

4. Smith MS. *Between City and Suburb: Architecture and Planning in Boston's South End*. Providence, Rhode Island: Brown University; 1977

5. Everett E. *Letter*. To: Everett OB, 1855.

6. Bunting B. The Plan of the Back Bay Area in Boston. *The Journal of the Society of Architectural Historians* 1954; 13:19-24.

7. Seasholes NS. *Gaining Ground: A History of Landmaking in Boston*. Cambridge, Massachusetts: The MIT Press; 2003.

8. Cain LP. Raising and Watering a City: Ellis Sylvester Chesbrough and Chicago's First Sanitation System. *Technology and Culture* 1972; 13:353-72.

9. Shurtleff NB. *A Topographical and Historical Description of Boston*. Boston: City of Boston; 1871.

10. Wheeler M. *Ruskin and Environment: The Storm-cloud of the Nineteenth Century*. New York: St. Martin's Press; 1995.

11. Sammarco AM. *Boston's South End*. Dover, New Hampshire: Arcadia Publishing; 1998.
12. Everett O. *Letter*. To: Everett OB, 1851.

13. Goodman PS. *The Garden Squares of Boston*. Lebanon, New Hampshire:University Press of New England; 2003.

14. Potts L. *A Block in Time: A History of Boston's South End From a Window on Holyoke Street*. New York: Local History Publishers; 2012.

15. Wolfe AB. *The Lodging House Problem in Boston*. Cambridge, Massachusetts: Harvard University Press; 1913.

16. Boston Redevelopment Authority. *South End Environmental Assessment* 1979.

17. Neale J. The Allen House. *Newsletter of the South End Historical Society* 1989; 18:1.

18. Howley K. Old mansion returned to life. *Boston Globe* 1999 February 21.

19. Huse CP. *The Financial History of Boston from May 1, 1822, to January 31, 1909*. Cambridge, Massachusetts: Harvard University Press; 1916

20. Steven Cohen Team. *An Open Letter to South End Stakeholders*. 2014.

21. South End Historical Society. *Down Washington Street*: Visions of Past, Present, and Future. 1994.

22. Whitehill WM, Kennedy LW. *Boston: A Topographical History.* Cambridge, MA: Belnap Press of Harvard University Press; 2000.

23. Seasholes NS. *Walking Tours on Boston's Made Land.* Cambridge, Massachusetts: The MIT Press; 2006.

24. Smith MS, Moorhouse JC. Architecture and the Housing Market: Nineteenth Century Row Houses in Boston's South End. *Journal of the Society of Architectural Historians* 1993; 52:159-78.

25. Everett E. *Letter.* To: Everett OB, 1858.

26. Card RO. Boston's South End: *An Urban Walker's Handbook.* South End Historical Society. 1992.

27. Shannon HJ. *Legendary Locals of Boston's South End.* Charleston, South Carolina: Arcadia Publishing; 2014.

28. Pertronella MM. *Victorian Boston Today.* Boston: Northeastern University Press; 2004.

29. Hale RB. A Brick Block. In: Putnam JW, ed. *A Picture of the South End. Boston.* South End Historical Society; 1968.

30. Sullivan L. *The Autobiography of an Idea.* New York: Press of the American Institute of Architects, Inc.; 1924.

31. Lynch K. *Image of the City.* Cambridge MA: MIT Press; 1960.

32. Everett E. *Letter.* To: Everett OB, 1856.

33. Klein C. Strong Boy: *The Life and Times of John L. Sullivan, America's First Sports Hero.* Guilford, Connecticut: Guilford Press; 2013.

34. Sullivan JL. *Life and Reminisces of a Nineteenth Century Gladiator.* Boston: Jas. A. Hearn Company; 1892.

35. O'Connor TH. *Eminent Bostonians.* Cambridge, Massachusetts: Harvard University Press; 2002.

36. Marquard G. *The Late George Apley.* New York: Grosset and Dunlap; 1937.

37. Fodor's Travel Publications. *Fodor's Boston* New York: Random House; 2010.

38. Howells WD. *The Rise of Silas Lapham* Boston: Houghton Mifflin; 1885.

39. Bacon EM. *The Book of Boston: Fifty Years' Recollections of the New England Metropolis.* Boston: The Book of Boston Company; 1916.

40. Committee of the Hospital Staff. *A History of Boston City Hospital from its Founding until 1904.*

Boston: Boston Municipal Printing Office; 1906.

41. Haller J. *The History of American Homeopathy: The Academic Years, 1820-1935*. Binghamton, New York: The Haworth Press; 2005.

42. Huffman Z. Children's Hopital's Humble Beginnings. *Boston Courant* 2014 July 25.

43. Zaitzevsky C. Housing Boston's Poor: The First Philanthropic Experiments. *The Journal of the Society of Architectural Historians* 1983; 42:157-67.

44. Boston Co-operative Building Company. *Fourth Annual Report* 1875.

45. Boston Co-operative Building Company. *Seventeenth Annual Report* 1888.

46. Boston Co-operative Building Company. *Eighteenth Annual Report* 1889.

47. Woods RA. *The City Wilderness: A Settlement Study*. Boston: Houghton, Mifflin and Company; 1898.

48. Conwell RH. *History of the Great Fire in Boston*. Boston: B. B. Russell; 1873.

49. Howe MAD. *Boston: The Place and the People*. New York: The Macmillan Company; 1924.

50. Coffin CC. *The Story of the Great Fire, Boston, November 9-10, 1872*. Boston: Shepard and Gill; 1872.

51. Puleo S. *A City So Grand: The Rise of an American Metropolis, Boston 1850-1900*. Boston: Beacon Press; 2010.

52. Maxwell AH. The anthropology of poverty in black communities: A critique and systems alternative. *Urban Anthropology and Studies of Cultural Systems and World Economic Development* 1988; 19:171-91.

CHAPTER 3

The Age of Immigrants and Institutions: 1873-1920

E ven while the South End was a decaying and declining community, to
many it was home— "a vibrant, economically poor but culturally rich,
dynamic community."[1] Regardless, the decline did not happen all at once; it
was a slow process that took decades. For example, Robert Archey Woods'
1898 book on the South End, The City Wilderness, covers only the portion
of the neighborhood to the east of Brookline Street because relatively prosperous single-family homes still dominated the western portion of the neighborhood twenty-five years after the crash. Reports that the lodging house
district extended west to Northampton Street did not appear until 1913.

To explore the decline in the real estate market, Robert Benedict Wolfe
traced the history of fifty-three buildings on Union Park. The first lodging
house appears in 1873; there were ten in 1882, thirty-three in 1887, and forty-five in 1894.[2] These numbers suggest that though the decline of the area
north of Columbus Avenue may have begun right after the Financial Crisis of
1873, it didn't accelerate in Union Park until the mid-1880s.

Wolfe, Woods, and others stressed that the South End was not the poorest
neighborhood in Boston, nor was it the place where new immigrants chose to
settle first. For the decades prior to World War I at least, the South End was
a step up on the ladder of economic progress from gateway neighborhoods
like the North End.[3] As a result of its slightly elevated status, its demographics stood out from the rest of the city. Unlike other neighborhoods that hosted one particular race or ethnicity, the South End was a heterogeneous mix
of younger singles and immigrant families.[4] For many years, the Irish were the
largest group, making up 31 percent of the population and generally living in
single-family homes. Thirty percent of South End households included lodgers, 37 percent of whom were between the ages of twenty and twenty-nine;
27.5 percent were in their thirties. Female-headed households made up 28
percent of the total.[5] The lodging house residents tended to be native-born
Americans from the New England countryside, Canadian English, and Brit-
ish-born immigrants. Italians and Jews lived mainly in the New York Streets

area.[6]

The lodgers attracted special attention from those studying the neighborhood. The large numbers of young people living alone startled the new college graduates working in the settlement houses with many of the neighborhood's social ills blamed on this shocking and depraved way of life.[2] But for residents, the rooming houses provided vital economic and social services in the time after they left their family homes and before they got married, a period when they could live on their own before they could afford better housing. They supported a way of life that provided flexibility in an economy where work could be transient and unemployment benefits nonexistent. For this population, the South End was an accommodating landscape where the movement of people was constant. Rent increases, job loss, illness, or a family crisis could lead to a sudden change of address, but the weekly rent structure also made it easy to leave.[5]

While the rowhouses' exteriors didn't change, these lodgers nevertheless transformed the neighborhood. The original plan for the South End did not include space for commercial activities. To serve the neighborhood's working population, building owners renovated the first floors of rowhouses and apartment buildings into retail spaces, bars, cheap restaurants, and other support services—mostly located along the east-west arterials.[1] In 1913, Wolfe counted eighty-seven cafes and fifty-seven basement dining rooms. [2]

Many aspiring families sought to buy rowhouses, seeing ownership as a source of income and a sign that they had achieved a middle-class existence. For those who lacked sufficient resources, however, buying property was difficult and financially dangerous. Unlike modern-day homeowners who build up equity as they make each payment, South Enders during this time did not incrementally accrue equity or obtain clear title to their properties until completing their final payment. Furthermore, a single late installment resulted in the total loss of all payments to date and the complete forfeiture of the property. In the context of economic uncertainty, no unemployment insurance, and a volatile job market, losing everything was a constant risk.[6]

An economic downturn in the 1890s sent many residents into desperate conditions. Losing a job when there was no ability to save, given the cost of living and the prevailing wages of the era, meant starvation, an acute lack of clothing, and eviction.[7] There was no safety net and the authorities in charge of providing relief sought to weed out anyone considered chronically poor and undeserving. The Associated Charities, the city's main relief organization, wanted to help only those "who have not yet made the habit of dependence." But even in this stern context, about five hundred families received assistance at any one time, and about one sixth of all South End families were on relief at some point during a given year. Recipients had to work for assistance, and some were sent away to poor houses outside the area. Associated Charities did not directly provide relief; it acted as a gate keeper, taking applications and sending volunteers, mostly skeptical middle-class Protestant women, to check on eligibility for support. Those deemed worthy were referred to other organizations. Associated Charities also maintained records to ensure that no family received aid from more than one source.[6]

Applying for assistance was risky; deprivation was not considered sufficient grounds for relief if the family was morally suspect. Social workers repeatedly visited a tenement on Broadway, for example, noting that there was a drunk man asleep in bed during the middle of the day, and while the lady of the house, Mrs. Duffy, claimed to sew piecework, the apartment was dirty, causing the social worker to question her mothering skills The social worker acknowledged that the family needed money, but the unclean state of the children's underwear disqualified the family for charity. The mother was "too ignorant" to be worthy of help.[5]

At the end of the nineteenth century, the South End was generally safe with no one area singled out as a crime hot spot. While there were plenty of arrests for minor crimes including petty larceny and public drunkenness, the murder rate remained fairly low at a time when nationally it was quite high. There were also few burglaries because of the density of the population and the lack of anything valuable to steal.[6] However, this did not mean that outsiders viewed residents as peaceful and law abiding. Settlement house workers believed that every boy was a gang member, every gang had its street corner, the gangs were highly organized—each having between five and forty members, mostly teenage boys—and worse of all, the gangs were controlled by the Democratic machine. In reality, the gangs were fluid and informal, breaking up and reforming in response to police pressure or inner group conflict. Some members would continue to participate even if they moved out of the neighborhood, and many of the older gangs held dances, attracting "factory girls, nearly all of them are bold and vulgar."[6]

Environmental conditions in the neighborhood were grim, with single-family houses now sheltering as many as six to eight households.[3] Tenement rentals usually had three rooms but could have as many as six. They were almost always poorly maintained and often dismal. In one, "the kitchen is a twelve by fifteen room, lighted by a single window which overlook[ed] a five by eight back yard, odorous of the garbage barrel."[8] Newly arrived from Russia, Mary Antin described her living conditions on Dover Street: "Our new home consisted of five small rooms up two flights of stair, with the right of way through the dark corridors. In the 'parlor' the dingy paper hung in rags and the plaster fell in chunks. One of the bedrooms was absolutely dark and air-tight. The kitchen windows looked out on a dirty court."[9] Many lodging houses and tenements housed fifteen to thirty people at a time with but one toilet and no bathing facilities.[10]

There was a large variety of residential establishments, serving everyone from the genteel young away from middle class homes for the first time to the sick and poor of all ages. The quality of some of the houses was particularly desperate, with hot water scarce, towels dear, and the general appearance of the bathroom grubby from overuse. It was the custom to supply hot water only on Saturday or Sunday and to turn it off altogether in the summer. Many of the smaller houses had no bathrooms at all.[2] Personal cleanliness was difficult, and some buildings were described as "squalid and filthy to the extreme."[11] The South End House estimated that 25 percent of the neighborhood lived in "positively objectionable sanitary conditions."[12]

Outside circumstances were not much better. "In the street were apple cores, decayed peaches and tomatoes, cabbage stalks and corn husks, slices of fly-blackened watermelon, fishes' heads, a dead rat, broken bottles, dented tin dishes, rusty iron hoops, pasteboard boxes, crumpled newspapers, an un-wound broom-head, a piece of carpet, a leg of a chair, a wrinkled show-bill, a decrepit umbrella, a ragged black stocking, a lacerated section of window curtain, and a dismantled mop."[8] Antin wrote that "nothing less than a fire or flood would cleanse" Harrison Avenue.[9]

Over time, some reformers began to make large distinctions between the more genteel establishments that served middle-class customers and the plainer houses that rented to the poor and laboring classes. The middle-class reformers found the latter to be a particular moral evil. The settlement workers believed the lack of dining services in the lesser off houses to be a major problem. The establishments that catered to better off residents provided formal sit-down meals, and settlement workers thought that the proprietors and the meals helped socialize residents with middle-class values (clearly confusing cause and effect). But the lodging houses (also called rooming houses) only provided sleeping accommodations, forcing residents to take their meals in diners and bars. Reformers thought this exposed the residents to vice, crime, and moral degeneracy. This distinction placed the social workers at odds with many proprietors because not providing meals made establishments cheaper to operate.[13] Not serving meals also alleviated the need to set aside a dining room, allowing for additional rental income and reducing the need for kitchen facilities.

Some thought all rooming houses were suspect. Wolfe believed that the practice of men and women living next to each other led to prostitution and other crimes. He found much to dislike about lodging house residents and claimed they were socially isolated, lonely, and—most problematic—they were constantly entertaining members of the opposite sex in their rooms. The drinking and pairing up was distasteful to him; he preferred that residents socialize with each other in parlors. Trying to explain this lifestyle, Wolfe was scornful of the lodgers and complained that "both men and women come to value the pseudo-Bohemianism and the artificial excitements of city life."[2]

For many working-class households, running lodging houses, or at least renting out spare rooms, was an economic necessity. The rents helped pay mortgages and monetized women's housework, supplementing incomes, providing assistance for widows, and helping smooth over cyclical finances. It was a durable system that lasted for almost a century. It was only political, economic, and social changes in the mid-twentieth century that ended the era of lodging houses.

An entire industry developed as real estate brokers bought up buildings, reconfigured them as lodging houses, and sold them to operators. With forty real estate offices specializing in the purchase, sale, and rental of lodging houses, buildings were frequently transferred "whole" including furniture and tenants. Realtors used contract selling, requiring only a small down payment, but interest rates could be as high as 1.5 percent a month. Weekly payments were required, and every fee and expense was put on the buyer. Dealers were adept at using tricks, such as fake lodgers and unmentioned expenses, to cheat landladies, and as mortgages were paid down, the temptation to force a default increased. As a result, landladies were in a very precarious position; any setback could cause a default. If the boiler quit working, for example, tenants would leave, her income would drop, and with no money for repairs, she could end up losing her house and all her equity to the agent. Because the contracts stipulated that everything in a house would be forfeited in a default, landladies could lose all their personal possessions, including wedding rings. Sometimes lodgers would return home from work and find their trunks and clothes seized as part of a foreclosure.[2]

Despite these problems, some landladies were very successful and operated two or more houses; a few operated as many as eight. But many failed, turnover was high, and many were exploited or swindled by owners or agents. Economic pressures often led to skimping on upkeep or lowering the quality of tenants.[2] The result of these compromises was deferred maintenance and a slow deterioration of the quality of the neighborhood's housing market over the years.

"It has long been my desire, in common with many of the alumni and friends of the Seminary, to see the establishment in Boston of an Andover House, devoted to the special ends of Social Christianity"[14] With this call to service, Andover Theology Seminary's William Jewett Tucker launched what would become one of the South End's most enduring and important institutions, the South End House. The response to Tucker's call was enthusiastic, indicative of the level of desire among young, idealistic college-educated men and women of this era to help the people in the South End.[3] What was initially called the Andover House Association was Boston's first settlement house and only the fourth in the United States. It was organized on October 19, 1891 with one hundred members, and within a year, membership had grown to three hundred. First located at 6 Rollins Street and offering rooms for residents, household servants, and four rooms for general purposes, it was meant to be a home, not an institution, with its residents living as part of the neighborhood.[15] Andover House was renamed South End House in 1895 and merged into United South End Settlements (USES) sixty years later. Within a few years of its founding, the settlement house moved to Union Park where it would be a major presence until it relocated to the Harriet Tubman House in 1971.

There were other settlement houses in the South End that had similarly modest beginnings and ambitious goals. Four young women volunteering to look after the children of men attending a temperance meeting would establish Lincoln House, later merged into USES.[16] In 1895, Dr. Edward Everett Hale enlisted several young men to take up residence in a house near the former location of his church on Union Park Street. Eventually named Hale House, in 1908 it became strongly associated with the Theodore Parker Memorial and moved its operations to the building at the corner of Berkeley and Appleton Streets.[16] It, too, merged into USES.

The settlement house movement resulted from concerns about the social and living conditions of the poor and the belief that the educated elite could materially, socially, and morally impact the mass of immigrants moving to cities. By example and education, settlement residents (mostly well-off whites) would restore proper American social norms to the hegemony they once enjoyed. The founders "believed immigration and industrialization had destroyed the city's ethnic and cultural homogeneity, had sharply divided the city into hostile classes, and had increased the likelihood of violent economic and ethnic conflict."[17] In response to this crisis, the settlements sought to reunite cities by encouraging everyone to adopt upper-class Protestant values.

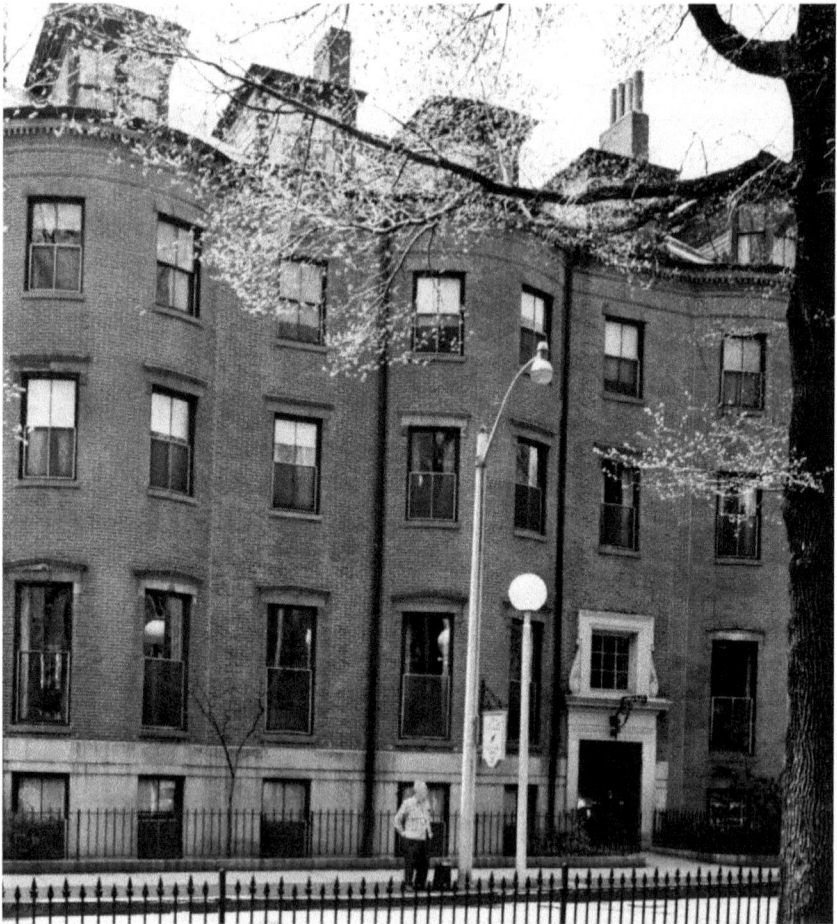

3.1 THE SOUTH END HOUSE IN 1974

US reformers had been inspired by the English settlement house movement. In 1867, Edward Denison, just out of Oxford, moved to London's
East End to address its tremendous poverty and social ills, saying it was the
obligation of England's college-educated elite to advocate for housing and
environmental reforms. Denison died young. But he influenced another
young man, Arnold Toynbee, to pick up the advocacy banner, and then Samuel Barnett established the university settlement house that came to be called
Toynbee Hall. By creating a clublike atmosphere where the privileged and the
poor could meet, his aim was to reduce the class inequities he thought were
driving poverty in Victorian England. Oxford students, who were disappointed in traditional charity and relief organization, enthusiastically welcomed

the project, and it attracted visits from Americans including Woods and Jane Addams.[3]

The South End House was home to a series of clubs in which more than one hundred boys and young men participated. They were divided into groups with two residents assigned to each to get to know them on a personal basis. There were no formal programs, though each group was encouraged to meet at the house one night a week. A typical gathering would begin with games, then readings, and "usually the evening ended with the singing of college songs."[15] Girls' club evenings usually began with sewing and ended with games. The house had a lending library and a savings bank and hosted public lectures and musical performances by students from the nearby New England Conservatory of Music.[15] The original idea was to have only volunteers staff the settlement, but founders soon realized they needed to pay senior management and provide stipends and scholarships to the line staff. There were four to seven men in residence at any given time who stayed for an average of eight months.[18] Each settlement house worker took a personal interest in a particular group of families, visiting them in their homes to gauge the families' needs and status without using the formal methods of social workers. Staff went to an average of seventy homes per week in what they called "friendly visits."[3]

The settlement houses had few, if any, neighborhood representatives working or managing them. Of the council that oversaw the South End House, only Woods and William Cole lived in the neighborhood (both in the house itself), while eight gave downtown business addresses, three had suburban addresses, and one person listed a New Hampshire address.[19] Similarly, only six out of three hundred members of the Association, each of whom contributed at least three dollars to the house, lived in the South End; a substantial number lived outside of Boston, and one resided in Japan. [20]

The outcomes of the day-to-day interactions between staff and neighborhood people—buying food, observing entertainment, walking the streets, and so forth—were mixed as there was culture shock when college-educated young people visited poor immigrant families. Many of these young men and women had never seen the conditions in cold water tenements where there were no servants to maintain cleanliness.[3] Settlement workers often exhibited disturbing prejudice and sometimes made sweeping generalizations about different ethnic groups including their work habits, personal morality, and the propensity to commit crimes.[6]

Despite sometimes abrasive exchanges, many immigrants found participating in settlement house programs to be a life-changing experience, setting them up for all the wonderful opportunities their new country had to offer. Mary Antin, for example, believed that attending clubs and activities at Hale House provided her access to the education and personal growth she could not have had if she had stayed in Russia. Antin authored a book, The Promised Land, as an ode to assimilation and the opportunities in the New World. In it, she described life in Russia as constricted by anti-Semitism and strong constraints on women and detailed how the United States gave her the opportunity to go to school and become an author.[21] She believed attending Hale House activities gave her a chance at a better life, and she enjoyed the libraries, classes, and other opportunities that were open to her.[22]

For several decades, the South End House was run by Robert Woods, one of the neighborhood's strongest advocates of any era. Born in Pennsylvania into a family of devout Presbyterians, Woods left for Amherst College when he was sixteen years old. After graduating, he attended Andover Seminary where he took courses in constitutional history, political economy and social- ism, and Biblical theology.[3] Woods would be the public face of the neighbor- hood until his death at the age of fifty-nine in 1925.

The City Wilderness, the 1898 book that Woods and his fellow South End House residents wrote about the neighborhood, was one of the major influences on how outsiders viewed the South End. The book was an import- ant social document of its time and helped humanize what many thought was a frightening neighborhood of godless immigrants and unsupervised young people. But the title also became a shorthand way to denigrate the South End. If the neighborhood was a wilderness, then its people were savages, and its landscape needed to be cleared for civilization.[23] The South End's reputation would take decades and large-scale urban renewal to recover, and the book would help seal the fate of the neighborhood fifty years later.

The South End had become synonymous with vice. Its lodging houses, brothels, dance halls, and barrooms suggested the neighborhood was a "mor- al no-man's land." Bostonians of this era didn't just deem the women in cafes, theaters, and other working-class establishments to be wicked; they suspected any woman employed in a dress shop, department store, grocery, factory, and other non-residential places where these women worked or gathered to be a den of iniquity. Because these places were situated throughout the South End, they contributed to critics painting the district to be foul and evil.[5]

Woods thought the neighborhood was a moral wilderness but also con- sidered it to be a community of promise where enterprising Protestant mis- sionaries could rescue the souls of the deserving poor. It was a place of opportunity for Christian evangelization and a fertile terrain for the estab- lishment of a white Protestant centered civilization. The disconnect between middle-class social mores and South End living conditions and social arrangements helped Woods to consider the area a dark, corrupt place. To him and other settlement workers, the working women and men of the South End were less civilized than the affluent Protestant boys and girls from Harvard, Wellesley, and other prestigious colleges coming to rescue the neighborhood. The South End was not the only territory described as a wilderness in this era. Woods' attitude paralleled the chauvinistic ideology used by other white Protestant men to justify European colonization in Africa, imperialism in South America, and exploitation in Asia. This perspective framed the treatment of non-white people around the globe.

Interestingly, the educated women, many of whom held views similar to Woods, who went to work in the settlement houses to transmit traditional values to the poor were themselves breaking loose from the mainstream social mores of their time because they were independent wage earners living apart from family. They may have sought to impose strong conventionality on their tenement neighbors, but for themselves, living in a settlement house was liberating. "They changed the recipe of possibilities and even the urban infrastructure of schools and services, laws and landscapes, for themselves and for the men in the city."[5]

One example of the energy and ambition of these women is Vida Scudder of Denison House. She grew up in the Back Bay, attended Girls Latin, and studied at Oxford, where she became familiar with Toynbee Hall.[3] Denison House was one of a group of settlements founded in New York, Philadelphia, and Boston by women from Wellesley, Smith, Vassar, and other women's colleges under the auspices of the College Settlements Associations. Residents paid board, worked for a minimum of four hours a day, and performed housekeeping services while a paid director managed the house. Though she was Denison House's administrator for twenty years, Scudder herself mostly lived in Wellesley where she was a professor.[3] Working in the tenement districts among the poor satisfied her intense personal need to remedy the ills of the turn of the century industrial system.[24]

The founding of Denison House was the direct result of a network of lesbian relationships based at Wellesley College. Scudder had a passionate, romantic, intellectual, and spiritual relationship with fellow Wellesley professor Florence Converse, who was another Wellesley graduate, social activist, and woman of letters. Their activism also helped connect Katherine Lee Bates, the poet and author of the words to "America the Beautiful," to her lover, Katharine Coman, the dean of Wellesley College. Denison House grew out of discussions between Coman, Bates, and Scudder. When the three conceived of the idea of the College Settlement Association in 1890, it was Coman who found a sponsor in her friend Cornelia Warren, a member of the well-known Beacon Hill family.[25] Dennison House moved to Dorchester in 1942. Today, it is remembered as the place where Khalil Gibran met people who encouraged his poetry skills, and for its employment of Amelia Earhart shortly before she achieved global fame as the first woman to cross the Atlantic in an airplane.

The settlements never attracted more than a fraction of the neighborhood. The Catholic Church distrusted them and warned parishioners against their aggressive Protestant perspective.[17] Not surprisingly, the local parish priest discouraged Denison House from contacting his families.[3] Hale House had a large Jewish presence, while South End House tended to serve less religious Jews who were not concerned with the Christian focus of the institution.[6] Many of the working-class targets of the houses were suspicious of the middle-class Protestant settlement workers. They ignored the workers' overtures out of fear of being morally judged or being turned in to social workers and others policing the neighborhood. The settlement workers offered assistance at the price of outside scrutiny while many families wanted independence and dignity.[5] Nor did the houses, with their emphasis on personal responsibility, ever directly address the root causes of poverty: discrimination, poor wages, and other systemic issues.

World War I split the national settlement movement between pro-war leaders like Woods and peace advocates such as Addams. After the war, settlement houses declined as government and other charities began to provide similar services. In the 1920s, funders in Boston, as elsewhere, consolidated philanthropy and social service organizations into large networks so they could control the flow of money into local agencies. As the settlement houses traded independence for financial stability, pressure from the philanthropists who controlled the purse strings diminished any social justice components of settlement house programming. In addition, the houses shifted away from using volunteer, amateur, and untrained college students to deliver services towards paid professional social workers who did not want to live in poor neighborhoods. In the South End, there was the additional issue of racial change as the movement of young white Protestants into the neighborhood from rural New England ebbed; settlements found it difficult to work with Black residents who were now flocking into the lodging houses.[3] As will be seen, the South End's remaining settlement houses would merge and adopt a new model of social service provision under the pressure of the urban renewal.

The original goal of developing the South End was to preserve the city's native Protestant majority, but that quickly failed as they became a permanent minority. By the 1870s, the Irish were on their way to dominating the city's politics. Boston's first Irish mayor was Hugh O'Brien, who managed to bridge the gap between his fellow immigrants and the Brahmin aristocracy. Serving from 1885 to 1889, he had been born in Ireland but was not seen as a threat to the Yankee Protestant establishment that approved of his parsimonious administration.

In 1895, Josiah Quincy, scion of two earlier Quincys who had served as mayor, was elected to the office. A coalition builder, Quincy succeeded in attracting the support of organized labor, immigrants, and even Woods, who became the Commissioner of Public Baths in Quincy's administration.[26] But as the Irish grew more powerful after the turn of the century, their need to cooperate with the Brahmins declined, and they consolidated their control over the political life of the city, putting further pressure on the settlement houses.

As a group, the settlement house workers were dismayed by the politics of the South End. As opponents of the Irish Democratic machine, they believed the political structure of the neighborhood contributed to its moral poverty.[6] Therefore, settlement workers tended to support reform candidates and oppose Irish and ethnic-based politicians, pitting them against their neighbors. In 1905, for example, Woods worked to defeat John "Honey Fitz" Fitzgerald, an American-born Irishman and grandfather of President John Fitzgerald Kennedy, who captured the imagination of working-class Bostonians.[27] Five years later, South End settlement house leaders launched an even larger campaign in support of mayoral candidate James J. Storrow who represented the Protestant establishment's efforts to reform city government.[28] Storrow had impeccable Yankee credentials: Harvard, banking, philanthropy, and he had been instrumental in creating the Esplanade along the Charles River. Nevertheless, he was narrowly defeated by Fitzgerald's emotional ethnic campaigning.[29] Fitzgerald's victory disillusioned settlement house workers. Afterwards, Woods decided it was better to cooperate with the ward bosses than to try to defeat them. He moved away from politics and began to work with local leadership; together they secured city support for a number of vital services.

The growing city needed modern facilities, several of which were in the South End. One of the more significant buildings was the jointly housed Boston Latin School and English High School, occupying the block behind the Clarendon Street Baptist Church. "The structure is of brick with sandstone trimmings, and exterior ornamentation, from designs of T. H. Bartlett, the sculptor, consisting mainly of terra-cotta heads in the gables of the dormer windows and terra-cotta frieze courses."[30] Comprised of three sections, the facility was large enough for a drill hall, libraries, and an amphitheater. Its two schools had separate entrances: the Latin School on Warren Avenue and English High School on Montgomery Street. Long ago demolished, the McKinley School now occupies the site.

The city opened its Girls High School on West Newton Street in 1870. To its students, the school was both fascinating and scary as "pleasing terrors, like those excited by ghost stories, hung about certain corners and pervaded the cellars. Low ceilings, blind turnings, disused stairways, mysterious trapdoors, tempted the adventurous."[31] The O'Day playground now occupies the site.

There were also several private institutions constructed in the neighborhood including the Working Girls Home near Harrison Avenue which provided Irish Catholic women laboring in factories or in private homes with a safe place where they could learn job skills and socialize. The nearby Catholic Union included a library, billiard room, and a bowling alley.[32] Other important institutions were the Home for Little Wanderers, the Boston Female Asylum, the St. Vincent Orphan Asylum, the Home for Aged Men, and the Wells Memorial Workingman's Club.[33]

Given the lack of bathrooms in many tenements and lodging houses, the public bath house on Dover Street was especially important to the neighborhood. After much lobbying by Woods and others to the city, the bath house was built and became the pride of the neighborhood. "The building is simple and substantially constructed of brick with stone trimming. The interior is a scheme of marble and mosaic, the partitions, stairways, and walls all being constructed of durable stone. The best equipment in Gegenstrom sprays, open plumbing, and nickel-plated trimmings has been installed." More than two hundred thousand people used the facility each month.[34]

A visitor took a number, waited to be called, then was issued soap and a towel. Baths lasted a specified time and were calibrated to use a predetermined amount of water, which was hardly warmer than tepid; the maximum temperature was set at 73 to discourage lingering.[35] The building was demolished in the 1960s after a controversy regarding whether the long-closed building should be used as a shelter for men with alcohol problems.

One group that left a lasting architectural legacy in the South End was the First Corp of Cadets, who built their armory at the corner of Arlington Street and Columbus Avenue in the 1890s. The First Corp traced its history back to 1726, when it provided an escort to the Royal Governor of Massachusetts. Primarily a social organization, it was made up of men from the most prominent families in the state; one early commander was John Hancock.

The cadets arrayed themselves in lavish uniforms provided at their own expense and held drills on Boston Common. In response to the threat of immigration and the need for more formal meeting places than the taverns they were using, the Corps decided to construct a permanent headquarters and armory. Corps members believed that if the city's Irish immigrants were to rise in riot and mob violence, it would be up to them to help restore order. Thus, the prejudices of the era would lead to the construction of one of the neighborhood's iconic buildings.

3.2 THE SOUTH END ARMORY

William Gibbons Preston designed the armory.[36] Two hundred feet long with a six-story head house, the structure was built for defense against the Irish with massive stone walls, thick wooden shutters and doors, and a draw-bridge over a moat-like surrounding. To raise money for the building, the Corps held a series of theatrical performances and minstrel shows, as many of its members had been part of the Hasty Pudding club at Harvard. In keep-ing with the tradition of Harvard shows, men dressed in drag to perform the female roles.[37] Though the Corps assisted in the Boston police strike twenty years later, it was never called upon to suppress an Irish rebellion, and eventually the armory was abandoned. It now houses a restaurant in its basement with the upstairs is used for special events. In keeping with its theatrical roots, the Boston Lyric Opera used the armory for special productions in 2010 and 2013.

The South End continued to be a major center for medicine, though care in this era was often ineffective. But because of extreme overcrowding of the poor, it was vital to build places where sick people could recuperate. So to enhance its role in protecting the public's health, Boston City Hospital was granted powers of eminent domain by the legislature in 1889. Two years later, the hospital expanded and eliminated East Springfield Street between Harrison Avenue and Albany Street. Over time, the campus added buildings for pathology, morgues, libraries, chapels, laundries, and other services. In the summertime, male patients were often housed in tents, which were lined with wooden floors to prevent moisture penetration and carefully tied down to shelter patients from wind and rain.[38]

The standards for disease control were in flux. By the 1890s, Louis Pasteur's revolutionary ideas that germs caused disease were being rapidly adopted, prompting Boston City Hospital to tear out older, wood-paneled surgical units to prevent infections. But at the same time, the number of seats in the hospital's new surgical amphitheater was expanded to 174. Though there were two adjoining sets of bowls for washing and sterilizing instruments, there was also seating for twenty visiting medical personnel next to the operating table, providing tremendous opportunities for infection. Yet the staff blamed sewer gas from the Roxbury canal for the high rates of hospital acquired disease.[38]

There were other medical institutions in the South End. Waltham Street had a home for alcoholic men with thirty beds. St. Elizabeth's Hospital was founded in 1868 at 28 Hanson Street. It moved to Waltham Street, then to 61 West Brookline where it had one hundred beds. Finally, it relocated to Brighton in 1914.[40] At 3 Worcester Square was Boothby Surgical Hospital, a private facility.[41] In 1908, Dr. Cornelius Garland opened the Plymouth Hospital, the city's only medical facility owned and operated by African Americans, on East Springfield Street. "Like many small hospitals in the area, such as Children's and Deaconess, which had started nearby, also in row houses, the operating room was on the top floor to benefit from the light, which meant staff had to cart patients up the stairs. House calls were made by horse and carriage."[42] Though it faced opposition from within the Black community (some advocated for integration over the establishment of independent institutions) as well as hostility from whites, the facility survived until 1928.

The southern third of the neighborhood below Washington Street was a major center for industries using lumber, coal, and other materials transported by barge to the Albany Street docks. In 1902, there were eleven piano and organ factories, forty-four woodworking companies, sixteen metal working establishments, nine laundries, and thirty-eight other types of establishments for a total of 118 in the district. Collectively they employed more than two thousand people including seven hundred in the piano industry with about a third of the workforce living nearby. There was a broad range of incomes with the piano companies rarely paying less than ten dollars per week. Some skilled workers earned more than thirty dollars per week while laundry workers, mostly white women and Chinese men, earned as little as $3.50 per week.[43]

Women had severely restricted employment opportunities, mostly working as domestics, laundry workers, or in the needle trades. Another source of income for women was owning or operating small businesses that served the neighborhood; many sold alcohol in the small diners and kitchens they operated. In the eyes of the middle-class women at Denison House, these establishments were hardly distinguishable from saloons, but they provided income to their proprietors and places where women could gather to socialize and create connections to help them navigate an often-hostile city.[5] Most neighborhood men worked as laborers, in factories, for the railroads, or at the docks. A few were in more skilled professions and worked as clerks and low-ranking employees downtown.

The South End was most famous for its piano factories. At peak production, the Chickering Company on Tremont Street built four thousand pianos a year, Hallet and Davis on Harrison Avenue had a capacity of 2,500 pianos annually, and Vose and Sons at Washington and Waltham Streets produced four thousand per year.[44] The Emerson Piano Factory produced 7,500 pianos annually.[45]

With the invention of the record player and changing tastes, the public turned away from owning pianos. So many brands went out of business in the years around 1930 that it has been called the "Great Extinction." Many of the companies that were once based in the South End merged into what became the Aeolian Piano Company, and afterwards, many brands were discontinued or heavily reduced in quality.[46] By midcentury, there were no more piano makers left in the neighborhood

There are a few legacies from the piano era. A faded painted sign for Emerson Piano's Chicago showroom graces the mill complex at 560 Harrison Avenue. The former Chickering facility on Tremont Street is now a large housing complex for artists, and many of the surviving piano factory buildings have been converted to upscale housing.

Another landmark from the South End's Industrial Era is the old Boston Elevated Railway Company Powerhouse on Harrison Avenue, designed by William G. Preston. When it opened in 1892, it was one of the largest power plants in the world with a capacity of fourteen thousand kilowatts that supplied electricity for trolleys across the city. The plant closed in 1911 when the city converted the trolley system to alternating power.[40] The building has been restored for event space and the SOWA Open Market.

3.3 INTERIOR, CHICKERING PIANO FACTORY

In addition to bringing jobs to the area, these industries posed a fire danger. A building at Bristol and Albany Streets, which housed piano manufacturers, veneer finishes, sewing machine storage, and other businesses, burned in 1890.[47] Nearby, at the corner of Sharon and Albany Streets, a spectacular blaze destroyed a building that was home to several woodworking companies in 1891. Firefighters had such a tough time controlling it that at one point, they feared for the nearby rowhouses on East Brookline Street and the city stables on Albany Street. The fire had so unnerved the fire department that afterwards the firefighters called the whole area a dangerous district.[48] A fire in an Albany Street lumber yard in 1899 almost destroyed the Dover Street bridge when a burning shed floated down Fort Point Channel.[49] A 1910 fire destroyed twenty buildings, burned nine acres, and at one point threatened the headquarters of the fire department itself.[50]

On the other side of the neighborhood, a fire destroyed the South End Grounds on May 15, 1894. The park was the home field of the Boston Red Stockings—not to be confused with the Red Sox—baseball team that eventually became the Atlanta Braves. They played there from 1871 to 1914 in three different stadiums before moving to Commonwealth Avenue. A spectator started the fire when he dropped a cigarette into piles of rubbish below the stands during a game. The blaze caused a commotion in the stands as fans began to jump out of the bleachers to get away from the smoke and flames. Boston's right fielder ran over to try to stomp it out while a policeman kept others away, hoping to extinguish the fire himself. But a lack of water, a stiff wind, and the mass of trash proved too much, and, in less than forty-five minutes, the ballpark burned to the ground. The fire jumped to the surrounding residential blocks and destroyed wooden tenements on Cunard, Walpole, Coventry, and Burke Streets. Altogether, twelve acres burned and 1,900 people were left homeless. A school and firehouse went up in flames as well.[51]

In the 1870s, Robert Treat Paine led a new effort to build affordable housing for working people in the extreme northwest corner of the South End. Like many of his patrician peers who were involved in charities and social welfare, Paine was openly distrustful of the poor and prone to blame them for their poverty. At the same time, he also acknowledged the inequality of the era and suggested that the ultimate way to improve the lives of the poor was through higher wages.[52,53] He combined stern theories regarding public assistance with an astute understanding of the causes and consequences of poverty.

The project created several blocks of modest single family row houses near Tremont Street. Paine acquired the properties in 1874, but it would take him twelve years to build its two hundred units. Each cost $2,500, and families needed a down payment of $1,000 to receive a mortgage from Paine's organization at 5 percent for five years. In keeping with the neighborhood's demographics, buyers were clerks, laborers, grocers, and other unskilled workers.[54] Paine subdivided the lots, and his architect, George W. Pope, designed two houses per lot, separated by a rear alley. Typically, the first floor had a front parlor and a rear dining room with two bedrooms and a central bathroom upstairs. There were skylights and transoms to bring in light, and the kitchens were in the basement, opening into a small garden.[55] Many of the houses have been lost to renewal and other land takings but seventy-seven remain. Mayor James Curley renamed the area Frederick Douglas Square on February 14, 1917 to honor the centenary of the abolitionist's birth. The square would be the setting for a number of outdoor addresses over the next century by famous people including Coretta Scott King, Duke Ellington, Dinah Washington, and Senators Edward Brooke and Edward Kennedy. William Monroe Trotter's newspaper offices were at 977 Tremont Street.[56]

The South End was a major center of labor activism in the late nineteenth century as three-fourths of trade unions in the city, about one hundred, were headquartered or met in the neighborhood. Woods and the other settlement house leaders approved of unions, since they considered membership a sign that a family had proper middle-class values with an emphasis on self-improvement.[6] At times, settlement workers would intervene in labor issues. At the request of the union, for example, the South End House arbitrated an end to a steamfitters strike.[11]

One of the more prominent South End labor leaders was Mary Kenney, who was born in Hannibal, Missouri in 1864. Kenney completed the fourth grade and then entered the workforce when her father died. She tried dressmaking, then went to work as a bookbinder, first in Hannibal and eventually in Chicago. There she was confronted by sexist pay scales where women earned seven dollars per week to a man's twenty-one dollars for the same job, and her experiences led her to labor organizing. These efforts caught the attention of Hull House, and—through Jane Addams—she met Samuel Gompers, president of the American Federation of Labor (AFL). Impressed by her intelligence and energy, Gompers asked her to go to Massachusetts to organize female workers.

Once she arrived in Boston, Kenney met John F. O'Sullivan. Born in Charlestown, he was both a labor leader and a reporter, a combination that led to his being hired by the Boston Globe in 1891 to cover the city's growing union movement. The intelligent, handsome O'Sullivan and the smart, attractive Kenney fell in love immediately. Even so, she returned to Chicago to work with garment workers and be closer to her mother. When the governor of Illinois appointed Florence Kelley chief factory inspector in 1893, a landmark event in labor history, Kelley recruited Kenney to be her deputy.

The romance between the Kenney and O'Sullivan captured the imagination of the women of Denison House; it combined social activism with profound affection. Kenney finally married O'Sullivan in a civil ceremony in New York City in 1894 with Gompers as a witness. Back in Boston, a dinner in their honor was held at Denison House with Woods in attendance.[57] In one of their first actions as a married couple, they worked to support silk weavers in a Newton strike, winning the dispute in two weeks. The couple next turned to the garment industry, where a strike had been going on for months. They were again successful, and the union soon had almost a thousand members.[32]

The couple's house in the South End became a gathering place for labor activists and other progressives, including Louis Brandeis, who was making his transition from corporate lawyer to social progressive. Kenney later related that she had worked long and hard to nurture his sense of social justice.[32]

She seemed unstoppable. For example, when Kenney was in the hospital after giving birth during the 1895 garment workers' strike, worker committee representatives met with her doctor to communicate with her.

The couple suffered personal tragedies when their first born died of diphtheria and their house on Carver Street burned down. They were too poor to hire servants, and the demands of running a household and Kenney's additional pregnancies limited her ability to contribute to the labor movement. Then in September 1902, O'Sullivan was killed in a streetcar accident, leaving behind Kenney and their three children, the oldest of whom was just four years old. Kenney used the funds donated by friends and supporters to move her family to the suburbs where she continued to be an important labor leader, supporting causes across Massachusetts and contributing to the national effort to unionize women.[57] In 1996, The Massachusetts State House recognized Kenney's contributions by installing a plaque in her honor outside Doric Hall.

By the early years of the twentieth century, much of what the South End is today was in place. It was a neighborhood with institutions that demonstrated their founders' commitment to social justice and a community that welcomed those who were unconventional or uninterested in social norms. Though the wealthy had abandoned it, the poor and working people of the community found ways to optimize their meager incomes and maximize their ability to live independently in the face of daunting adversity. The always unstable demographics, however, were about to change once again.

1. South End Study Committee. *Report of the South End Study Committee on the potential designation of the South End in part as a Landmarks District*. Boston; 1983.

2. Wolfe AB. *The Lodging House Problem in Boston*. Cambridge, Massachusetts: Harvard University Press; 1913.

3. Streiff M. *Boston's Settlement Housing: Social Reform in an Industrial City*. Louisiana State University; 2005.

4. South End House Association. *Seventh Yearly Report*. 1899.

5. Deutsch S. *Women and the City: Gender, Space and Power in Boston 1870-1940*. New York: Oxford University Press; 2000.

6. Woods RA. *The City Wilderness: A Settlement Study*. Boston: Houghton, Mifflin and Company; 1898.

7. Distress. Distress At South End: Many Deserving People in Need, Says Rev W. S. Kelsev.

Boston Globe, 1896 December 27.

8. Sanborn AF. *Moody's Lodging House, and Other Tenement Sketches*. Boston: Copeland and Day; 1895.

9. Antin M. *The Promised Land*. Boston: Houghton Mifflin; 1912.

10. Tayvon JS. *Neighborhood-based Services for the Poor: Re-examining Morgan Memorial and the Settlement House Movement*. Cambridge, Massachusetts: Massachusetts Institute of Technology; 1993.

11. South End House Association. *Fifth Yearly Report of the Settlement*. 1896.

12. South End House Association. *Eighth Annual Report* 1900.

13. Peel M. On the margins: Lodgers and boarders in Boston, 1860-1900. *The Journal of American History* 1986; 72:813-34.

14. Tucker WJ. *Letter*. 1891.

15. Andover House Association. *Report of the Work of the House at the End of the First Official Year*. 1892.

16. Boer A. *The Development of USES: A Chronology of the United South End Settlements 1891-1966*. Boston: United South End Settlements; 1966.

17. Shapiro ES. Robert A. Woods and the settlement house impulse. *Social Service Review* 1978; 52: 215-26.

18. Woods RA. University settlements: Their point and drift. *The Quarterly Journal of Economics* 1899; 14:67-86.

19. South End House. *South End House: A University Settlement, 1892-1899*. Boston; 1900.

20. South End House Association. *Fourth Yearly Report of the Settlement*. 1895.

21. Antin M. *From Plotzk to Boston*. New York: Press of Philip Cohen; 1899.

22. Tuerk R. The youngest of America's children in "The Promised Land". *Studies in American Jewish Literature* 1986; 5:29-67.

23. Lloyd WJ. Understanding late nineteenth-century American cities. *Geographical Review* 1981; 71:460-71.

24. Scudder V. *A Listener in Babel*. Boston: Houghton Mifflin and Company; 1903.

25. Schwartz J. Yellow Clover: Katherine Lee Bates and Katherine Coman. *Frontiers* 1979; 4:59-67.

26. Blodgett GT. Josiah Quincy, Brahmin Democrat. *The New England Quarterly* 1965; 38:435-53.

27. South End House Association. *Fourteenth Annual Report*. 1906..

28. Davis AF. Settlement workers in politics, 1890-1914. *The Review of Politics* 1964; 26:505-17.

29. Burns CK. The Irony of Progressive Reform, 1898-1910. In: Formisano R, Burns CK, eds. *Boston 1700-1980: The Evolution of Urban Politics*. Westport, Connecticut: Greenwood Press; 1984.

30. Bacon E. *Boston Illustrated*. Boston: Houghton, Mifflin Company; 1886.

31. Woods LR. *A History of the Girls' High School of Boston, 1852-1902*. Boston: Riverside Press; 1904.

32. Ryan DP. *Beyond the Ballot Box: A Soical History of the Boston Irish 1845-1917* Rutherford, New Jersey: Fairleigh Dickinson University Press; 1983.

33. G.W. Bromley & Co. *Atlas of the City of Boston, Boston Proper and Back Bay, from Actual Surveys and Official Plans*. 1902.
34. Stewart JA. Boston's experience with municipal baths. *American Journal of Sociology* 1901; 7:416-22.

35. Glassberg D. The design of reform: The public bathhouse movement in America. *American Studies* 1979; 20:5-21.

36. National Register of Historic Places - *Nomination Form. First Corps of Cadets Armory*. 1973.

37. Barnet A. *Extravaganza King: Robert Barnet and Boston Musical Theater*. Boston: Northeastern University Press; 2004.

57. Nutter KB. *'The Necessity of Organization': Mary Kenney O'Sullivan, the American Federation of Labor, and the Boston Women's Trade Union League, 1892-1919*: University of Massachusetts Amherst; 1998.

38. Committee of the Hospital Staff. *A History of Boston City Hospital from its Founding until 1904*. Boston: Boston Municipal Printing Office; 1906.

39. Hirschhorn N, Greaves I. Louisa May Alcott: Her mysterious illness. *Perspectives in Biology and Medicine* 2007; 50:243-59.

40. Card RO. *Boston's South End: An Urban Walker's Handbook*. South End Historical Society, 1992.

41. Burrage WL. *Boston 1630 1906: A Guidebook of Boston for Physicians*. Boston: The Merrymount Press; 1906.

42. Barnet A. Plymouth Hospital. *South End News*; 2012 October 11.

43. Phelps RF. *South End Factory Operatives: Employment and Residence.* Boston: South End House Association; 1903.

44. Sammarco AM. *Boston's South End.* Dover, New Hampshire: Arcadia Publishing; 1998.

45. Sammarco AM. *Boston's South End: Then and Now.* Charleston, South Carolina: Arcadia Publishing Company; 2005.

46. Piano Brands. 2013. (Accessed January 20, 2014, at http://www.marthabeth.com/piano_brands.html.)

47. Three alarms. Three Alarms! *Boston Daily*; 1890 January 23; Sect. 1.

48. Four Alarms. Four Alarms. *Boston Globe;* 1891 November 2.

49. Sight to See. Sight to See. *Boston Globe*; 1899 December 11.

50. Big Fire Scare. Boston has Big Fire Scare. *Boston Globe*; 1910 August 10.

51. Story of the Conflagration. *Boston Globe* 1894 May 16.

52. Saveth EN. Patrician philanthropy in America: The late nineteenth and early twentieth centuries. *Social Service Review* 1980; 54:76-91.

53. Paine RT. *The Inspiration of Charity.* Boston: W. B. Clarke Co.; 1905.

54. *Frederick Douglass Square Historic District.* Trust for Architectural Easements, 1996. (Accessed June 22, 2014, at http://architecturaltrust.org/easements/about-the-trust/trust-protected-communities/historic-districts-in-massachusetts/frederick-douglass-square-historic-district/.)

55. National Park Service. *National Register of Historic Places Registration Form.* 1996.

56. Boston Redevelopment Authority. *Frederick Douglass Square Historic District.* 1978.

57.Nutter KB. *The Necessity of Organization': Mary Kenney O'Sullivan, the American Federation of Labor, and the Boston Women's Trade Union League, 1892-1919*: University of Massachusetts Amherst 1998.

CHAPTER 4

A Community of Faith: Religion in the South End

Most South End buildings are less than fifty feet tall with the vast majority featuring varying shades of dark red brick. The main exceptions to this uniform streetscape are the South End's churches, which range in color from yellow brick to dark grey stone with spires that rise well above their surroundings. Though most are now deconsecrated, the surviving structures continue to dominate the neighborhood. A stroll down Tremont Street, for example, will reveal at least a half dozen churches. Most were constructed between 1850 and 1900, and their histories reflect the challenges posed by the South End's ever-changing demographics. A close look at these buildings and congregations enlightens the history of the neighborhood's people, institutions, and relationships with the outside world.

Some buildings have housed three or more congregations over the years; a complete account of the comings and goings of the neighborhood's churches and synagogues would fill a book of its own. Take the South Congregational Church on Union Park Street, for example.[1] Built in 1861, the church hosted Edward Everett Hale as its first pastor. In 1886, Temple Ohabei Shalom bought the building, and in 1925, it became the Greek Orthodox St. John the Baptist.

A few churches have had interesting alternative uses. The Hollis Street Church was converted into a theater; similarly, Edward Everett Hale's first church was turned into the Columbia Theater after serving as the temporary Roman Catholic Cathedral; and a church at the corner of Pine and Washington Streets was an aquarium before the Salvation Army moved in. It is not odd, in the context of South End ecclesiastic history, that the former Church of the Unity was at one point converted into the Jorge Hernandez Center, the site of theater, dance parties, and other entertainment.

Many churches have been preserved but rehabilitated into housing. The Shawmut Congregational Church hired Charles E. Parker to design a new church on Tremont Street that opened on February 11, 1864.[2] In the 1990s, developers used its abandoned shell for new condominiums. Then there are vacant churches. The building at the corner of Waltham Street and Shawmut Avenue, now empty, was originally the Zion German Lutheran Church, dedicated on Christmas Day 1847.[3] The congregation moved to West Newton Street in 1899 and then to the Back Bay in 1955.[4] The building was most recently the Sahara Restaurant, reflecting the area's Syrian population in the mid-twentieth century, but it has been vacant for decades.

Boston's history is marked by political, social, and physical conflict between its Protestant and Catholic residents. But the Protestants were not a monolithic block; the neighborhood's many Protestant congregations competed for souls and contributions using doctrine and programming. As elsewhere, there were important distinctions between denominations that often put them at odds with each other. They can be divided into two groups: those that were prominent in Boston before the revolution, including Unitarians, Congregationalists, and Episcopalians—called mainline denominations here—and those that became more active after Independence, including Baptists, Methodists, and others, referred to as evangelical churches in this narrative. Considered separately here are Catholic institutions, Jewish congregations, and Black Protestant churches.

Most mainline denominations built their South End churches in a period when there was optimism about the role of faith in society and a belief in the neighborhood's prosperity, but they struggled with issues of faith, mission, membership, and finances. For the most part, these churches identified with the higher income, native-born aristocracy of the city and often had financial support from downtown sponsors. However, they had difficulties relating to the multi-ethnic, downscale population of the South End. To connect to the neighborhood, they adopted a range of tactics. Some churches thrived, some declined, and some merged or moved. Churches were always in flux.

The rise and fall of the Berkeley Street Temple, a Congregationalist church, illustrates these challenges. It struggled during its early years on Pine Street, then moved to the corner of Berkeley Street and Columbus Avenue because its pastor, Henry Martyn Dexter, argued it was necessary to follow the movement of white Protestants out to the new South End. Inspired by his vision, the church opened in 1860 with a large debt but only three hundred active members to fill its two-thousand-person capacity building. To address this shortfall, the church broke with tradition by offering "free seats" rather than charging a pew fee to balance its budget. That effort was unsuccessful, and so it set out to connect to the neighborhood by addressing the social and economic problems of its residents through clubs, services, and charitable acts as it tried to solve its financial problems.[5] This was a new way to organize a church: save souls by addressing social needs and integrating faith into social action. By healing the social ills of the community, the church argued, it was acting the way Christ meant his followers to act. Implementing this strategy, the church became a community center, a place where anyone could come for services and—by connecting with the faithful—be saved.

4.1 CLARENDON BAPTIST CHURCH

The effort was initially successful; the church changed its name to People's Temple, doubled its membership, and by 1893 it had grown into the largest Congregationalist Church in the city. Seven Sunday services and numerous weekly activities attracted more than five thousand attendees, and the church finally was able to replace its pew fees with voluntary pledges. People's Temple became a model for other churches across the country as it codified its philosophy and agenda into what was called the Institutional Church or the Social Gospel Movement. The church expanded and opened a training school for social workers and missionaries, founded orphanages, and even considered establishing a lodging house. Among its lasting contributions was a program that took sick children out to Boston Harbor to give them access to fresh air and recreation. This effort led to the establishment of the Floating Hospital for Children, now part of Tufts Medical Center.

The People's Temple sharply declined after 1895 as the deaths of key personnel, financial problems, and a loss of focus doomed it. The Institutional Church model failed to provide financial stability because the young people it attracted did not make sufficient contributions to pay for services, and its dependence on outside donors proved risky. Another problem was that the large number of activities drew attention away from the central church administration. The talents of the faithful were consumed by running hospitals, orphanages, and schools rather than addressing maintenance and other issues. In 1906, these difficulties forced People's Temple to merge with the nearby Union Church.[5]

Other churches would be paralyzed by their refusal to accommodate Black worshipers. Emmanuel Church, an important Back Bay Episcopal institution, founded the Church of the Ascension in the South End in the 1880s to conduct outreach to the poor. In 1890, it moved to 1901 Washington Street where its leaders discouraged the growing number of Black Episcopalian immigrants from the West Indies from attending the church using quotas and other methods. The church's leadership feared that white congregants would leave if too many Blacks used the building; it even fumigated the sanctuary after it was used by Black congregants.[5] Outraged, Blacks stayed away but so did whites, and the church spiraled downwards. After it closed, the Grant AME Zion church, a Black congregation, purchased the building.

The few pro-slavery clergy in the neighborhood faced opposition from Boston's staunch abolitionist establishment. In 1870, the Union Congregational Church, designed by Alexander R. Estey, was constructed at the corner of Rutland Square and Columbus Avenue. In contrast to the significant role the building would play in the civil rights movement, its first pastor, Nehemiah Adams, was a notorious supporter of slavery. After he wrote an 1854 pro-slavery book called A South Side View of Slavery, his critics called him "South Side Adams" until his death in 1878.[1] The church thrived for several decades after it merged with the remnants of the People's Temple but eventually succumbed as well, and in 1949, the congregation joined the Old South Church in Copley Square. The Fourth Methodist Episcopal Church bought the building and changed its name to Union United Methodist, which occupies the building to this day.

Some churches had decades of success before their decline. At one point, the Shawmut Congregational Church was one of the most well-attended churches in the neighborhood. Though its members lived as far away as Chicago in the early 1880s, well over 90 percent of dues-paying members were from the South End.[6] But it went into decline a few years later and closed in 1892. Its building, formerly used by several other congregations, is now condominiums.

One particularly important church was the South Congregational Church. Founded downtown in 1827, it moved to Union Park Street by way of Washington and Castle Streets in 1862.[1] Its pastor was Edward Everett Hale. While most known today for his novel A Man Without a Country, in his time, he was one of the city's greatest Protestant preachers. A few years after he moved his congregation out of the neighborhood, Hale was famously quoted by Robert Woods as saying that the South End was "the most charitied place in Christendom."[7]

Most of the remaining mainline churches declined after World War I because they were rooted in a religiosity that conflicted with the neighborhood's values and demographics. The South End gradually lost its native-born Protestants, who were the target audience of these churches, replacing them with residents who found the churches' upper-class theology and conservative political positions alienating.[8] Unable or unwilling to attract Blacks, Catholics, or Jews, the mainline churches moved, merged, or shut down.

The various Protestant denominations had distinct theological and social differences that shaped how they intersected with the neighborhood. The split between mainline and evangelical churches reflected profound disagreements over the relationship between God and humanity. Perhaps the most prominent of the evangelical churches was the Clarendon Street Baptist Church, whose congregation believed that the second coming of Christ was near and conducted door-to-door proselytizing in the neighborhood as part of a last attempt to save residents' souls. In contrast to other Protestant denominations, the church reached out to other religious groups; there were even meetings at the church to strategize on how to convert Jews. It also held services in Chinese.[9]

The church was located near the intersection of Clarendon and Tremont Streets. As part of an effort to increase Baptist outreach to the city, it laid its cornerstone on October 31, 1868 and held the first services in the building on April 25, 1869. Its architect was Samuel J. F. Thayer, the designer for

Providence City Hall, a library at Dartmouth, and the original Jordan Marsh department store.

Like many churches, Clarendon Street was highly dependent on charismatic leadership. Ironically, its greatest minister, Adoniram Judson Gordon, was its third choice, but he agreed to leave his pulpit in Jamaica Plain to become the church's first pastor, serving from 1869 to 1895.[10] Through Gordon's work, it became one of the largest Baptist congregations in Boston. It peaked at 1,200 members a few years after Gordon's death but had fallen to five hundred members in 1908 and three hundred in 1920. Clarendon Street's decline in membership was reflected in the physical decay of its building. In 1961, the church took down the steeple because it was unstable, and for years, deferred maintenance and vandalism plagued the church.[11] After the 1982 fire that was the church's final death knell, developers incorporated remains of its façade into an upscale condominium building.

Religion was not limited to the South End's formal churches. In 1877, D. L. Moody of Chicago held a large-scale revival meeting in a temporary brick structure known as Moody's Tabernacle on the corner of Tremont and Clarendon Streets. He was a media-savvy, nationally prominent evangelist who used the popular press to draw audiences that averaged between six thousand and seven thousand people each night.[13] Moody also marshaled an impressive door-to-door campaign; a highly motivated network of churches and volunteers visited ninety thousand Boston households. He had planned the event for years with a fundraising budget that included $30,000 for construction costs alone. Moody also had extensive support from mainstream clergy, including Phillips Brooks, the great rector of Boston's Trinity Church, and Henry Durant, who hosted Moody's family during the revival.

The tabernacle was one of the most elaborate structures in Boston with six grand entrances, special gallery seating, and an auditorium that was 140 by 204 feet with massive pine timbers and buttresses. Its design was supposed to reflect revival meetings and the "big tent of ecumenicalism".[9] Moody believed in the strict veracity of every word in the bible, quoting long passages in detail, and he preached that the love of God would save only those who repented their sins before Christ's return. It was a very narrow view of Christianity; those who did not share this perspective were not welcome. Despite a call for people of all faiths to participate, speaker after speaker used their time at the podium to condemn the Catholic Church, and the Archdiocese ignored the revival. Moody preached more than one hundred sermons, and more than one million attendees, many repeats, passed through the doors of the Tabernacle in the thirteen weeks of the revival. Not everyone who came was impressed, however. Walt Whitman called the building a "heavenly hippodrome" and was put off by Moody's poor grammar and countless references to himself and God.[13]

Unfortunately, the revival did not fulfill its ambitious goals. News leaked that fundraising had fallen short by $21,000, and local churches were unable to close the deficit. Then the public learned that Moody was filling seats by buying railroad tickets and reselling them at half price to suburbanites, further increasing the budget shortfall. In the gloom of recession, some criticized the revival's luxuries, and complaints about Moody's theology and methods grew. But as the revival neared its end, a frenzy gripped the city; people waited hours to get inside, supporters opened charities including a soup kitchen in Faneuil Hall, and Moody himself was flooded with personal appeals for help to achieve salvation. Afterwards, New England churches reported twenty-one thousand new attendees, with many converting to the evangelical faith for the first time.[13] Its builders demolished the Tabernacle after the revival was over. In 1884, the Cyclorama rose in its place.

In contrast to the ephemeral Moody Tabernacle, Henry Morgan founded one of the South End's most enduring institutions. Morgan came to Boston in 1859 as an unknown, unordained minister.[14] Born in poverty in Connecticut in 1825, he was an advocate for the disadvantaged, referring to himself as "Henry Morgan, Poor Man's Preacher." He was penniless but ambitious; he rented the Music Hall downtown and charged ten cents admission to hear him preach. Fired by faith, his thunderous sermons and strong condemnations of immorality and licentious behavior attracted a large following, enabling Morgan to purchase the Church of the Disciples in 1868 and move his base of operations to the South End.[15]

Morgan used highly publicized acts of faith to his advantage. Along with two associates, he publicly challenged an old Boston law prohibiting preaching on the Common and created an uproar that brought increased attention to his church.[12] Furthering his mass appeal, he published several novels that featured lurid plots in which lascivious priests corrupted innocent young women while young men triumphed over adversity because of their strong moral compasses. Morgan was vehemently anti-Catholic and used all the bigoted rhetoric of the day to denounce morally corrupt clergy, the political dominance of local Bostonians by the pope, and other alleged Catholic abuses. He proclaimed that in Boston the "aristocracy bows to the Roman yoke and Beacon Hill kisses the Pope's toe. Tools of the Catholic Church finger the taxes, manage the appropriations, deliver the votes and sell to the rich corporations all the privileges they want."[16]

4.2 MORGAN MERMORIAL AND CHURCH OF ALL NATIONS, 1930

Morgan died of tuberculosis in 1884, awkwardly leaving his church to the Unitarian City Mission Society with instructions to hire a Methodist minister. Finding a successor was difficult, and the church went through five pastors in the eleven years after Morgan's death. It almost collapsed, having lost more than half of its parishioners, and its chapel decayed to the point of condemnation by the city.

Edgar Helms rescued the church. After studying at the Boston University School of Theology, he and his wife Eugenia wanted to be posted as missionaries to India. But the Methodists only allowed single men to become missionaries and required a five-year commitment. So Helms stayed in Boston where he was recruited to take over the struggling congregation in 1895. Helms renamed the church Morgan Memorial and then The Church of All Nations as he focused on both the families and single men of the neighborhood, bridging the gap between institutional churches and settlement houses. Morgan Memorial was motivated by faith and a sense that people can be improved by paying attention to their individual circumstances.[14] Helms sought to redeem the poor of the South End through spiritual and social renewal.

Most famously, Helms believed that honest labor could promote moral growth. As he spent time among the poor of the neighborhood, his idea of employing people to further their salvation slowly grew. He first collected old clothing and furniture and asked volunteers to repair and sell them in church-owned stores. Then Helms started paying people to mend these items, a system he called industrial evangelism. As the enterprise grew, the business side was separately incorporated as Morgan Memorial Cooperative Industries and Stores in 1905. In 1913, Helms secured funding to open a factory, and in 1915, an organization in Brooklyn opened a center called House of Goodwill modeled on Morgan Memorial. It eventually changed its name to Goodwill Industries; under this name, the movement spread across the country as Helms changed the name of his church-run business to Morgan Memorial Goodwill Industries. By the late 1930s, Goodwill Industries faced problems from unions and minimum wage laws and found it could no longer employ the urban poor at very low wages. The solution was to turn to the training and employment of people with disabilities, a mission it continues to this day.

Helms did not ignore his South End roots. His Church of All Nations had English, Italian, Syrian, and Portuguese ministries, a Black minister, and it even attracted a small number of Catholics and a few Jews.[15] Though Morgan Memorial survives, almost all its original buildings were taken for the Massachusetts Turnpike Extension in the 1960s or were destroyed by a spectacular fire after the buildings had been emptied for acquisition. The Church of All Nations built a new home at the corner of Charles Street South and Tremont Street designed by Bertrand Goldberg, who is most famous for his Marina City twin towers in Chicago. It continued to hold services until 2000, when it finally succumbed to declining attendance and now stands vacant.

Strong, intelligent women who challenged the dominant parameters that defined acceptable female behavior dominate the South End's history. The controversial Mary Baker Eddy was one such woman. This late-nineteenth-century religious leader was the founder of the Church of Christ, Scientist. While Phillips Brooks and others were sympathetic to the new religion, A.J. Gordon ridiculed Eddy and her faith, calling it "spiritual malpractice" and "transcendental misbelief".[17] Eddy's supporters saw her as integrating science and spirituality, bringing rationality to many of the pressing issues of her time by promoting the healing power of faith. Her detractors accused her of stealing her ideas, running an autocratic organization, and relying on a theoretical construct that had no basis in reality.[17]

Born and raised in New Hampshire, Eddy endured many trials over her life, including repeated illnesses, the death of her husband while she was pregnant with their only child, and the limited economic prospects available to women at the time. In what must have been a particularly traumatic act, her son was taken away from her and told she was dead. Searching for solace, she became interested in spiritualism. In 1862, she came to study under Phineas Parkhurst Quimby, a former mesmerist who was to strongly influence Eddy's philosophy.

Undeterred by critics who questioned both her competency and her right to be a spiritual leader, in 1881, Eddy opened the Massachusetts Metaphysical College in Lynn to train practitioners in her system of mental therapeutics. The next year, recovering from a schism among her followers, she moved her organization to 569 and 571 Columbus Avenue in the South End, where its adherents shifted from working-class to more affluent followers.[18] Eddy had previously lived in the neighborhood, first at 551 Shawmut Avenue and later with two of her students at 133 West Newton Street.[3]

Eddy called herself a Professor of Obstetrics, Metaphysics, and Christian Science, simultaneously challenging two strictures against women at the time: higher education and the practice of medicine. Because of the opposition of outsiders and other issues, the college had a short life. In 1888, a manslaughter charge against a Christian Science practitioner split the church, causing Eddy to close the college.[19] The religion she founded has outlasted her death in 1910, a testament to the power of her faith.

Though a prime goal of the South End's development had been to maintain Protestant dominance of Boston, Irish Catholics flocked to the neighborhood. The bigotry they encountered in the nineteenth century was staggering.[20] But the Catholic Church thrived, and its presence in the neighborhood was strong. Boston College, an important Catholic institution founded by Irish-born Reverend John McElroy, opened on Harrison Avenue in 1864 and remained there until 1913. McElroy first tried to build the college downtown, purchasing city land near present-day North Station, but neighborhood opposition, which included voracious anti-Catholic sentiment, forced him to abandon that site. McElroy encountered resistance in the South End as well, but on July 22, 1857, the City Council approved the sale of land on Harrison Avenue for construction of a school, and Boston College broke ground on April 7, 1858.[21]

Also in this corner of the South End is the Church of the Immaculate Conception. Designed by Patrick Keely, the architect of the nearby Cathedral, it was built of New Hampshire granite. The cornerstone was laid in 1859, and when the church opened two years later, it was one of the most beautiful in the city.[4] The church suffered from low attendance for much of the mid twentieth century until gay and lesbian Catholics revitalized it in the 1980s. In later decades, services were held in the basement chapel because the Jesuits were unable to maintain the building. When they deconsecrated and gutted the interior of the main church in 1986, preservationists and many devout Catholics objected.[22] In 2014, a housing developer bought the church.

Another Catholic institution was the Holy Trinity Church on Shawmut Avenue, built as a center for German Catholics. It was an era when US Catholic dioceses established parishes that catered to the special needs of immigrants, incorporating masses, religious instruction, and other activities in multiple languages into their programming. In the South End, these ethnic parishes included Our Lady of Pompeii in the New York Streets area (with a large Italian membership) and Our Lady of Victories near Park Square (a center for French Canadians).

The archdiocese founded the German-focused Holy Trinity church downtown in 1844. It was difficult to find German-speaking priests, however, so they recruited the Society of Jesus to staff the parish in 1848.[23] The congregation tried to build a church at the corner of Tremont and Canton Streets in 1850, but the cost and logistics proved overwhelming, and they abandoned the project. Rumors of misappropriations of funds and debt further discouraged the parish, and the construction site was foreclosed on and sold at auction.[24]

In the late 1860s, a new effort to build a church began, this time on Shawmut Avenue. With renewed fundraising, the congregation laid the cornerstone on November 10, 1872, the morning after the Great Fire had devastated downtown. John H. Keely designed the $250,000 building that could seat 1,200 in the main church and seven hundred in a lower-level room. The parish spared no expense. Its organ had 2,880 pipes and fifty-four stops, and its $1,500 bells came from an army occupied church in New Orleans. The church is physically imposing, standing out from the other architectural styles of the South End. Keely incorporated dark stone and elaborately decorated windows in a Gothic building with wood-carved statues from Aachen, Germany and stained-glass windows from Munich. [25]

Like many ethnic Catholic parishes in its day, the church provided a range of services and activities, including language instruction to children, a parish school, burial assistance, literary and debating societies, a cooperative bank, an orphanage, and an old age home.[25] A group of prominent musicians including Holy Trinity parishioners incorporated the Germania Orchestra, which later formed the nucleus of the Boston Symphony Orchestra in 1881. The Holy Trinity Church also takes credit for introducing the Christmas tree and the custom of sending out Christmas cards to New Englanders.[23]

Over many decades, the parish declined and the building decayed. When the Hurricane of 1938 damaged its ornate steeple, the church removed it, and a 1956 fire caused more extensive damage. Later that year, the administration of the church passed from the Jesuits to the Archdiocese of Boston, who closed the school and orphanage in 1961.[25] The church was deconsecrated in 2002 despite strong protest from its remaining parishioners. Today, it is the only surviving pre-renewal building in Castle Square, wedged between an abandoned telephone switching station and an empty nursing home. The archdiocese put the building up for sale and it is now a very upscale condominium development.

The most important Catholic institution—and one of the most imposing buildings in the South End—is the Cathedral of the Holy Cross. The seat of one of the country's premier archdioceses, it drew twenty-five thousand people to the laying of its cornerstone on September 15, 1867. The program included one hundred priests, seven bishops, a fifty-member orchestra, and a three-hundred-member choir as Bishop John Williams sprinkled holy water where the alter would be and chiseled three crosses into the building stones. Following a forty-five-minute address by John McCloskey, Archbishop of New York, selected officials went to nearby Boston College for a celebratory dinner.[26]

The Church had initiated plans for the building in 1860 but construction was delayed by the Civil War. It then redoubled its efforts after deciding to concentrate its major institutions in the then fashionable South End near the Church of Immaculate Conception and Boston College. But no one foresaw the neighborhood's looming decline. After the Civil War and years of construction, the Cathedral's 1875 dedication came at a time when the South End was a vastly different neighborhood.

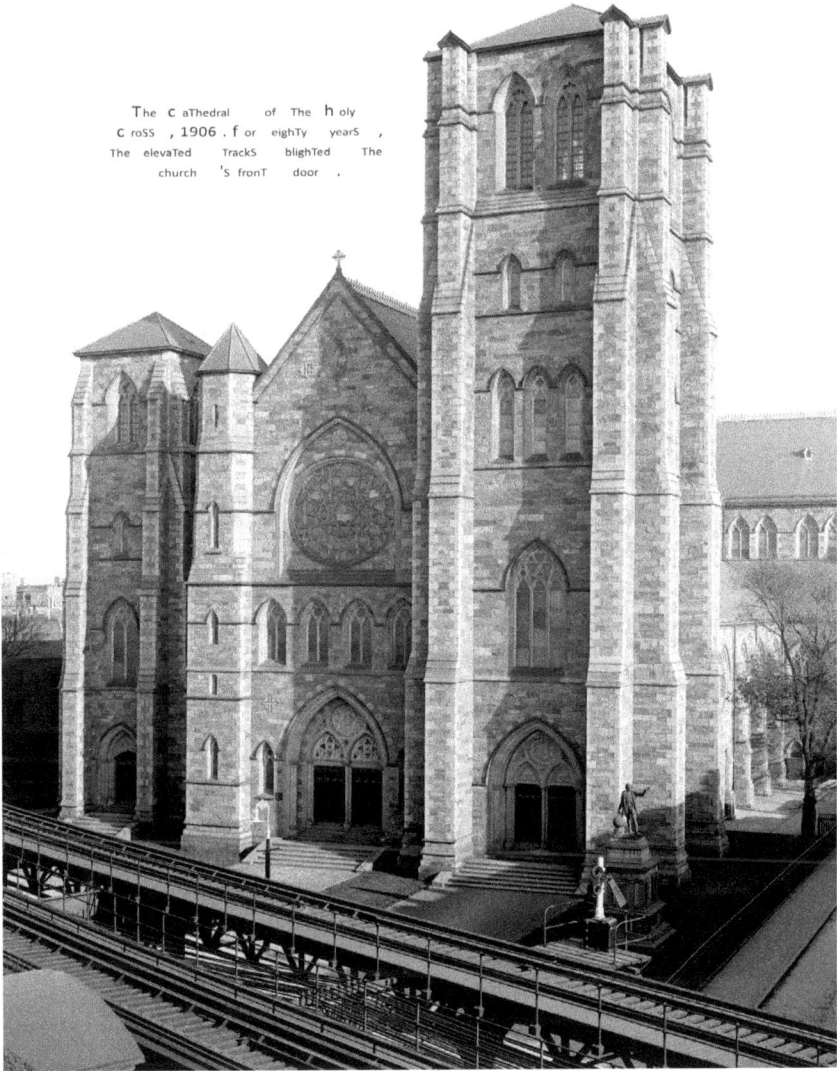

The Cathedral of The holy Cross, 1906. for eighTy years, The elevaTed TrackS blighTed The church 'S fronT door.

4.2 THE CATHEDRAL OF THE HOLY CROSS, 1906

The building was an expression of faith as well as an assertion of Catholic rights in a city noted for its Protestant opposition. For example, the archway over the front door of the Cathedral includes bricks from Charlestown's Ursuline Convent, salvaged after an 1834 mob burned it down. The taller tower is higher than the Bunker Hill monument, and if the spires had been completed as planned, the structure would have been as prominent as the State House. The church is 364 feet long, ninety feet wide, and can sit 1,700 people.[27]

The country's first Black priest performed a now underappreciated role in the construction of the Cathedral. The Cathedral's rector (essentially its parish priest) from 1870 to 1875, Alexander Sherwood Healy, was the son of an Irish plantation owner and a Black slave. When he was born in 1836 in Georgia, the law prohibited his parents from marrying, and he was a slave. It appears, however, that his parents lived together as openly as they could and sent Healy and his siblings to Massachusetts for an education. Several of the children became priests and nuns. Healy enrolled at Holy Cross College in Worcester in 1854 but left before graduation to go to Montreal to study for the priesthood; he could not enter a seminary in the US because they would not admit Blacks. Showing promise, church leaders sent Healy to Rome and Paris where he was ordained at Notre Dame in 1858.

Finding a place for him in the US Catholic Church was difficult. As the country marched towards Civil War, it was unsafe for Black men. Though considered for a position teaching American priests, prejudice made it difficult for white seminarians to defer to him. The Church sent Healy to Boston to work in a Catholic orphanage, making him the only Black priest in the country. Soon, his talents were so recognized that he began to work at the diocese office. His intelligence, preaching skills, and singing talent prompted Bishop Williams to rely on him more and more. This relationship in turn led to his appointment as rector where Healy was visibly Black in a parish and city that were overwhelmingly white.

Healy was critical to building the Cathedral; he organized a campaign through which Catholics contributed fifty cents a month toward its financing. At a fair to raise money for the building, Healy's Rector's Table brought in $6,500, the highest single contributor of money at the event. At the same time, Healy provided all the functions of a parish priest: confessions, baptisms, weddings, deathbed absolutions, personal counseling, fundraising, and so forth. Despite the extreme prejudice of the era, Irish, Italian, French, German, and other racial groups that made up the nineteenth-century Boston Catholic church accepted him. In 1875, the bishop transferred Healy to be the leader of nearby St. James Parish, but he died in October of that year.

He is buried in St. Augustine's Cemetery in South Boston in what was then a whites-only cemetery.[27]

Despite growing numbers of Black Catholics, diocese leaders were reluctant to create a Black parish.[28] The archdiocese eventually set aside a mass for them at St. Patrick's on Northampton Street, but many chose to attend services at St. Phillip's, located at Lenox Street and Harrison Avenue, instead. Saint Patrick's was one of the most austere churches in the South End, if not all of Boston. Its exterior was plain with only two small windows fronting the street; its interior was without decoration except for the altar.[29] The Church built St. Patrick's in the 1830s when anti-Catholic hysteria was strong and the threat of mob violence constant. Its very existence can be credited to the faith and devotion of Boston Catholics. On its fiftieth anniversary, people recalled that the men of the parish had to stand guard at night to protect the building from arson.[30] Both St. Phillip's and St. Patrick's churches have been demolished.

The neighborhood never achieved the prominence that was forecast when the Church was building its new institutions in the mid-nineteenth century, and later, the diocese suffered from a lack of land for expansion. Archbishop William O'Connell began moving Catholic institutions to the Brighton/Newton area in 1913. Boston College High School moved to Columbia Point in the 1950s, and developers converted its old building into condominiums in the early 2000s.

During renewal in the 1960s, the BRA proposed creating a plaza in front of the Cathedral, and it briefly considered condemning the buildings across Washington Street to enhance the area. That idea fell through, but the BRA gave the church the blocks to the east of the Cathedral. Post-renewal, the church built a gym to support Cathedral High School, a small modern architectural gem designed by Childs Bertman Tseckares, and the Archdiocese's Urban Planning Office built Rollins Square, the award-winning, mixed-income development.

For many years, El Centro de Cardenal, the Cardinal Cushing Center for the Spanish Speaking, was a major provider of social services to Boston's Latino community, operating out of the old Penny Savings Bank on Washington Street. But demographic change, the South End is now distant from most Hispanic neighborhoods in the city, and funding issues led to El Centro's closing down and the building being sold for condominiums. Reflecting the strong role of Latino immigration in church demographics, however, services at the Cathedral continue to be in English and Spanish.

The period after 1990 was a trying time for the Boston Archdiocese. The child sex abuse scandal shook the support of many Catholics, and attendance at mass and the church's influence on political and social issues declined. The Cathedral became the site of frequent protests by supporters of the victims of abuse, who called upon the Church hierarchy to explain actions that protected priests facing accusations. Others gathered in front of the Cathedral to protest the Church's opposition to same sex marriage and its advocacy of other conservative positions.[31, 32]

For many decades, the Archbishops of Boston had preferred to live in Brighton, and their mansion on Lake Street was the seat of their power and influence. But Cardinal Sean O'Malley moved back into the South End in 2003, preferring a simpler lifestyle in the rectory connected to the Cathedral over the relative opulence of Brighton. The move was symbolic of an attempt to reconnect to the poor, immigrant, city-dwelling population that was becoming the core of church membership.[33]

The Cathedral played a special role in the wake of the 2013 terrorist attack at the Boston Marathon when it was the site of an interfaith prayer vigil with President Barrack Obama in attendance. The televised gathering of clergy, lay people, first responders, politicians, and others featured performances by famed Cambridge-based cellist Yo Yo Ma and a children's choir. As the city's largest religious building, it was part of the process by which Boston gathered itself together to mourn.[34]

For a few decades before 1900, it appeared that the South End might become a major center of Boston's Jewish community. But though there were several large congregations in the neighborhood at one point, most of the Jewish population moved out in the first decades of the twentieth century as living conditions deteriorated. Like the transitory nature of Protestant churches, Jewish institutions often split, combined, closed, and moved.[35]

One of the most influential synagogues in the city was Adath Israel, a spinoff of Boston's first Jewish congregation, Ohabei Shalom. Reflecting the rising status of Boston's Jews, more than three-quarters of its men were retailers and 10 percent were manufacturers. In 1885, most of Adath Israel's families lived in the South End's row houses with six living on the small block of Holyoke Street. The men had businesses selling cigars, liquor, shoes, and men's clothes.[35]

By 1883, Adath Israel had sufficient resources to build a new synagogue on Columbus Avenue west of Massachusetts Avenue—additional evidence this portion of the South End took longer to decay than more easterly sections of the neighborhood. Designed by the firm of Weissbein and Jones, it had a seating capacity of 850 and "was the most impressive Jewish structure built in nineteenth century Boston ... of brick, with brownstone and terra cotta trimmings."[36]

Adath Israel's Rabbi Solomon Schindler, a South End resident, was friendly with Unitarian and other prominent Protestant clergy and served six years on the Boston School Committee. His sermons were so popular with outsiders that gentiles sometimes outnumbered Jews in the audience. Schindler and the congregation were prominent leaders of Reform Judaism; among their modernization efforts, they promoted the use of English during services, banned the wearing of yarmulkes, and advocated for cooperation with people of other faiths.[37]

There were Jewish institutions across the neighborhood. In the mid-1870s, Adath Israel used the Theodore Parker Meeting House on Berkeley Street for its Sunday school, the Young Men's Hebrew Association (YMHA) met at Deacon Hall on Washington Street, and there were several congregations in the New York Streets area. The Mount Sinai Hospital Association dispensary opened in 1902 to serve patients on an outpatient basis.[35]

Growing intolerance in Russia in the late 1800s set off a new wave of immigrants, leading to a substantial increase in Boston's Jewish population. Many Russian immigrants settled in and around the New York Streets area, prompting German Jews to move to Roxbury or the western edge of the South End.[35] One famous new South Ender was Louis B. Mayer, who was born in 1884 in what is now Belarus. He immigrated to the United States in 1887 and moved to 17 Rochester Street in 1904. Mayer married Margaret Shenberg, who lived across the street, and the couple settled at 7 Rollins Street. They departed to Haverhill where Mayer began to buy up movie theaters on his way to becoming a famous Hollywood studio chief.[38]

Local Jewish numbers declined as many left their traditional neighborhoods of the North, West, and South Ends for Roxbury, Dorchester, and other communities.[35] Ohabei Shalom had moved to Union Park Street in 1887. By 1898, however, most of its members were living outside the South End, and it eventually moved to Brookline. In 1895, Shaarey Tefila merged with Mishkan Israel, and two years later, it purchased the former South End Tabernacle at the corner of Shawmut Avenue and Madison Street, on the very western edge of the South End. Then in 1906, a deal was struck to sell the building to the Twelfth Baptist Church. Many of the remaining Jews in

Lower Roxbury organized another temple, Atereth Israel, on Northampton Street.

As Black congregations moved into former Jewish and Protestant houses of worship in the South End and Roxbury, they sold their existing buildings in the West End and Beacon Hill to Jewish congregations accommodating a large influx of Jews into those neighborhoods. For example, Twelfth Baptist Church sold its Phillips Street church to the Vilna Shul in 1906, Anish Lihabitz purchased the African Meeting House in 1905, and the former AME Zion Church on North Russell Street also became a synagogue. Profits from sales of buildings to Jewish congregations in the West End/Beacon Hill area were used by Black churches to buy the physical assets of Jewish groups in the South End and Roxbury. Adath Israel sold its Columbus Avenue facility to the AME Zion Church in 1903 and moved to Commonwealth Avenue.

Reflecting the movement of Jews out of the South End, the YMHA moved to Roxbury in 1911.[35] There were synagogues in the New York Streets area that survived for several decades, but urban renewal destroyed all evidence of the once-large Jewish presence there. Jewish people have continued to live in the South End to this day. Adath Israel, now renamed Temple Israel and located on the Riverway, for example, had a major program to connect to young Jews in the South End and other parts of Boston beginning in the 1990s. The era when the South End was a Jewish neighborhood, however, has been over for a century.

One of the major characteristics of the South End in the twentieth century was its many Black churches. White Protestants and Jews retreating out of the neighborhood created opportunities for Black people of faith to own buildings and worship as they wished, free from discrimination. Many of these congregations remained in the South End well after urban renewal had displaced their members out of the neighborhood. On Sundays, the streets around these churches overflowed with double-parked vehicles and cars parked in the medians, setting up the churches for conflict with their neighbors.[39] Eventually, however, many of the churches sold their buildings to developers and moved to other parts of the city or the suburbs. Black churches offered spaces safe from racism, where values such as volunteerism, respectable clothes, and family ties were nurtured and reinforced. Despite the sometimes long commutes, members who returned to the church on multiple days and nights during the week found vital sustenance in a hostile city.[40]

The most important church for the West Indian population was St. Cyprian's Episcopal Church on Tremont Street. St. Cyprian's traces its history back to 1910 when a group predominately made up of Jamaicans and Barbadians began meeting in the home of Ida Gross at 218 Northampton Street. The group had grown to more than fifty people by 1920, and it met at the nearby Church of the Ascension until racist policies led the group to create a separate church. By 1940, there were almost seven hundred adults and four hundred children committed to the church, and many more participated in more informal ways; some who attended other churches would go to St. Cyprian's for social activities, training, or help to find housing and employment.[41] St. Cyprian's remains a major presence on Tremont Street to this day.

Another surviving, predominately Black church is Union United Methodist. In 1948, the New England Methodist conference purchased the Union Congregational Church on Columbus Avenue where for a time, the congregation resembled the divisions within Boston's Black community: Black Brahmins sat up front, West Indians were on the right, and southerners on the left.[42] The church played an important role in the national civil rights movement in 1950 when the National Association for the Advancement of Colored People (NAACP) held its national convention there.

One of the more famous pastors at Union United was Charles Stith, whom President William Clinton appointed Ambassador to Tanzania in 1998.[43] Stith was also a prominent politician and a leader in the effort to defeat the 1980s Mandela secession movement that would have created a new city out of Boston's minority wards. His wife, Deborah Prothow Stith, was well-known for her work on health disparities at the Harvard School of Public Health.

There were other Black churches that thrived even through the upheavals caused by urban renewal after 1960. Many southern Blacks attended services in the neighborhood's Baptist congregations, as native Boston Blacks did not always accept southerners. New Hope Baptist was particularly known for providing a welcoming place for people from the South.[41] There were numerous storefront churches and small Pentecostal Black and Hispanic congregations in the neighborhood that often had stronger faith than finances; many only lasted for a few years. Over time, their numbers have declined, though Leon de Judah, a Hispanic evangelical church on Northampton Street, has been one of the largest and most enduring of these.

Ultimately, each South End congregation rose and declined for its own reasons. Many moved out to follow their congregants, others closed following the loss of a charismatic leader, and only a few of the churches and synagogues that once were active in the neighborhood are still used for religious purposes. Of the two dozen churches built in the nineteenth century, about half were already abandoned by the 1960s.[44]

The ups and downs of the real estate market were a major driver of change. In the 1960s and 1970s, falling property values and dwindling congregations caused many to abandon their buildings, leaving them vulnerable to the elements and arson. After 1980, rising prices proved too tempting to several remaining institutions, which found that developers would provide much needed cash to purchase and rehab properties outside the neighborhood. The South End is approaching the point where there are more churches that have been converted to condominiums than are being used for religious purposes, but the buildings are reminders of how South Enders once placed a high priority on faith.

1. Bacon EM. The Book of Boston: *Fifty Years' Recollections of the New England Metropolis.* Boston: The Book of Boston Company; 1916.

2. Card RO. *Restoration Notes* Undated.

3. Card RO. *Boston's South End: An Urban Walker's Handbook.* South End Historical Society. 1992In:

4. Pertronella MM. *Victorian Boston Today.* Boston: Northeastern University Press; 2004.

5. Dorn JA. *"Our best gospel appliances":* Institutional churches and the emergence of social Christianity in the south end of Boston, 1880-1920. Cambridge, Massachusetts: Harvard University; 1994.

6. Officers and Members of the Shawmut Congregational Church. *Shawmut Church.* Boston: Beacon Press; 1881.

7. Woods RA. *The City Wilderness: A Settlement Study.* Boston: Houghton, Mifflin and Company; 1898.

8. White GC. Social Settlements and immigrant neighbors., 1886-1914. *Social Service Review* 1959;33:55-66.

9. Hartley BL. *Evangelicals at a Crossroads: Revivalism and Social Reform in Boston, 1860-1910.* Durham, New Hampshire: University of New Hampshire Press; 2011.

10. Clarendon Street Baptist Church. *Centennial Celebration.* 1969.

11. South End Historical Society. The Clarendon Street Baptist Church: A New Lease on Life. *Newsletter* 1986 September/October Sect. 6.

12. Bendroth ML. *Fundamentalists in the City: Conflicts and Divisions in Boston's Churches, 1885-1950.* New York: Oxford University Press; 2005.

13. Evensen BJ. "It Is a Marvel to Many People": Dwight L. Moody, mass media, and the New England Revival of 1877. *The New England Quarterly* 1999; 72:251-71.

14. Dorion ECE. *The Redemption of the South End: A Study in City Evangelization.* New York: The Abingdon Press; 1915.

15. Tayvon JS. *Neighborhood-based services for the poor: Re-examining Morgan Memorial and the Settlement House Movement.* Cambridge, Massachusetts: Massachusetts Institute of Technology; 1993.

16. Morgan H. *Boston Inside Out.* Boston: American Citizen Company; 1895.

17. Cunningham RJ. The impact of Christian Science on the American Churches, 1880-1910. *The American Historical Review* 1967; 72:885-905.

18. Johnson WL. *Hawthorne Hall: A historical story, 1885.* Dorchester, Massachusetts: The Homewood Press; 1922.

19. Hicks RR. Religion and Remedies Reunited: Rethinking Christian Science. *Journal of Feminist Studies in Religion* 2004; 20:25-58.

20. Klein C. Strong Bloy: *The life and times of John L. Sullivan, America's First Sports Hero.* Guilford, Connecticut: Guilford Press; 2013.

21. Dunigan DR. *A History of Boston College.* Milwaukee, Wisconsin: The Bruce Publishing Company; 1947.

22. Immaculate Conception. Jesuits' Dismantling Of 1861 Sanctuary Spurs Anger In Boston. *New York Times,* 1986 October 26.

23. Weisner FX. *Holy Trinity Parish Boston, Mass 1844-1944.* Boston: Holy Trinity Church; 1944.

24. Nopper FX. *Concerning the History of the Catholic German Holy Trinity Parish in Boston, Mass.*

Boston: P. L. Schriftgiesser & C0.; 1886.

25. Engler MC. *Holy Trinity Church*. Boston: Goethe Society of New England; 1981.

26. O'Connor T. *Boston Catholics: A History of the Church and Its People*. Boston: Northeastern University Press; 1998.

27. O'Toole JM. Portrait of a Parish: Race, Ethnicity, and Class in Boston's Cathedral of the Holy Cross, 1865-1880. In: O'Toole JM, editors DQ, eds. *Boston's Histories: Essays in Honor of Thomas H O'Connor*. Boston: Northeastern University Press; 2004.

28. Leonard WC. A parish for Black Catholics in Boston. *The Catholic Historical Review* 1997; 83:44-68.

29. Sammarco AM. *Boston's South End*. Dover, New Hampshire: Arcadia Publishing; 1998.

30. Beatty J. *The Rascal King: The Life and Times of James Michael Curley (1874-1958)*. Reading, Massachusetts: Addison-Wesley Publishing Company; 1992.

31. Paulson M. Catholics observe Good Friday with protests, prayer both inside and outside cathedral, abuse issue cited. *Boston Globe*; 2002 March 30.

32. Weiss J. Near cathedral portals, voices of protest and support street becomes arena for debate on archdiocese. *Boston Globe*; 2002 July 31.

33. Paulson M. Archbishop will leave manse. *Boston Globe*; 2003 August 9.

34. Wangsness L. To calls both resolute and reflective, a city unites. *Boston Globe*; 2013 April 19.

35. Sarna JD, Smith E, Kosofsky S-m. *The Jews of Boston*. New Haven, Connecticut: Yale University Press; 1995.

36. Gamm G. Urban Exodus: *Why the Jews Left Boston and the Catholics Stayed*. Cambridge MA: Harvard University Press; 1999.

37. Dwyer-Ryan M, Porter SL, Davis LF. *Becoming American Jews: Temple Israel of Boston*. Waltham, Massachusetts: Brandeis University Press; 2009.

38. Shannon HJ. *Legendary Locals of Boston's South End*. Charleston, South Carolina: Arcadia Publishing; 2014.

39. Kaufman J. S. End changes spawn Sunday parking squeeze. *Boston Globe*; 1984 July 13.

40. Deutsch S. *Women and the City: Gender, Space and Power in Boston 1870-1940*. New York: Oxford University Press; 2000.

41. Johnson VS. *The Other Black Bostonians: West Indians in Boston, 1900-1950*. Bloomington, Indiana: Indiana University Press; 2006.

42. Lukas A. *Common Ground: A Turbulent Decade in the Lives of Three American Families*. New York: Vintage Books; 1986.

43. Black C. Rev. Stith completes envoy preparation Returns to Hub to await Senate confirmation hearing on Tanzania ambassadorship. *Boston Globe*; 1998 May 1.

44. Atkinson JL. History and Development of the South End. In: Putnam JW, ed. *A Picture of the South End*. Boston: South End Historical Society; 1968.

CHAPTER 5

The Middle Years: 1900-1945

O ver time, the most visible demographic group in the South End shifted from Irish to Black. Neither group was ever close to a majority, but both shaded outsiders' perceptions of the neighborhood. While the heavy Irish presence made the neighborhood "a wilderness" in the nineteenth century, the Black population in the twentieth century gave outsiders the impression that the area needed radical urban renewal. In both cases, the fact that the South End integrated these populations into the fabric of the neighborhood so seamlessly is indicative of its welcoming nature. No single group claimed the neighborhood as its own—a sharp contrast to other parts of Boston. But that unique quality was invisible to outsiders.

Boston's Black population first lived on the back side of Beacon Hill. It was there and in the nearby West End that many important events took place, including William Lloyd Garrison's anti-slavery work, Frederick Douglass's efforts to promote freedom, and Robert Gould Shaw's recruitment efforts for the Massachusetts 54th regiment.[1] But by the 1890s, the Beacon Hill/West End area was considered too poor for respectable Black Brahmins, as the city's Black elite was often called, and a growing Jewish and Italian immigrant population was pushing Blacks out of these neighborhoods. At the same time, new laws in the 1880s allowed Blacks to own property. Higher-income Blacks began to seek out the rowhouses and small tenement buildings in the South End, which were once owned by Irish and Jewish immigrants. There, they met streams of Blacks from the South and the West Indies looking to the city for a better place to live.[1]

For decades, the South End would be in continuous transition with some Black families moving out to Roxbury and Dorchester as others moved in from elsewhere.[2] After 1890, the South End was a major center of Boston African American culture and a place where striving Black families found energy to cope with an increasingly prejudiced society.[3] It sheltered politicians, entertainers, activists, and artists because its housing was open to all at a time when most of the city was off limits to people of color. Illustrative of the complicated position of the neighborhood, in Dorothy West's 1948 novel

The Living is Easy, which is about Black life in Boston in the first decades of the century, West's heroine lived with her family in the South End in a house her businessman husband owned, but she longed to move out in order to proclaim her high-class status.[4]

Nineteenth century Boston Blacks may have initially been better off than those in other cities, but over time, their status declined. Throughout the twentieth century, as Boston's Black population increased, so did segregation. In Boston, however, the push against Black residents was less a reaction against population growth and more the result of deteriorating race relations around the country.[5] Locally, Black men and women found employment opportunities blocked by low-skilled Irish immigrants and their children, who dominated the female domestic and male longshoreman occupations. As Boston's economy stagnated after World War I, the racial competition for jobs grew fierce.[6] Also in new conformity to national trends, theaters and other public spaces began to segregate.[7] Black Bostonians responded to these challenges by establishing their own institutions, which provided the advocacy they needed, addressed specific issues, and provided an oasis of calm in increasingly tense times. In addition to Black religious institutions, the community established settlement houses, unions, social clubs, and entertainment venues.

At the beginning of the twentieth century, Protestant-focused South End settlement houses were finding it difficult to provide programs for Black residents. Unlike many settlements, they did not formally exclude Black people, but they were perplexed on how to serve them. Were they traditional immigrants like those from Eastern and Southern Europe? Did they need special programming to assist them to overcome the unique legal and social restrictions placed on them? What could be done to improve their employment and living conditions? To help guide its work, the South End House commissioned a 1904 report by John Daniels, who used a Harvard Fellowship to devote time to study Black issues. He "adopted the mode of procedure of a good Yankee" for his work, which was based on extensive interviews. Daniels found the community to be poor, mostly employed in low-skilled jobs, and living in deplorable housing.[8] In response, South End House helped establish the Robert Gould Shaw House for Blacks in Lower Roxbury. Despite the acute needs of Boston Blacks, however, the South End House was reluctant to have any activity focused on one particular ethnic group.[9]

Black South End women addressed these issues by founding the Harriet Tubman House, which was initially meant to provide housing for young,

Black women who had moved to Boston.[10] It began when the Harriet Tubman Crusaders, a temperance group, established a lodging house on Holyoke Street in 1904.[2] The group included Julia Henson, a friend of Harriet Tubman, and in honor of one of Tubman's many visits to the house, its founders named it after her.[11] Over time, it expanded its services, offering classes on a wide range of topics and helping struggling families access assistance. Unlike white settlement houses, however, the Harriet Tubman House could not rely on white charities, so the women had to be resourceful. They raised money "by means of teas, bazaars, suppers, concerts, and the like."[12] The settlement merged into USES in the 1960s and lent its name to a new building constructed in the 1970s to house the combined organization. Many were devastated when USES sold the property in 2020 in order to consolidate operations on Rutland Street.

5.1 HARRIET TUBMAN STATUE

The Harriet Tubman House was not alone; local groups established other homes for Black women in the early 1900s, including the Women's Service Club at 464 Massachusetts Avenue and the League of Women for Community Service at 558 Massachusetts Avenue.[13]

One of the most influential Black Bostonians in the early twentieth century was William Monroe Trotter, who forced a profound shift in national civil rights tactics through a public confrontation with Booker T. Washington in the South End. Trotter's activism grew out of his background as an elite Black Brahmin. The city and its extensive social network of Black Brahmins provided a strong education for its youth, a tradition of advocacy for social justice, and a safe place to launch protests.[14]

Trotter inherited his activism from his father, James Monroe Trotter, who had been born a slave in Mississippi in 1842 and made his way to Cincinnati before the Civil War. The elder Trotter traveled to Massachusetts to volunteer for the Union army, rising to second lieutenant. After the war, he worked for the post office until he resigned in protest against racial discrimination.[2] The younger Trotter was a gifted student who attended desegregated schools and graduated from Harvard, but he could not find employment in downtown firms. It was the money from his father's real estate investments that made him well off.[7]

The end of the nineteenth century saw a serious decline in the status of Blacks across the United States, particularly in the South. Energized by the end of Reconstruction, racist whites systematically disenfranchised Blacks, stripped them of basic human rights, and instigated a terrorizing regime of violence.[15] As this affected the lives and livelihoods of all Blacks, a coordinated national strategy was critical.

The most prominent Black figure at this time and the man who would shape the initial response to the crisis was Booker T. Washington. He was born a slave in 1856, grew up in West Virginia, and attended the Hampton Normal and Agricultural Institute in Virginia. Indicative of his intellect and the depth of support he had among white philanthropists, at twenty-five he became head of the newly founded Tuskegee Institute in Alabama. It quickly became the country's premier Black institution, and for the twenty years after 1895, "Washington was the most powerful Negro in the United States." He received honorary degrees, summered on Martha's Vineyard and New York, and shared meals with Queen Victoria and President Theodore Roosevelt.[16] Both Blacks and whites looked to Washington for leadership against the rising violence and repression.

Washington articulated his response to growing violence and segregation in his 1895 Atlanta Compromise. In this historic speech, he proposed that in return for access to basic "industrial" education and minimal tolerance, Blacks would not agitate for civil rights or struggle against the encroaching restrictions on their freedom. To reward this approach, white philanthropic interests would fund Black institutions, such as Tuskegee, to assist Blacks in improving themselves over time. Washington argued that this compromise was necessary to protect Blacks from violence and represented the best way to help his race deal with a society overwhelmingly arrayed against it.[17] Washington and his supporters, often called Bookerites or the Tuskegee Machine, advanced this agenda through tight control over the Black media and a monopoly on funds from white philanthropists. To oppose Washington could mean isolation, unemployment, and bankruptcy.[16]

The man who would break Washington's compromise and lay the groundwork for the twentieth century civil rights movement was W.E.B. DuBois. He was from western Massachusetts and attended Harvard a couple of years before Trotter. DuBois and Trotter had a long, complicated relationship, both personally and professionally. DuBois had dated Geraldine Louise Pindell, who would eventually marry Trotter, and they both lived and operated within the same political and social milieu. Both shared the objective of fighting rising racist oppression and were against Washington's accommodationist policies.

They had vastly different temperaments, however. Trotter strenuously attacked racism and discrimination no matter whom he alienated, relishing his solo activism. DuBois was more cerebral and deliberate as he sought to build a national coalition to confront racism and discrimination.[18] DuBois didn't like the brutal efficiency of Washington's machine, but it was difficult for anyone to oppose the Atlanta Compromise's policy of accommodation, and premature opposition could have meant silence and defeat, so DuBois hesitated to publicly break with Washington.[19]

Trotter's fiery activism made compromise and circumspection impossible. To advance his more confrontational strategy, Trotter and George Forbes, an assistant librarian at the Boston Public Library, began publishing The Guardian on November 9, 1901. This weekly paper cost five cents per issue (or $1.50 for a year's subscription) and mostly reprinted news and gossip from papers in other cities. But its opinion page was a national challenge to Washington, boasting the motto, "For every right with all thy might." A typical issue, for example, had a headline calling for a meeting at Faneuil Hall to promote voting rights in the South; articles on social events in Worcester, Brooklyn, and Pittsburg; advertisements for tailors, dentists, and music lessons; and an editorial against Blacks establishing their own hospital in Boston. Trotter was against self-segregation and insisted on complete integrated equality.[20] In another example of Trotter's unwillingness to compromise his ideals, he refused ads for alcohol despite the revenue they would bring to his struggling paper.[21] The paper quickly attracted a small but influential readership, though no one except Trotter and a few allies was willing to openly challenge the Atlanta Compromise.

Despite Trotter's strong opposition of his platform, Washington had no reason to fear going to Boston. He had delivered an uneventful address at the Hollis Street Theater in 1899 and had launched his National Negro Business League in the city.[14] Though Trotter had tried to incite Washington into doing something foolish to force a break with DuBois, Washington avoided being baited. Even after Trotter called him a coward, Washington held back. But on the night of June 30, 1903, Washington visited Boston and was met by chaotic protests from Trotter and his allies. The resulting incident, dubbed the Boston Riot, would lead to DuBois publicly breaking with Washington and drive him to join what eventually would become the NAACP.

The gathering was at the AME Zion Church on Columbus Avenue. So many people tried to get into the large church that they overflowed into the street, hindering effective crowd control. The anti-Bookerites struck first, hissing at pro-Washington comments from the podium. George Fortune, the editor of the pro-Washington newspaper The New York Age, then denounced Trotter and his allies using thunderous rhetoric. Enraged, a Trotterite in the audience rose to protest, but security forcibly removed him from the hall. Next, someone threw cayenne pepper at the stage, agitating both sides. Then when Washington at last stepped up to the podium, pandemonium took over.

Washington's security people pulled Trotter outside, but he rushed back into the chaos as fistfights broke out in the aisles and one man was stabbed. As the meeting became even more surreal, Trotter stood on a chair, shouting a list of insinuating questions at the stage, but no one could hear him amidst the uproar. Summoned by Washington supporters, the police arrested Trotter and his sister, who was accused of trying to stab a policeman with a hatpin. Trotter's mother had to bail them out of the East Dedham Street station house. Eventually, police and security forces restored peace long enough for Washington to give his speech.[16] Prosecuted by the authorities at Washington's insistence, Trotter was fined fifty dollars and jailed for a month.[7]

Enraged, Washington retaliated by trying to destroy Trotter and The Guardian. He attempted to buy up the paper's debts and hired secret agents

to infiltrate his Boston opponents' meetings.[16] Seeking to silence the growing resistance, Washington attacked DuBois for not controlling Trotter, even
though DuBois was not in town during the riot, and Washington's strong
reaction convinced DuBois that it was imperative to organize a counter-
movement. In the end, Washington's display of power after the riot pushed
a reluctant DuBois into leading those opposed to Booker's accommodationist policies to publicly break with him. DuBois made one more attempt to
reconcile the two camps later that year but concluded that a split was inevitable.[23] He and Trotter helped organize the Niagara Movement, which was
dedicated to actively opposing segregation and anti-Black violence, in 1905.
A few years later, the organization was folded into the NAACP.

After the fallout from the Boston Riot, Trotter continued his desegregation efforts, even challenging president Wilson at a meeting in the Oval
Office, but to little avail. Over time, his relationship with DuBois soured. His
pugnacious attitude lost him many allies, his newspaper failed, and he had
to sell off his father's real estate to cover his growing debts. Nevertheless,
when he died in 1934 by jumping off a building in the South End, throngs
of people came to pay their respects at a memorial service for Trotter held at
Faneuil Hall.[24] The funeral at People's Baptist Church attracted 1,500 people,
so many that speakers had to be placed outside for the overflow crowd.[25]
DuBois authored a stirring obituary for Trotter in the NAACP's The Crisis,
proclaiming that Trotter "was a man of heroic proportions and probably one
of the most selfless of Negro leaders during all of our American history…
He had in his soul all that went to make a fanatic, a knight errant."[26]

A prominent and influential Black institution in the 1920s was the Universal Negro Improvement Association (UNIA), which Marcus Garvey
founded in Jamaica in 1914. He brought the group to the United States
when he immigrated to New York in 1916; UNIA set up a Boston branch
three years later. The group's strong ideology focused on entrepreneurship,
respectability, and social activities. Its highly disciplined structure included
female and male presidents, ladies' clubs, and a youth auxiliary. As was the
case nationally, Boston's UNIA was mostly West Indian; its local headquarters was across the street from St. Cyprian's.[6] Its membership included many
influential Bostonians, such as the South End businessman and activist John
Bynoe, and Elma Lewis, who would make important contributions to the
city's arts scene.

The Boston chapter was closely tied to the more well-known and flam-
boyant New York chapter. While it focused on social and economic issues

rather than political ones, it did share the larger group's rhetoric and love of pomp and costume.[6] Unfortunately, Garvey's involvement in the Black Star Line, a shipping company that worked to advance Black economic power, led to legal issues. Even though he was deported and died penniless in London during World War II, his group helped many Blacks cope with disappointment and discrimination. The UNIA also influenced other movements, including the Nation of Islam, in later decades.

The UNIA was not alone in its love of glamour. On August 24, 1924, for example, a national gathering of Black Shriners, a Black fraternal organization, paraded from the headquarters of its Boston chapter in Douglas Square through the South End on their way to City Hall. They passed a reviewing stand that included the Governor, and a deputy mayor said of the parade: "The costumes were of the most brilliant sort, reveling in yellows, greens, blues and purples, and various combinations thereof, and the wearers wheeled and executed maneuvers on the route, danced part of the time, and played "peppy" music on shrine bands."[27] In this and other ways, Boston's Blacks found ways to demonstrate their pride and celebrate their community.

Due to its location between downtown Boston and the mainland, the South End bore the brunt of the city's transportation needs. In the first half of the nineteenth century, omnibuses—horse drawn coaches serving multiple passengers—had regular service down Washington Street. Soon railroads arrived, passing through the Back Bay and the downtown edge of the South End. A major advancement was the development of faster and more reliable streetcars, and horse-driven trolleys replaced carriages and omnibuses in the 1850s. After the city introduced electrification in the 1880s, the annual citywide number of passengers vastly increased with eighty million rides annually by 1885.[28]

Building a streetcar line to Roxbury was controversial enough that South Enders circulated a petition against its construction because they feared it would create a hazard on Washington Street.[29] The petition failed to stop the line, however, and construction quickly began. An unfortunate side effect was that construction ended the neighborhood pastime of sleigh racing during the winter. Crews who shoveled the snow to keep the tracks clear ruined the long runs needed for the races.[30] By 1895, there were east-west trolley lines on Columbus, Tremont, Shawmut, Washington, and Harrison, with north-south lines on Dover/Berkeley, Dartmouth, and Massachusetts/Northampton Streets (to respect Chester Square, the line jogged a block west).[31]

Unfortunately, trolleys caused congestion. Lines from around the metropolitan region, including most South End trolleys, converged on Tremont and Washington Streets downtown, blocking the passage of pedestrians and trucks and creating chaos and traffic jams. In 1891, the State Legislature tried to fix the problem by adopting a new transportation plan for the region that consolidated railroad operations at North and South Stations, constructed a streetcar subway under Tremont Street downtown, and extended elevated and subway lines to Charlestown, Cambridge, Roxbury, and Dorchester. As a result of this plan, the Elevated would blight Washington Street for most of the twentieth century.

5.2 THE WASHINGTON STREET ELEVATED

George A. Kimball, a respected civil engineer who had been involved in the planning of the metropolitan sewage system, oversaw the Elevated's design and construction. Together with J.A.L. Waddell, who had designed the Chicago Elevated, they developed preliminary plans to connect downtown with Roxbury. With final approvals given on April 29, 1898, construction began on January 23, 1899. It was not easy to build the Elevated in the dense neighborhood, and to keep the electric trolleys running during the day, construction took place at night. The materials arrived after 7 PM and most of the work occurred between midnight and 5 AM.

The stations on the new Elevated were beautiful. The Northampton and Dover Stations were sheathed in copper with dormer windows and Beaux-Arts cupolas. "At the first landing, the passenger entered an arched double door with diamond-paned lights and semi-circular transom. The second flight of stairs led directly to the waiting room lobby, where the passenger purchased his ticket at the ticket office." The ticket booths were octagonal with elaborate detailing and ironwork, and the stations' amenities included wooden benches, porters' closets and restrooms.[28]

But the effect on the neighborhood was traumatic. For the next eighty years, the Elevated was a dark, noisy, and frightening divide between the residential area to its north and the primarily industrial/institutional district to the south. Providing a cover for crime and prostitution and dripping mystery liquids on pedestrians and cars, the Elevated would have tremendous negative effects on the South End for decades.

The high number of lodging houses led to the rise of an extensive infrastructure with the appearance of cafeterias, bars, cheap clothing stores, and many other commercial establishments that met the needs of working residents. In 1897, there were two hundred establishments licensed to sell liquor in the South End along with many illegal establishments. Usually owned or controlled by breweries, these barrooms were often in basements or first floors of residential buildings. Most were small with no place to sit and limited areas for standing; patrons came in, finished their drink, then either had another or left. Drinking in bars was for men; it was illegal for women to patronize them.[32]

There were also theaters and spectacles in the South End with the area along Tremont Street between Berkeley and Clarendon Streets a center of activity. Most prominent was the Cyclorama, built in 1884 to display Paul Philippoteaux's four hundred by fifty-foot painting of the Battle of Gettysburg. Visitors entered the exhibit from Tremont Street and climbed a circular staircase to the viewing platform where mounds of dirt, trees, cannons, fences, and remnants of campfires between viewers and the painting made the tableaux more realistic. The painting, now slightly reduced in size, is on display in Pennsylvania. Over the next decades, the Cyclorama staged other major dioramas, then in the 1920s, the Flower Market moved in. The large brick buildings on the site also provided space for manufacturing. In 1906, for example, Albert Champion developed the spark plug there, a vital invention for the internal combustion engine. He moved his company to Roxbury two years later and eventually sold it to General Motors.

Another entertainment district clustered around the corner of Dover and Washington Streets. The area had begun to attract theaters as early as 1855, when Williams Hall was "filled up with panoramas, pictures, music affairs, ice cream tables, etc." Higher-income residents worried that the price of admission—only 12.5 cents—could attracted a low class of attendees.[29] During the early twentieth century, the tawdry nightlife lured a young Harvard student, Thomas Stearns Elliot, who regularly attended theatrical performances in the area and often drank the night away in neighborhood bars. The historian Douglass Shand-Tucci speculates that Elliot's South End experiences would eventually contribute to his famous poem, "The Waste Land."[33]

Three thousand people could fit in the Grand Opera House, which charged twenty and thirty cents for its seats and presented vaudeville between acts of such plays as The Ensign, The Galley Slave, and All the Comforts of Home. The management claimed the opera house attracted as many as fourteen thousand customers a week with entertainment "fit for women and children as well as men."[32] A few steps down Washington Street, the Columbia charged twenty-five cents for its cheapest seats and hosted more than ten thousand people each week. The Columbia was part of a chain that extended to New York, Philadelphia, and Pittsburg; men from Chicago owned the Grand Opera House.

A few blocks away, the Castle Square Theater presented shows that included Aida, Carmen, HMS Pinafore, and The Pirates of Penzance. At first, the Castle Square Theater aimed to produce musical performances at affordable prices. But grand operas were more successful than light ones, then after 1897, the theater shifted to straight plays.[32] John Craig, Mary Young, and their theater company moved to the Castle Square Theater in 1908 and operated the facility until 1916. The couple divorced in 1930, and Craig died a year later. Young moved to Hollywood, where her most famous role was as a dance instructor in An American in Paris with Gene Kelly.[34] The National Theater on Tremont Street was built in 1911. On opening night, September 18, the enthusiastic crowd was so taken by Irving Berlin's new hit, Alexander's Ragtime Band, that they demanded multiple encores.[35] Most of the Castle Square Theater was torn down in 1933; its hotel annex survived as the Chandler Inn, and the Animal Rescue League moved to the site in 1956. The National was demolished to make way for the expansion of the Boston Center for the Arts in 2002.

As Boston segregated its theaters and other public venues, some South End Blacks found ways around these new racial barriers. One such entrepreneur was Edward Price, a former vaudeville star, who bought the Old Crown Theater at 390 Tremont Street in 1910. A master of marketing, he changed the name of the theater to the Peking to take advantage of the fame of a Black-owned chain of theaters in the Midwest. He also had a strong commitment to social justice and was a member of the Colored Vaudeville Benevolent Association (CVBA), a national organization that worked to improve conditions for Black actors. Price hosted benefits for Black performers and made his theater the home of the local branch of the CVBA. Later, Price moved his operations to the larger six-hundred seat Back Bay Theater located at the corner of Dartmouth Street and Columbus Avenue. There, he sponsored talent contests, organized tryouts, and promoted local talent.[36] These theaters allowed Blacks to socialize and participate in group activities free from the prejudices and restrictions of white-owned theaters. The presence of these theaters in the South End also helped cement the neighborhood as a center of Black nightlife in Boston and New England. This would contribute to the great flowering of Black entertainment in the South End after 1930.

For decades, the South End was the largest rooming-house district in Boston, home to 3,200 of the city's five thousand licensed lodging houses in 1918. As in the nineteenth century, these tended to house working people. Poorer individuals were more likely to sleep in cheap hotels, many of which were in the neighborhood as well. We may never have known much about these often destitute residents if it were not for one of Boston's greatest tragedies. The Arcadia Hotel Fire in 1913 cost twenty-eight men their lives. The fire was caused by a poorly insulated furnace under the stairs. Located at the corner of Laconia and Washington Streets, the Arcadia had been turned into a residential hotel that hosted some of the humblest men in the city.

In the aftermath of the fire, there were investigations into the hotel's living conditions, where officials learned that the Arcadia sheltered up to 170 men on any given night. A five-story brick building with a saloon on the first floor and rooms above, the hotel covered most of its lot with a main building fronting on Washington Street with a rear annex accessible only through the main building. There was only one interior stairwell serving all rooms, a design that had tragic consequences during the fire. On the fourth and fifth floors, there were rows of iron frame bunk beds, each about two feet from its neighbor, allowing thirty or more men to sleep in a single room. The second and third floors were divided by partitions that ended two to three feet from the ceiling. These exceedingly small rooms (eight by six feet) were off one long hallway. Only a few had windows, but because these rooms afforded some privacy, they were more expensive, costing twenty-five cents per night. Cots on the fourth floor went for twenty cents, fifth floor beds fifteen cents, and managers often let the poorest sleep in the lobby for whatever they could pay. On the night of the fire, there were seventy-four men registered to sleep in the fifteen-cent beds, fifty in the twenty-cent beds, and seventeen in the twenty-five-cent beds. There were signs indicating emergency exits, but rather than leading to safety, they led to dead ends or to corner rooms that lacked fire escapes. Many died there while others perished from jumping out of upper windows.[37]

After the fire, there were renewed efforts to create better housing in the South End, including the redevelopment of the Franklin Square House to provide accommodations for female residents. Reverend George Lander Perin of the Shawmut Universalist Church spearheaded the conversion of the former St. James Hotel from Conservatory Building to women's housing after he polled his parishioners about the needs of single, working women. He found they often labored ten hours a day, six days a week for a dollar a day. Given that housing and food cost about five dollars a week, these women had no money for decent housing and no time for moral living.

Perin wanted to provide safe, affordable housing in a setting free from temptation, so he turned to what had been the St. James Hotel near his church. The Boston Conservatory of Music, founded by Eben Tourjee, a well-connected musician and educator, had taken over the building. Through his efforts, the Conservatory grew into an institution with almost two thousand students and nearly one hundred faculty and administrators. It had practice rooms and rehearsal halls, but no venues for recitals. Instead, most of the building was given over to residences; Tourjee's family lived on the top floor, and five hundred young women rented rooms on the lower floors. After Tourjee's death, the school's leadership sought a new location with a concert hall, and they offered to sell the building to Perin for $250,000, which he raised from philanthropists.

In keeping with Perin's priorities regarding morality, one interesting feature of the Franklin Square House was that its first floor had a series of parlors where residents could entertain male visitors in an atmosphere of propriety and semi-privacy.[38] The building would go on to house thousands of women over the next several decades until rising costs and falling demand created problems in the 1960s. After renovations, it is affordable housing for the elderly today.

World War I brought both hardship and prosperity to the South End, in part because many of its working-class families and lodgers had such limited incomes, they could not afford rising rents. In contrast, rapid wartime inflation enabled some families to purchase row houses by using increasing rents to pay mortgages, but most did not reconvert them back into to single-family homes. Instead, the buildings were turned into tenements, packed with as many families and boarders as possible to meet the burden of contract payments. Wartime deprivation also created problems. In 1918, there was a coal shortage that caused so much distress, the South End House sought to secure supplies and keep speculators from driving up prices even more.[12]

Post war, the neighborhood continued to be a major home for Boston area unions, and it was not surprising the city's police launched their 1919 strike here. In a room above J.J. Foley's bar on Dover Street, officers voted to walk off the job because of deteriorating work conditions and poor pay. The department was controlled by the state, and Governor Calvin Coolidge reacted harshly to the strike. He refused an offer by Samuel Gompers to mediate and ultimately authorized the hiring of a new police force. The strike failed and the fame of his stern response propelled Coolidge to national office.

Because the neighborhood was close to Back Bay and South Stations, the integrated and welcoming South End housed many Black railroad workers and their unions located in the neighborhood as well. In the 1920s, before A. Phillip Randolph organized the Brotherhood of Sleeping Car Porters, they earned sixty-seven dollars for laboring 240 hours a month. By the end of World War II, thanks to wartime scarcities and union advocacy, wages had risen to $175 per week, not including tips. This increase made these jobs highly desirable for low-skilled Blacks, and porters became highly respected members of the community. Another important South End-based Black railroad union was Dining Car Waiters Local 370, affiliated with the Hotel and Restaurant Union, which won its first contract with Pullman in 1937. In the 1950s, the union fought to desegregate the cafeteria cars, and it filed one of the first cases with the Massachusetts Commission Against Discrimination.

Railroad work was not easy. A worker reported to the Back Bay or Albany Street yards and was dispatched across the country, sometimes not returning for weeks at a time. Finding housing in Boston between trips could be difficult as well, and thus, several South End lodging houses specifically catered to Black railroad workers. Many lived on West Springfield Street or the side streets along Columbus Avenue.[39] These Black-dominated unions faded after World War II as cars and airplanes replaced railroads. The last union headquartered in the South End was the Hotel Workers Union on Berkeley Street; it moved to Chinatown around 2010.

In the 1930s, the South End House organized the Boston Rooming House Association. With three hundred members, most were located between Massachusetts Avenue and Waltham Street and Columbus and Shawmut Avenues. Landladies boasted that they had no locks on their doors, neither to the street nor to individual rooms, because they based their businesses on the careful selection of their tenants. To survive, landladies had to be salespeople, convincing reliable people to room in their houses while keeping guard against troublesome or deadbeat lodgers. One landlady noted her profession needed "patience, taste, and a great deal of diplomacy."[40] Some tended to be strict, others more relaxed, and individual landladies acquired reputations and followings. Some tenants rented rooms for years in a specific house.

5.3 JJ FORLEY'S

There were landladies who avoided renting to students, the elderly, or others who tended to be around all day and needed to have their rooms always heated. Some preferred to rent to women, some to men, while others had unique house rules regarding both sexes. For example, The Midtown Journal, a weekly scandal sheet covering the South End, reported on a landlady who smelled smoke early one morning and checked each floor to find two of her lodgers in bed together along with a dog. Angered by this egregious rule breaking, she evicted the lodgers. The landlady did not allow pets in her building.[41]

Some lodging houses had a sink in every room, but most had just one single toilet/shower room in the building. The City's standard was one bath for every fifteen residents, though some of the better residences had twice that ratio. One constant was managing tenants to make sure they did not take too much time cleaning themselves. Many of the district's older furnaces could not heat above the third floor, so the cold upper floors were cheaper. The financial returns continued to be modest, however; in 1930, rooms rented from $3.50 to $7.00 a week, and it was often difficult to keep a rooming house in business on the rents collected, particularly during slow times. Many landladies relied on their husbands or worked jobs that could supplement household expenses when rooms were vacant. A cleaning woman might come in two to three days a week, but for the most part, the landladies kept the buildings clean and maintained them themselves.[42]

The Rooming House Association lasted at least through the end of World War II. During the war, it held black-out drills and organized the civil defense of the neighborhood. The landladies sold bonds, planned evacuation drills (boasting that they had alternative housing for 100 percent of South End residents in the event of an emergency), and learned first aid. The members supported each other emotionally, traded tips on how to manage a house, and lobbied the city for services.[43]

In every era, Boston Blacks sought political power and elective office to advance their community and protect themselves from discrimination, and sometimes, they were successful.[44] Mayor John F. Fitzgerald, for example, courted the Black vote. In a speech to a Black audience at Faneuil Hall, he criticized President Theodore Roosevelt for his response to an August 1906 incident in Brownsville, Texas, a major national issue in its day.[45] After the shooting of a white bartender, the police had accused a group of Black soldiers, with many fearing they were being framed. When the soldiers refused to incriminate any of their number, Roosevelt waited until after the November election and then discharged the entire regiment without honor, sparking complaints and demonstrations across the country.[14] In Boston, many Blacks endorsed John Fitzgerald's mayoral reelection with the slogan, "Remember Brownsville!"

For the most part, unfortunately, Black issues were exacerbated by the racist attitudes of Boston's progressive politicians. Mostly Republicans who dominated downtown business interests, progressives refused to adopt policies to address the community's needs or halt the increasing segregation hemming in Boston's slowly increasing Black population. Thus, Boston Blacks were reluctant to join Good Government campaigns and began to shift to the Democratic Party well in advance of their counterparts in other cities. For example, after progressive James Storrow promised not to hire Black teachers at any school with more than fifty white children, Blacks further rallied around Fitzgerald.[6]

Boston politics continued to be dominated by the fight between Irish Catholics, who were a majority in the city, and suburban-based Yankee Protestants, who dominated the legislature and statewide offices. For much of the twentieth century, this conflict was personified by one man, James Michael

Curley, who was an overwhelming force in Boston politics in part because of his success in polarizing the electorate to defeat his Yankee Republican opponents. He was a native South Ender, born on Northampton Street, and he lived at several addresses in the neighborhood in his youth. In his memoirs, he writes of coping with sewer contaminated flooding from the Roxbury Canal, selling newspapers under the Washington Street Elevated, and walking up multiple flights of stairs in the area's row houses.[46] Over the course of his career, he was elected congressman three times, mayor four times (1914-18, 1922-26, 1930-34, and 1946-50), and governor once. Relishing his rapscallion reputation, he was imprisoned twice, the second time during his final term as mayor, paving the way for John Hynes to assume the office.

In the South End, the large numbers of Irish families and owners of lodging houses helped the neighborhood access the city's ethnic-based political spoils system for a while. But as the percentage of Irish in the neighborhood began to fall and Blacks, Jews, Syrians, and others moved into the neighborhood, the South End's leadership became increasingly dominated by anti-Irish settlement house workers such as Robert Woods. Demographic change and the unwillingness of Irish City Hall politicians to work with Blacks led to the decline of the South End's influence. Ultimately, this distance between City Hall and the South End ushered in the political climate that almost destroyed the neighborhood through urban renewal.[47]

Though the South End was securely Curley territory, its residents rarely received the rewards they deserved for their support. Curley consolidated his spoils system of municipal jobs and services for the benefit of his Irish base who were increasingly dependent on public sector jobs as Boston's economy declined, and it became harder for Blacks to convince the city's political establishment to advance their agenda. For example, even though Trotter and others made a significant effort to force City Hospital to employ Black nurses and doctors, most other city jobs remained closed to them. Decade by decade, the position of Boston's Blacks declined.

Prohibition forced the many bars and taverns in the South End to become secret clubs that endured sporadic attempts at enforcement. A series of raids in May 1930, for example, hit forty-three speakeasies in the South End and Bay Village, but the crackdowns had little lasting impact. There were said to be four hundred barrooms in the South End during Prohibition.[48]

One prominent bootlegger who controlled many of the illegal venues in the neighborhood was Charles "King" Solomon. He was noted for his tailored suits, slicked back hair, and the beautiful women he escorted around town. He diversified his business empire into theaters, hotels, loan companies, and real estate as he ruled his empire through intimidation and violence. Though he was never convicted of murder, he was associated with mobsters such as Meyer Lansky, Dutch Schultz, and Bugsy Siegel who were known for their lethal ruthlessness. Solomon came to a bad end on January 3, 1930 at the Cotton Club on Tremont Street at 3:30 AM. When he rose from his table to go to the restroom, he was gunned down by an unidentified group of men sitting at a nearby table. Thousands gathered to mourn at Solomon's Brookline home, and crowds lined the streets between the funeral home and the cemetery. Hundreds were at the gravesite.[48]

After Prohibition ended, bars—which were newly co-ed— came out in force in the South End, some licensed, some not. Much of the neighborhood's raw life was chronicled in the Midtown Journal, published by Frederick Shibley under the pseudonym Ibn Snupin. Shibley was a former vaudeville actor and dancer who turned to writing after serving a jail term for robbery. Published from 1938 to 1966, the journal's breezy accounts of crime and sex often scandalized proper Bostonians.[34] The paper would report people being intimate in local theaters, alleys, cars, benches, and on front steps as well as in lodging houses, where everyone knew when someone visited.[41] Shibley enjoyed writing about anything tawdry or salacious and causally detailed fights, muggings, and robberies.

The level of violence in the neighborhood, often fueled by alcohol abuse, was disturbingly high. Men regularly assaulted women, and there was a constant parade of arrests for women fighting women and men fighting men.[41] The police announced a crackdown on crime and drinking in the South End after Lieutenant Governor Horace Cahill's brother was attacked near the corner of Washington Street and Massachusetts Avenue in 1937. It was accompanied by descriptions that called the neighborhood shabby, the center of the narcotics trade in New England, and "the residence of a large number of the city's law violators, many of whom have no home or even a room in a dingy rooming house, but sleep on in hallways, alleys and refuse-littered backyards."[49]

For much of the twentieth century, the South End was one of the poorest neighborhoods in a declining city. As Boston's economy collapsed and a smoldering civil war between Irish Catholics and Yankee Protestants sapped its vitality, the city seemed on the verge of chaos with the South End suffering terribly from neglect. The neighborhood became infamous for low-class entertainment, dive bars, and places for immoral behavior. Many Bostonians felt the South End needed rehabilitation and a thorough scrubbing to cleanse it of vice. If that did not work, their solution was to bulldoze the neighborhood altogether and start fresh. Unfortunately for the South End, that would soon be the official city plan as well.

1. Klimasmith B. Race, Politics, and Public Housekeeping: Contending Forces in Pauline Hopkin's Boston. *Trotter Review* 2009; 19.

2. Hewitt JH. A Black New York newspaperman's impressions of Boston, 1883. *The Massachusetts Review* 1991;32:445-63.

3. Dowdy ZR. Farrakhan's Boston roots Early days in black community here, friends say, helped shape leader. *Boston Globe*; 1994 July 27.

4. West D. *The Living is Easy. New York*: The Feminist Press; 1948. 108   109

5. Ballou RA. Even in "Freedom's Birthplace"! *The Development of Boston's Black Ghetto, 1900-1940*. Ann Arbor, Michigan: University of Michigan; 1984.

6. Johnson VS. *The Other Black Bostonians: West Indians in Boston, 1900-1950*. Bloomington, Indiana: Indiana University Press; 2006.

7. Hayden RC. William Monroe Trotter: A One-Man Protester for Civil Rights. *Trotter Review* 1988; 2.

8. South End House Association. *Thirteenth Annual Report*. 1905.

9. Streiff M. *Boston's Settlement Housing: Social Reform in an Industrial City*. Louisiana State University; 2005.

10. Deutsch S. *Women and the City: Gender, Space and Power in Boston 1870-1940*. New York: Oxford University Press; 2000.

11. Potts L. *A Block in Time: A History of Boston's South End From a Window on Holyoke Street*. New York: Local History Publishers; 2012.

12. Boer A. *The Development of USES: A Chronology of the United South End Settlements 1891-1966*. Boston: United South End Settlements; 1966.

13. Knight L. *Interview with Kessler Montgomery*. 1991.

14. Schneider MR. *Boston Confronts Jim Crow, 1890-1920*. Boston: Northeastern University Press; 1997.

15. Woodward V. *The Strange Career of Jim Crow*. New York: Oxford University Press; 1955.

16. Fox SR. *The Guardian of Boston: William Monroe Trotter*. New York: Atheneum; 1970.

17. Cummings M. Historical setting for Booker T. Washington and the rhetoric of compromise, 1895. *Journal of Black Studies* 1977;8:75-82.

18. Green DS, Smith E. *W.E.B. DuBois and the Concepts of Race and Class*. Phylon 1983; 44:262-72.

19. Chaffee ML. William E. B. DuBois' concept of the racial problem in the United States:

The early Negro education movement. *The Journal of Negro Education* 1956; 41:241-58.

20. Trotter WM. *The Guardian;* 1903 February 14.

21. Worthy W. South End Memories. *Boston Globe;* 1971 December 5.

22. Trotter WM. Booker Washington Speaks Under a Cordon of Police. *The Guardian;* 1903 August 1.

23. Rudwick EM. Race Leadership Struggle: Background of the Boston Riot of 1903. *The Journal of Negro Education* 1962:1.

24. Memorial Services. Held for Negroes' Champion. *Boston Globe;* 1934 May 29.

25. William Trotter Funeral. William Trotter Funeral Tuesday: One of Outstanding Negro Leaders in Nation. *Boston Globe;* 1934 April 8.

26. DuBois WEB. William Monroe Trotter. *The Crisis;* 1934 May.

27. Colored Shriners. Colored Shriners In Most Brilliant And Snappy Parade. *Boston Globe;* 1926 August 26.

28. Zaitzevsky CR. *Historical Documentation Boston Elevated Railway Company Washington Street Elevated Mainline Structure (MBTA Orange Line).* 1987.

29. Everett E. *Letter.* To: Everett OB,.1855.

30. Everett E. *Letter.* To: Everett OB, 1859.

31. Cheape CW. *Moving the Masses: Urban Public Transit in New York, Boston, and Philadelphia, 1880-1912.* Cambridge, Massachusetts: Harvard University Press; 1980.

32. Woods RA. *The City Wilderness: A Settlement Study.* Boston: Houghton, Mifflin and Company; 1898.

33. *Dover Street Rag: The Grand Opera House.* 2014. (Accessed June 15, 2014, at http://www.backbayhistorical.org/blog/archives/1032.)

34. Shannon HJ. *Legendary Locals of Boston's South End.* Charleston, South Carolina: Arcadia Publishing; 2014.

35. Some History *Behind the Buildings of the Boston Center for the Arts.* 2013. (Accessed January 20, 2014, at http://www.southendhistory.org/.)

36. Garcia DJ. Subversive sounds: ethnic spectatorship and Boston's nickelodeon theatres, 1907-1914. *Film History* 2007; 19:213-27.

37. Carberry JW. Lured into Death Traps. *Boston Globe;* 1913 December 4.

38. Hinchliffe B, Smith BH. *The House that Love Built.* Boston: Franklin Square House Foundation; 2012.

39. Green JR, Hayden RC. A. Philip Randolph and Boston's African-American Railroad Worker' *Trotter Review* 1992; 6.

40. Careful. Careful What You Say About The Old South End Nowadays: Militant Landladies Have Redeemed It and Will Not Rest Until They Have Made It Over Into Spotless Town. *Boston Globe;* 1931 April 19.

41. Snupin I. *Reeling Around Boston*. Journal Publishing Company; 1945.

42. Landlady A. Takes A Diplomat Nowadays To Manage A Rooming House Well: Also Patience, Good Taste, a Business Head and Personality, says One Woman Who Goes In For Light and Real Home Feeling. *Boston Globe*; 1931 January 4.

43. Mahoney M. South End Has Unique Club of Rooming House Keepers. *Boston Globe*; 1945 July 19.

44. Jones HE. Introduction. In: Jennings J, King M, eds. *From Access to Power: Black Politics in Boston*. Cambridge, Massachusetts: Schenkman Books; 1986.

45. Ryan DP. *Beyond the Ballot Box: A Social History of the Boston Irish, 1845-1917*. Rutherford, New Jersey: Fairleigh Dickinson University Press; 1983.

46. Curley JM. *I'd Do It Again*. New York: Arno Press; 1976.

47. Connolly JJ. Reconstructing ethnic politics: Boston, 1909-1925. *Social Science History* 1995; 19:479-509.

48. Schorow S. *Drinking Boston: A History of the City and its Spirits*. Boston: Union Park Press; 2012.

49. Purge Planned. Purge Planned For South End. Criminals There Face Six Weeks' Drive Plainclothes Men to Conduct War on Drinkers' Assailants. *Boston Globe*; 1937 March 1 ;Sect. 1.

CHAPTER 6

The Run Up to Urban Renewal: 1940-1960

In the decades before and after World War II, the South End was a target for comprehensive urban renewal, one of many urban neighborhoods across the country threatened or destroyed by large-scale redevelopment. Nationally, the need for renewal was first articulated in the 1920s as immigration ceased, suburbanization grew, and cars transformed how people lived.[1] This combination threatened to depopulate cities as no new residents were available to replace those moving to the urban periphery to enjoy car-based lifestyles. Shoddily constructed to hastily meet the great immigration wave that crested before World War I, by now, many buildings needed renovations to bring them up to modern standards. US cities looked shabby, dirty, and unfit for industry and clean moral living. The gathering urban exodus threatened city budgets and struck fear in the banks, developers, and others with property investments, not to mention that the distasteful politics of the poor urban masses terrified the wealthy. Eyeing old road networks and nineteenth-century architectural forms, many thought that cities were outmoded and unable to compete in the modern economy.[2] Even successful urban areas were thought to be at risk, as some believed that rising traffic and congestion were bad for health.[3] Boston, one of the most troubled cities in this era, was seen as particularly in need of radical rebuilding. The worst urban places, in the view of many theorists and administrators, were working-class tenement districts such as the South End. Ideas and beliefs were about to severely damage cities across the country.

This rapidly accelerating crisis prompted new theories regarding healthy urban design, and many influential architects and planners advocated for new forms of development. The more urban-focused visionaries, including the Paris-based architect Le Corbusier, proposed the idea of the skyscraper in the park to concentrate activity in large, high-rise buildings surrounded by open spaces and connected by highways. Modernist architects and planners argued this would give everyone access to sunlight, ventilation, and nature as well as allow for the efficient provision of services. In one breath taking example of Modernist planning, Le Corbusier proposed demolishing the Right Bank of Paris and replacing it with cruciform towers set in broad parks.[4] These theories would dominate urban design in the postwar United States, which built public housing projects such as St. Louis's Pruitt Igoe and commercial developments including San Francisco's Embarcadero Center.[5] It would also shape part of the South End, particularly the designs for Castle Square, the New York Streets, and the Cathedral development. By the 1950s, these ideas would even provide the framework for proposals to demolish and reconstruct the entire neighborhood.

Others proposed suburban-focused alternatives aimed to do away with cities altogether and spread the population out into single-family dwellings, each on its own substantial parcel of land, so families could live independently as if they were yeoman farmers. This idea had many advocates, including Frank Lloyd Wright, whose Broadacre City would be one prototype for post-World War II suburbia in the United States.[6,7] Others, including the influential mid-twentieth-century urban theorist Lewis Mumford, promoted garden cities and a rationalization of chaotic urban development as a way to address the crime, social pathology, and mental illness they associated with urban living.[8] Though the South End was never rebuilt as detached single-family homes (one city plan for the neighborhood did come close to adopting this ideal) or radically demolished to meet the designs of the garden city movement, the fact that people were advocating these ideas added to the perception that the neighborhood was dated and unhealthy. City officials, business leaders, journalists and others misunderstood how the South End functioned, and their values and assumptions influenced how Bostonians viewed this unique neighborhood. The fact that the South End even survived despite this bias against it is a testament to the beauty of its architecture and the resourcefulness and courage of its residents.

In the 1930s, Boston was declining economically, hemorrhaging middle-class residents, and facing bankruptcy. While banks, law firms, and insurance companies had their offices downtown, they invested in the suburbs. Eyeing the city from the safety of their suburban homes, they believed Boston was corrupt and crowded. Every city in the country suffered in the 1930s, but Boston's decay had started at the end of World War I. It had missed the prosperity of the roaring twenties and failed to reverse itself as the national economy revived at the end of the Depression.[9] The debate over how to save the city became particularly important during this crucial time in the South End's history.

Boston's urban renewal efforts began with a large-scale public housing program in the 1930s and accelerated with a 1940 planning initiative. An advisory board set up to oversee the development and implementation of a comprehensive plan included banking and insurance company representatives, labor leaders, charity directors, real estate professionals, the League of Women Voters, and the deans of the area's major architecture schools. Critically, it did not include neighborhood residents.[10] The motivation for the plan was 1930s federal legislation that launched forty years of federal support for low-income housing and urban renewal. To receive funds, the federal government required cities to adopt general plans and create specialized agencies. In response, Boston established the City Planning Board and Boston Housing Authority (BHA). The Planning Board developed the first renewal plans for the South End while the BHA served as the city's official housing and urban renewal agency until renewal powers were transferred to the newly created Boston Redevelopment Authority (BRA) in 1957.

6.1 CORNER OF CASTLE STREET AND SHAWMUT AVENUE, 1938

The Planning Board used a biomedical metaphor to describe the need for urban renewal, calling Boston the "diseased heart of the metropolitan region."[11] It noted that the South End, given its strategic location in the center of the city, proximity to the main commercial areas of downtown and Back Bay, social problems, and deteriorated housing stock, had to play a major role in the rebuilding and revitalization of the city. Thus, the South End was a city priority more than twenty years before the first plan for its renewal was formally released.

The Board used the framework of neighborhood change developed by Earnest Burgess and Robert Park to justify the need for renewal: urban neighborhoods are initially built for the wealthy and well maintained, but over time, all will decay and need to be redeveloped. Other sources of distress, the Board pointed out, were decentralization and suburbanization, which prompted the movement of people out of the city and left the neighborhood unwanted and ill-suited for "desirable living."[11]

In the view of city administrators, the issues in the South End were a concern for all of Boston because the neighborhood generated a high demand for services while not producing enough taxes to pay for them. With chronic municipal budget deficits and rising debt pushing the city to insolvency, this viewpoint transformed issues inside the neighborhood into threats to the vitality of the entire city, if not the state. From this perspective, renewal of the South End was imperative to save Boston and the region.[10]

This mindset had grave consequences for the South End and similar neighborhoods across the country. Because they were thought to be outmoded and unhealthy, the United States government and private financial companies withheld mortgages and credit from their residents and investors. If decline was inevitable and irreversible, as Burgess and Park forcefully predicted, then any investment in these areas was doomed. This extreme pessimism permeated both government and the private sector and would destroy communities home to millions. In response to the collapse of the housing market caused by the Great Depression, the Roosevelt administration created a range of new mortgage products and guarantees, but their regulators and administrators prohibited their use in neighborhoods like the South End, even going so far as to draw maps of every city and town in the country outlining in red where loans were to be categorically denied. As a result of these destructive policies, after 1929, it became extremely difficult to get mortgages for properties in poor neighborhoods or areas that housed Blacks, Mexicans, Asians, or any other undesirable population. In the South End, as elsewhere, this discrimination forced owners to continue to rely on the exploitive contract lending system put in place in the 1870s even as suburban areas began to enjoy the benefits of new forms of mortgages. Without credit, decline accelerated.

Despite the urgent need for renewal, Boston lacked the ability to administer a comprehensive citywide redevelopment plan or even address the South End's entire neighborhood physical conditions. So in 1943, the city narrowed its focus to the New York Streets area, seventeen acres of tenements, warehouses, churches, bars, and theaters between Dover, Albany, and Washington Streets and the railroad tracks.[12] During the war, city planners put forth several proposals for this area, including one designed by the celebrated Bauhaus architect, Marcel Breuer. All these plans called for completely razing the area, bulldozing every building, and constructing new housing on large superblocks, which would be set off from new streets in a Modernist vision of an efficient neighborhood. Some plans called for limited retail uses and some restricted new development to entirely residential uses, but none would have been affordable to current residents. The plans particularly failed to address the special housing problems of the area's Black renters, who would be displaced. Fortunately, as the country endured World War II, the city put all plans on hold.

After the war, Boston's economic decline accelerated even as the country reached new heights of prosperity. As defense spending and new entrepreneurship sparked the founding of a preeminent technology cluster that for a while rivaled Silicon Valley, Boston's suburbs blossomed.[13] But this expansion outside the city only served to highlight Boston's failures and decay as centripetal loss added to the growing sense of despair.[14] As commerce followed the population outward and new development moved to the suburbs, the great postwar urban crisis in the United States began, particularly in Boston. The downward spiral would take years to reverse itself. Even in the late 1970s, one analysis rated Boston as more distressed than Detroit, Saint Louis, or Cleveland.[15]

South End old timers, particularly those who were children in the 1940s and 1950s, look back at the neighborhood as a place that nurtured them. They remember a close-knit community with a high degree of social capital. One displaced resident, for example, recalled roller skating and playing hopscotch and baseball while her parents watched with other parents from the stoops.[16] Another wrote of the wide mix of stores that served people of many different ethnicities.[17]

None of these experiences mattered; city planners were informed by a bias against urban living or any neighborhood that was home to the poor.[18] From 1940 to 1970, the city released a series of studies documenting the South End as being in such a desperate situation that it needed to be cleared. City planners had an extraordinarily strong incentive to denigrate the neighborhood: the city could hardly expect to receive tens of millions of dollars of federal aid for a neighborhood that was basically sound and only needed a superficial upgrade. "Planners had to project an image of [the South End] so pathologically disorganized as to require social surgery."[19]

City administrations believed the South End was a very poor neighborhood occupying potentially very valuable property; the land was near downtown and Back Bay, but as currently occupied, it was worthless. Because it was so close to the central core, in the eyes of influential Bostonians, it would have tremendous value if its low-income residents could be evicted. One reason the city prioritized renewal here was that, though it was low income, the South End "occupied a strategic location in the geopolitical competition for central-city land."[19]

Racial animus motivated planners and politicians as well. In the opinion of many, the fact that the neighborhood was a mixture of Blacks, native whites, and immigrants who all lived together without conflict was a problem that needed to be fixed. "In the minds of many socially conservative Bostonians, the locations where the lives of Blacks and whites converged stood out as spaces of aberrant behavior; a netherworld of moral degeneracy and social perversion."[20]

The South End's demographics were not the only thing that needed "fixing." Nearly a century after its nineteenth-century development, construction problems and the lack of civic investment in the neighborhood's infrastructure were becoming clear. The 1850s plan for the South End, for example, neglected to include open space beyond its few squares. The Rotch and Carter Playgrounds were on the periphery of the neighborhood, and there were very few recreational opportunities near its residential blocks, making it hard for neighborhood children to find places to play. The city had failed to address this problem for generations; it never built parks in the community even when it had opportunities to do so. Frederick Law Olmstead's great plan for an Emerald Necklace of green spaces around Boston, for example, ignored the South End.

For many, the worst aspect of living in the neighborhood was its housing conditions, which were well below contemporary or modern standards. Housing surveys consistently found large-scale problems. Renewal advocates visiting lodging houses "revealed terrible scenes of squalor, desperation, and loneliness. Most rooms were dark and gloomy, drapes pulled tight against cold, light, and the outside world. A dank, musty smell—reminiscent of cooking oil, sweat and garbage— hung in the air. Often a piece of cardboard was tacked over a broken windowpane. Chunks of ceiling plaster littered the floor. Gas burners roared perpetually to ward off the chill as the roomers huddled in ragged sweaters and thin overcoats."[21] The external environment was just as bad. "The main streets of the South End are sprinkled with the broken glass of a million wine and whiskey bottles. But it is the filth and decay of some of the side streets and back alleys that overwhelms you."[22] The city could have addressed these problems with code enforcement, better delivery of services, and so forth. But that would have required a commitment of money and effort it was not able or willing to make.

Boston's South End

After World War II, the demographics of lodging houses began to change. They were no longer home to young people moving to the city to seek their fortunes because those populations were now going to college while they lived in dorms, settling down in suburban homes, or choosing to live in modern apartment buildings on their own. Lodging houses were now the last resort for the poor, transient workers, addicts, elderly, and the disabled.[23] Though these people were simply trying to live as best as they could, given their desperate financial situations and other social, mental, and health problems, their very presence reaffirmed the biases of suburban, anti-urban, middle-class planners.[24] Because of racism, Black residents experienced the worst conditions. A 1963 public hearing by the Massachusetts Advisory Committee of the U.S. Civil Rights Commission found that Blacks faced profound discrimination in the Boston area housing market and were forced to live in appalling housing conditions.[25]

There was one positive result from this century of neglect: there was little new development to mar the nineteenth-century integrity of the neighborhood. "Architecturally, most of the South End remained frozen in a mid-nineteenth-century tableau."[21] This lack of investment and sound construction made the South End "the most elegant slum in the world."[26]

While downtown city planners were sowing the seeds of destruction, there was a final great flowering of Black culture in the western portion of the neighborhood. The area around Columbus and Massachusetts Avenues became known as a place for jazz and nightlife. The South End had long attracted Black musicians and other performers. Sammy Davis, Jr., for example, stayed at so many places during his periodic visits in the 1930s and 1940s that later residents made a game of speculating where he ate, performed, and lived.[27] The Western Lunch Box at 417 Massachusetts Avenue catered to then-unknown students like Martin Luther King and celebrities including Nat King Cole.[28] Charlie's Sandwich Shoppe, an eighty-year-old institution on Columbus Avenue, was fondly remembered not only for its food and the celebrities who ate there, but also because it served Black patrons when many other restaurants in the city would not.[29]

Though most of the clubs were owned by whites, a few provided opportunities for Black entrepreneurs. The Taylors were able to own the Pioneer Club on Westfield Street through their control of the local Democratic machine, for example. The building had been a rooming house and then a speakeasy; after the Taylors bought it in the 1940s, it became a venue where Blacks and whites socialized. It only seated fifty people but from 3 AM to 5 AM, it was often the best place for music in the city. Richard Vacca, who wrote a loving book on the history of Boston's jazz scene, noted that at the Pioneer Club, "all the royalty of jazz came through the door to relax and sometimes sit in: Miles Davis, Ella Fitzgerald, Erroll Garner, Dizzy Gillespie, Charlie Parker, Art Tatum, Sarah Vaughan, Dinah Washington, Lester Young, all of the Mills Brothers, and most of Count Basie's band somehow fit on and around that tiny stage."[28] The building was demolished in the 1970s.

Though most closed by the late 1960s, one club lasted into the twenty-first century. Its owner, Joseph L. Walcott, was born in Barbados and moved to Boston in 1908 as part of the great exodus of Caribbean Blacks. In a time when many other venues would only admit very light-skinned people of color as anything but hired help, Walcott wanted a place that welcomed everyone, so he secured his liquor license through the help of Mayor Curley and Wally's Paradise was born on January 1, 1947. In the 1960s, the club's name was changed to Wally's Café and Walcott remained involved in the club until his death in 1998 at the age of 101.[28] Operated by his descendants, it continues to thrive to this day even though declining interest in jazz doomed most other clubs.[28]

The mix of affordable entertainment and housing made the South End a biracial haven nestled in an increasingly segregated Boston. During these years, it was home to four people who would become some of the country's most famous black activists: Malcolm X, Coretta Scott, Dr. Martin Luther King, Jr., and Louis Farrakhan.

Malcolm Little, known to history as Malcolm X, left some of the most detailed descriptions of the South End in this era. Fifteen-year-old Malcolm first visited Boston in the summer of 1940 at the urging of his half-sister Ella, and he quickly gravitated to the South End. In January 1941, he returned to Boston and lived in Roxbury,[30] but spent much of his time in the South End. Rolls Little, another of Malcolm's half-sisters, worked in a store she owned with her family at the corner of Lenox Street and Shawmut Avenue, and Ella eventually bought 486 Massachusetts Avenue.[31] Little began to hang out in the South End with its "world of grocery stores, walk-up flats, cheap restaurants, poolrooms, bars, storefront churches, and pawnshops." He was fascinated by city living and Boston's racial climate and was amazed to see whites and Blacks strolling arm in arm.[32]

He plunged into the area's nightlife and did everything he could to act and dress the part of an urban sophisticate. Little described his first zoot suit as "just wild: skyblue pants thirty inches in the knee and angle-narrowed down to twelve inches at the bottom, and a long coat that pinched my waist and flared out below my knees." He finished the outfit with a leather belt, which had a buckle with an "L" on it, a blue hat with a four-inch brim and a feather, and a gold-plated chain "that swung down lower than my coat hem."[32] So dressed, he spent his nights out in the South End. Little eventually became involved in a robbery ring, and was arrested, convicted, and imprisoned. He found Islam in prison and opened the a Nation of Islam Temple in 1952 at 405 Massachusetts Avenue. He later moved it to 9 Wellington Street. After his time in the South End, he was called to lead a temple in Harlem.

Coretta Scott moved to Boston in 1951 to attend the New England Conservatory of Music at a time when Black women were not allowed in college dorms. Scott first lived in a lodging house on Beacon Hill, but after she met Martin Luther King, she moved to the League of Women for Community Service lodging house at 558 Massachusetts Avenue. Meanwhile, King was studying at the Boston University Divinity School. "Students who visited … usually found him surrounded by a stack of books four feet high".[33] King and Scott had a swift courtship that began with a first date at a cafeteria on Massachusetts Avenue. After they were married, the couple lived at 395 Northampton Street while King finished his dissertation.[34]

King had a triumphal return to the South End in April 1965 when he led a march from Carter Field to the Common via Columbus Avenue and Copley Square to protest segregated schools, poor housing, and other issues. It was a cold, drizzly morning, but there were so many people waiting for King on Columbus Avenue that the parade start was delayed for more than two hours as police and march organizers tried to sort out safety and logistic concerns.[35] Downtown, King delivered an address to the legislature while Mayor Collins and School Committee Chairwoman Louise Day Hicks uneasily awaited his arrival. During the riots that followed King's assassination in 1968, police barricaded Massachusetts Avenue, though most of the violence in the city, limited compared to the unrest in other communities, was elsewhere.

Gene Walcott performed at Eddie's, located at 435 Massachusetts Avenue, from 1953 to 1954, where he was noted for his calypso music. In 1954, Walcott and his wife lived in an apartment a few doors down from Martin Luther King, and between sets, he would dash into the Chicken Lane for a quick meal. It was there that he first met Malcolm X.[30] Walcott quickly dropped out of the music scene, changed his name to Louis Farrakhan, and eventually became head of the Nation of Islam.[28]

Though Boston Housing Authority's initially built traditional public housing in South Boston to accommodate the needs of whites, it soon sited developments in the South End. Approximately one-sixth of twenty-first century affordable housing units in the neighborhood are in BHA housing, many dating back to the period between 1940 and 1951. Lenox Street was one of the first four public housing developments built in the city and the only one that was open to Blacks. By then, Lower Roxbury had large numbers of Black residents, many living in dilapidated conditions. The blocks cleared for the Lenox Development covered 4.6 acres housing seven hundred people in 436 dwelling units. Prior to clearance, their average annual income was $834 and the average monthly rent was $13.11. This was very low-quality housing with 17.8 percent of units lacking a flush toilet, 28.2 percent had no hot water, and 96.3 percent were without central heat. To replace these units, the BHA built 306 units at a cost of just over $2 million in 1940.[36] Camden was the next development in the neighborhood. Located adjacent to Lenox Street, it also housed Blacks when its seventy-two units opened in 1949.

6.2 RUTH BARKLEY HOMES (CATHEDRAL PROJECTS)

The land for the Cathedral projects, once formally known as the South End Development, had been cleared in 1941, but the groundbreaking for the new housing was delayed until 1949.[37] Vacant for years, "Mayor Curley compared the interim result to an ugly shell-hole in a bomb-wrecked European city, and deplored the treatment of former site tenants who were simply turned out into the streets." He made the construction a major priority of his administration, and it opened in 1951.[38] Though at first glance Cathedral may look like a typical Modernist housing development, its yellow brick design is one of the most distinctive of any low-income housing project in the country. The central building is the tallest, with four slightly shorter buildings connected to the center by second floor arches. The heights are stepped down to two story buildings at the periphery, and the whole development is reminiscent of a cathedral spire. Residents are proud of its distinctive design, and—despite its troubles over the years—they fought against proposals to demolish any buildings or replace them with more conventional designs. Reflective of this activism, the development was renamed in honor of long-term resident Ruth Barkly in 2013.

All three developments housed Blacks at a time when the BHA was highly segregated. As urban renewal plans began to take form in the late 1950s, Cathedral was integrated with about half of its units available to Blacks while the other two BHA developments were all Black. In the 1960s, there were a total of 886 units in the BHA's South End inventory with just four vacancies. Almost all the BHA developments outside the South End prohibited Black families, a practice that continued in many BHA properties until the mid-1980s. As renewal loomed, there would be few apartments for displaced residents.

The first section of the South End the city targeted for demolition was the New York Streets (NYS) neighborhood. It was architecturally distinct from the core rowhouse district; its history predated the main era of development. A particular concern for city planners was its demographics: the area had a mix of races and ethnicities. A 1940 city analysis (based on a census tract that was larger than NYS) reported that 506 residents (12 percent) were Black, 2,369 (56 percent) were native-born whites, and 1,312 (31 percent) were foreign-born whites. Rather being seen as an advantage or something to be protected, however, this racial mixing horrified planners. Another concern was that the neighborhood had a range of land uses and was not strictly residential.[12] The neighborhood had several movie theaters and many stores, while the land along its southern edge was mostly warehouses, lumberyards, and auto repair shops; electrical supply companies, hardware wholesalers, and garages were scattered among the residential blocks. There were churches, boys and girls clubs, and social service providers in the neighborhood as well.[39] Though the non-residential land uses were not particularly noxious, mixed-use areas were considered to be bad for families and children, and their presence contributed to the perception that the community needed to be cleared and rebuilt. In addition, its fine-grained street network was considered obsolete. In 1952, the city described the neighborhood as a "menace to housing and a barrier to proper business development."[40] The city ignored the social ties and family relationships in the neighborhood. Downtown planners were unconcerned that the area provided sustenance for many who couldn't afford higher income neighborhoods and that its tenements sheltered very vulnerable people who would be pushed aside by these proposals for renewal.[41]

n eW y ork S TreeTs , 2010 . f ifTy yearS afTer iT WaS deSTroyed by urban reneWal , The neighborhood WaS moSTly vacanT . T he area finally aTTracTed neW developmenT in 2014 .

6.3 NEW YORK STREETS AREA 2010

There was an important change in the nature of proposals for the NYS area following the passage of the Federal Housing Act of 1949. The new law encouraged urban renewal for business uses over housing and so Boston planners now focused on creating economic development.[42] Taking advantage of a surge in funding, the BHA signed a contract with the Housing and Home Finance Administration in September 1950, and federal funds were advanced to pay for planning, preliminary surveys, and administrative costs of the NYS project.[43]

The city prepared a new proposal for NYS, released in 1952.[40] Under this plan, demolished housing would not be replaced with new units. Instead, all NYS residents would be moved to make way for a manufacturing zone with large superblocks amidst broad arterials. Promoting this change in focus, a

1953 marketability study suggested that building industrial space in NYS was of vital importance to the regional economy.[44] The BHA approved the land takings in November 1952, and plans were well underway by 1954.[45]

A January 1955 publication soliciting bids from developers pointed out the advantages for industrial uses in the area: access to downtown, highways, airports, railroads, and docks; level land suitable for urban manufacturing; and in-place utilities. The brochure promised that the first stage of acquisition by eminent domain would be complete by June, and the land would be cleared and ready for conveyance by December 1955.[46] Implementing this hasty timeline brutally displaced residents.

Throughout this long planning period, the knowledge that the city wanted to acquire and demolish everything in NYS made further decay inevitable. No one would invest in a property that the city might take by paying only a fraction of its worth. Confronted by the chaos of owners refusing to maintain their buildings during the uncertainties of eminent domain, residents moved out in advance of the actual land acquisition. Over sixty percent (563 of 931) of the families remaining in the neighborhood in 1954 were gone in 1955, when relocation formally began. Despite promises, the BHA provided very little assistance to those displaced, spending only two dollars per family.[47] There were other problems caused by the lag between the announcement of takings and the time people actually moved. "This led to extensive vandalism to vacated units, tenants refusing to pay rent, and the cancellation of fire insurance."[48]

Urban renewal was a process that began with the development of a plan, proceeded through land acquisition, and ended with the sale of the acquired parcels to a developer (or another entity that would build the replacement land use).[49] For the NYS project, the BHA wanted to sell the entire consolidated parcel to a single developer rather than resubdivide the land.

Just as bids were due in the summer of 1956, there was a last-minute flurry of activity when William Zeckendorf proposed to incorporate the NYS area into a 750-acre, $250 million development project that would stretch from South Station to the heart of the South End and require the demolition of Chinatown, the Leather District, and other blocks in the vicinity. Zeckendorf, the developer of the United Nations Plaza in New York City and later, Century City in Los Angeles, proposed a two-story retail center and "lots of parking" on the NYS land.[50] He first formally communicated his plans to Mayor Hynes via a letter in July 1956, delaying the awarding of a contract for NYS redevelopment for five months.[51]

The BHA considered Zeckendorf's offer but ultimately granted the land to Corel-Druker, a development firm co-owned by the head of the Boston

Real Estate Board. The developers sold part of the land to a newspaper plant, which planned a one hundred thousand square foot $5 million building and a seven-hundred-car garage.[52] The newspaper took 6.2 acres (45 percent of developable land) for its facility, though it never built the garage, while another 40 percent was uncommitted. An electrical supply company was in negotiations to take most of the remaining land.[48]

By 1964, the city considered the NYS project complete. The redeveloped neighborhood consisted of one- to two-story industrial buildings with few ground floor windows. These buildings were set back from the street and surrounded by large, mostly underutilized parking lots and chain-link fences. A mostly vacant Harrison Avenue was widened; other roads were replaced by a few cross streets, some of which were used for commuter bus parking during off hours but were otherwise empty. A bank branch settled in the neighborhood in 1964, and in 1981, a high-technology firm built a midrise research and development facility with an adjoining parking garage. The bank was replaced by an Asian grocery store around 2000, the technology company moved out in 2009, and several blocks were eventually fenced off and not used at all. Lawrence Kennedy, in his 1994 book on the history of city planning in Boston, called NYS an "industrial no man's land".[9]

For the next sixty years, the NYS area would be an ugly scar between the South End and Downtown. Despite the glittering promise of city brochures, there was no demand for urban manufacturing and little need for warehousing so close to the center of the metropolitan area. In fact, the land was almost worthless. Over time, the area grew increasingly bleak and when the newspaper closed its printing plant, the gloom increased.

Then in 2015, developers finally took an interest in the area, not for industry but for housing. Suddenly, luxury residential towers, an upscale supermarket, and trendy restaurants were built, though some parking lots remain. The new NYS is less integrated than it was pre-renewal even as the city as a whole has a much higher percentage of people of color in 2020 than it had in 1950. Since the 1980s, Boston has required developers to either build a certain number of affordable units onsite or pay into a fund for the construction of affordable housing elsewhere in the city. NYS Developers chose the offsite option, and thus there is no hint of the vital low-income, mixed-race community that once occupied this land.

The city and state contributed to the South End's problems; much of its decline can be traced to government actions. The 1950s demolition of Scollay Square in preparation for the Government Center project, for example, pushed many of its homeless and addicted to the area around Dover

Street.[21,53] The area sagged under the pressure.

One of the city's most infamous actions in the pre-renewal era was the destruction of Chester Park when they pushed a road through the middle of the open space to make way for faster vehicular traffic from the new Southeast Expressway to Back Bay. The area between Albany Street and Fort Point Channel, with its lumber yards, decaying wharfs, and semi abandoned factories, provided cheap land for the Expressway's route into downtown. The South End, however, posed a barrier between the highway and Back Bay that slowed commuters; the state and city sought a fast, unhindered path to the Charles River. Given that Chester Square's history and architecture were underappreciated, the state had no qualms building a four-lane road through the park and rechristening the block Massachusetts Avenue. By destroying one of the South End's original squares, the city sacrificed integral parts of the neighborhood to improve outsiders' travel needs.

6.4 CHESTER SQUARE 2014

The city and state did not tell residents about the project until it was too late for opposition. The notices went out to the neighborhood for the public hearing on the destruction of the park on May 27, 1952, four days after it was held.[54] Residents had no chance to resist the proposal, and they were surprised by the speed of its implementation.[55] Eventually, Bostonians recognized the demolition of Chester Square as a tragedy, and there have been half-hearted attempts to at least partially remedy its destruction. In the 1990s, there were proposals to move Massachusetts Avenue underground to restore some of the Square, but these never advanced beyond the discussion phase as the cost and technical aspects were daunting. In 2013, there was a partial restoration with new plantings and fountains. Afterward, the square was a bit more pleasant, but the roar of speeding traffic and the division of the Square into two sides continues today.

Residents vacated buildings in many parts of the South End in advance of renewal and highway clearings, sometimes decades before land was formally taken because even proposing a building or block be demolition promoted disinvestment and decay. Furthermore, well before renewal began the BRA was heavily involved in acquiring and demolishing buildings. Russell Traunstein, Director of the South End Urban Renewal Project, told his new superiors that a great deal of demolition was already completed in June 1961, five years before a project plan was adopted.[56] A 1962 report indicated that "800 properties had been demolished over the past ten years" in what was to be the South End urban renewal district, the area to the west of Berkeley Street.[57] As a result of these takings and demolitions, people fled the area in droves in the 1950s. The neighborhood's population had increased by three thousand from 1940 to 1950, and the number of Blacks almost doubled in the decade before renewal became public. From 1950 to 1960, however, after the South End was targeted for renewal, the total population of the neighborhood plummeted by 38 percent and its Black population fell by 24 percent. The city would then cite this decline as a justification in its 1960s urban renewal applications, even though most of the loss was caused by planned or actual clearances for the New York Streets and Castle Square developments, the Massachusetts Turnpike Extension, and the Inner Belt construction. The taking of housing for the NYS project alone displaced at least four thousand people, almost all out of the neighborhood.

The artist, Allan Crite, lamented the demolitions along Shawmut Avenue in the 1940s as he "watched the bulldozers and cranes reduce the wooden houses into jagged splinters and the brick houses into clouds of rubble." He noted "this bit of massive destruction of street after street, once filled with people, alive with children and the busy chatter of black people, the cries of vendors of fruits and vegetables and fish, and ice and wood and coal and oil."[58]

Renewal was episodic, proceeding in bursts and stops, but the overall goal was always to get rid of this troublesome district. After it cleared the NYS area, the city began to look at demolishing the remainder of the South End, and it set in motion policies that would cause a crisis in the neighborhood a decade later. One such policy was how the city calculated potential alternative housing units for displaced households: it considered all units that turned over each year as available for relocation. For example, citywide, all 1,500 BHA annual turnovers were counted as being ready to house those displaced by renewal. But this turnover rate is irrelevant because it represents the natural year-to-year reshuffling of the population, not extra available housing for those displaced. Giving a unit to a relocated household would mean another needy household would lose that spot. It was not the number of turnovers but the number of vacancies that was important. Overall, the BHA had only a handful of units vacant and uncommitted at any given time. These were very scarce; the city estimated there were about 222,000 total units in Boston (public and privately owned combined) with a 1.5 percent vacancy rate. This very tight rental market meant there were only 3,300 units available for relocation citywide, but even this number is a vastly optimistic statistic as it includes units in the process of being sold, vacant for rehabilitation or so decayed they were uninhabitable or otherwise not for rent. But the city continued to use this flawed methodology for calculating units available for relocated residents through the 1960s. The lack of decent, affordable housing for those displaced by renewal would radicalize many in the South End.

Slowly pushing ahead, the City Planning Board produced a South End-wide urban renewal plan in December 1959. They never shared it with the neighborhood but many of its elements would eventually be incorporated into the 1962 and 1964 plans, which were made public. The 1959 plan included, for example, a proposal to build a fifteen-to-twenty-acre Blackstone Field and redevelop the surrounding blocks into low-income housing. The complex included a swimming pool, hockey rink, gym, playing fields, new school, and community center. The City Planning Board claimed the complex would reduce the South End's density while providing open space and stimulating the rehabilitation of the surrounding community. This Blackstone Field proposal was not just an afterthought; according to the city, it was central to the plan.[59] The proposed destruction of what became Parcel 19 would incite major resident activism in 1968.

The 1959 plan called for the remainder of the neighborhood to be bulldozed and every single row house demolished because "ultimately the South End, except for public housing and certain institutions, must be entirely rebuilt" in the Modernist style. This architectural style emphasized housing as machines for living and glorified industrialized concrete building modes. Many of its features would eventually be incorporated into a design known as Brutalism, which would have meant replacing the South End's graceful Victorian architecture with plain concrete buildings devoid of ornamentation and character.

The plan also wanted to change the street pattern into superblocks, with two-to-four-story walk ups and garden apartments set back from the streets. Columbus Avenue was to be reconfigured to bring in traffic downtown, and the NYS industrial area would have been extended to Tremont Street, creating a quarter mile barrier of warehouses and factories between the South End and downtown. The plan would have reduced population density so that there would be about ten thousand dwelling units housing about twenty-five thousand people. Approximately fifteen thousand people would have had to move out. Urban renewal was to take five to ten years and cost $10 to $20 million of public and private money.[60]

Union Park Street was to be cleared and sold to the Cathedral for a plaza. In addition to the new Blackstone Field, the plan proposed to build a new open-space facility in the area inside Dartmouth, Tremont, West Newton, and Columbus Streets. The proposal said that sections of Appleton, West Canton, West Brookline, Montgomery, and Pembroke Streets could be "eliminated without any adverse effect on South End traffic flowage," even as it ignored the human impact of that scale of demolition.[59]

Altogether, this was a total rejection of Bulfinch's and Chesbrough's plans, an extreme repudiation of the South End's 1850s-era squares, and a radical statement against the neighborhood's rowhouses. The South End faced the greatest threat of its history because planners had taken to heart the idea the neighborhood was obsolete. Fortunately, the BHA was unable to advance the plan, though many of its elements would reappear in proposals for the neighborhood in the 1960s.

The city and state were also moving forward with plans to circle the neighborhood with highways. To the south was the new Southeast Expressway, which cut the neighborhood off from Fort Point Channel and eliminated the South End's waterfront. It would take an additional decade to construct the Massachusetts Turnpike Extension, but that road would eventually create a barrier between the South End and Back Bay and downtown. Finally, there was the Inner Belt, a highway that would connect a proposed extension of Interstate 95 to the Southeast Expressway along where Melnea Cass Boulevard is today, and the South End Bypass, an elevated or below-grade access road connecting the proposed highway to Copley Square. The City Planning Board enthusiastically approved these plans.[61] Though they were not to be built for decades, the city and state began implementing these plans in the 1950s, buying up buildings, assessing properties, and developing engineering studies. The South End was about to be rebuilt for cars.

As the 1950s ended, public agencies began aggressively purchasing land. Residents had experienced the displacement from NYS and saw families leaving Castle Square and Lower Roxbury before their homes were bulldozed for other projects, but overall, South Enders were unaware that the city wanted to demolish the neighborhood. The few who were familiar with the various redevelopment proposals, along with downtown interests in favor of renewal, were more concerned that the city was moving too slowly than with the destruction of the neighborhood. They would use the 1959 mayoral election as an opportunity to push the city, and the South End, into full-scale renewal.

1. Wilson J. *Urban renewal: The Record and the Controversy*. Cambridge, MA: MIT Press; 1966.

2. Anderson M. *The Federal Bulldozer*. Cambridge MA: MIT Press; 1964.

3. Lopez R. Public Health, the APHA, and Urban Renewal. *American Journal of Public Health* 2009; 99:1603-11.

4. Le Corbusier. *The City of To-morrow*. Cambridge MA: MIT Press; 1929.

5. Lopez R. *Building American Public Health: Urban Planning, Architecture, and the Quest for Better Health in the United States*. New York: Palgrave Macmillan; 2012.

6. Fishman R. Urban Utopias in the Twentieth Century: Ebenezer Howard, Frank Lloyd Wright, Le Corbusier. Cambridge MA: MIT Press; 1982.

7. Wright FL. Broadacre City: A New Community Plan. *The Architectural Record* 1938:243-55.

8. Mumford L. *The City in History: Its Origins, Its Transformations, and Its Prospects* New York: Harcourt, Brace & World; 1961.

9. Kennedy L. *Planning the City upon a Hill: Boston since 1630*. Boston: University of Massachusetts Press; 1994.

10. The Urban Planning Board. *Building a Better Boston*. Boston1941.

11. City Planning Board. *Building a Better Boston*. 1941.

12. Boston City Planning Board. *Rehabilitation in Boston*. 1943.

13. Saxenian A. *Regional Advantage: Culture and Competition in Silicon Valley and Route 128*. Cambridge, Massachusetts: Harvard University Press; 1994.

14. Bluestone B, Stevenson MH. *The Boston Renaissance: Race, Space, and Economic Change in an American Metropolis*. New York: The Russell Sage Foundation; 2000.

15. Bradbury KL, Downs A, Small KA. *Urban decline and the future of American cities*. Washington, DC: The Brookings Institution; 1982.

16. South End History, *Part III: Urban Renewal*. 2012. (Accessed July 30, 2012, at http://www.

southendhistory.org/2012/04/south-end-history-part-iii-urban.html.)

17. King M. *Chain of Change: Struggles for Black Community Development*. Boston MA: South End Press; 1981.

18. Smith MS. *Between City and Suburb: Architecture and Planning in Boston's South End* Providence, Rhode Island: Brown University; 1977.

19. Mollenkopf JH. *The Contested City*. Princeton, New Jersey: Princeton University Press; 1983.

20. Rose TF. *Civic War: People, Politics, and the Battle of New Boston, 1945-1967*. Berkeley, California: University of California, Berkeley; 2006.

21. Lukas A. *Common Ground: A Turbulent Decade in the Lives of Three American Families*. New York: Vintage Books; 1986.

22. Buchanan W. Everybody Is Somebody. *Boston Globe*; 1965 July 25.

23. United South End Settlements. *Lodging House Preservation in the South End: An Expansion Request*. 1984.

24. Pikielek F. *Boston's South End Past and Present*. Research Department BRA, 1974.

25. Shapiro L. Witnesses Paint Grim Housing Picture for Boston Negroes. *Boston Globe*; 1963 March 6.

26. Closeup of Neighborhood. Boston: A Closeup of Its Neighborhoods, Its People and Its Problems. *Boston Globe*; 1967.

27. Barnet A. Sammy's South End History. *South End News*; 2012 June 7.

28. Vacca R. *The Boston Jazz Chronicles: Faces, Places, and Nightlife 1937-1962*. Belmont, Massachusetts: Troy Street Publishing; 2012.

29. Baker B. Authentic to the Last Bite. *Boston Globe*; 2014 May 13.

30. Marable M. *Malcolm X: A Life of Reinvention*. Nwe York: Viking; 2011.

31. Hentoff N. *Boston Boy: Growing Up with Jazz and Other Rebellious Passions*. Philadelphia: Paul Dry Books; 2001.

32. X M, Haley A. *The Autobiography of Malcolm X*. New York: Random House; 1964.

33. Branch T. *Parting the Waters: America in the King Years 1954-63*. New York: Simon and Schuster; 1988.

34. MLK on Northampton Street. 2013. (Accessed June 15, 2014, at http://www.mysouth-end.com/index.php?ch=columnists&sc=south_end_character&id=143229.) 35. Levey R. A mile of marchers. *Boston Globe;* 1965 April 24.

36. Boston Housing Authority. *The First Year* 1940.

37. Boer A. *The Development of USES: A Chronology of the United South End Settlements 1891-1966*. Boston: United South End Settlements; 1966.

38. Vale L. *From the Puritans to the Projects*. Cambridge MA: Harvard University Press; 2000.

39. Boston, Massachusetts: *Sanborn Fire Insurance Map*; 1948.

40. Urban Redevelopment Division - The Boston Housing Authority. *The New York Streets Project (Preliminary)*. Boston 1952.

41. Barnet A. New York Streets. *South End News;* 2012 August 1.

42. A. van Hoffman. A study in contradictions: The origins and legacy of the Housing Act of 1949. *Housing Policy Debate* 2000; 11:299-326.

43. *Contract* - Boston Housing Authority and the Federal Housing and Home Finance Administration. 1950.

44. Urban Redevelopment Division - The Boston Housing Authority. *Marketability Studies - New York Streets Project*. Boston. 1953.

45. Boston Housing Authority. *Declaration of Findings Relative to the New York Streets Land Assembly and Redevelopment Project*. 1954.

46. Urban Redevelopment Division - The Boston Housing Authority. *Expressways to Everywhere*. Boston. 1955.

47. Committee SEPA. *Special Housing Committee Report*. 1975.

48. Bureau BMR. *Charting the Future of Urban Renewal*. 1959.

49. Brownfield L. The Disposition Problem in Urban Renewal. *Law and Contemporary Problems* 1960; 25:732-76.

50. Keblinsky JA. Would Erase Chinatown for South End Project. *Boston Globe;* 1956 August 22.

51. Hynes MJ. *Letter to William Zeckendorf*. 1956.

52. Herald-Traveler to Build Plant. Herald-Traveler to Build Plant in South End. *Boston Globe;* 1957 June 14;Sect. 24.

53. Atkinson JL. History and Development of the South End. In: Putnam JW, ed. *A Picture of the South End*. Boston: South End Historical Society; 1968.

54. City of Boston Board of Street Commissioners. *Notice of Public Hearing May 22 1952*. 1952.

55. Lazarus R. Community Organization in the South End: A Proposal for Coordinated Community Action at the Neighborhood Level. In: *Program D-MUS*, 1966.

56. Traunstein R. *Memorandum* to Rowland R. 1961.

57. Traunstein R. *Memorandum* to: Logue E.1962.

58. Crite AR. *An Autobiographical Sketch*. 1978.

59. Boston City Planning Board. *Urban Renewal of the Central South End*. 1959.

60. Barbour WE. *Notes Toward a General Plan for the South End*. Boston City Planning Board. 1959.

61. Boston City Planning Board. *Transportation Policy for Boston Expressways*. 1959.

CHAPTER 7

Plans, Pushback, and New Plans: 1960-1966

As the administration of Mayor John Hynes came to an end in 1959, there was a growing, desperate fear among the city's business leadership that urban renewal, Boston's last hope for revival, was not working and "had for all intents and purposes been a failure."[1] Though Boston had built substantial numbers of low-income public housing units between 1939 and 1954, these were already deteriorating, and while Hynes had ambitious ideas for rebuilding Boston into a modern city, he only launched two renewal projects. One, the West End, was an open wound in the city and a warning to other neighborhoods that urban renewal meant destruction and displacement. Furthermore, when the mayor granted the West End's development rights to a former aide, it smelled of corruption. The other project, the clearing of the NYS, was a major disappointment. Many Bostonians had held a poor opinion of the area and welcomed its demolition, but replacing it with a bleak landscape of vacant lots, warehouses, and a newspaper plant wasn't a great economic advancement for the city. Together with the stalled Prudential and Government Center projects, these failures reinforced the idea that the City of Boston was incompetent. To many Bostonians, there was a need for innovative ideas, large-scale plans, and powerful men to implement them.[2]

As efforts to launch redevelopment intensified, there were powerful political forces fighting for control of the city. One group, Boston's wealthy downtown interests, paternalistically treated South End residents as helpless charity cases they needed to evict, while the other, the Irish political establishment, disliked the neighborhood because of racist ideologies.[3] Lower-income white ethnics dominated city government, public sector jobs, and most unions, while wealthy white Yankees controlled the private economy. As a result, both marginalized the multiethnic South End.

To relaunch redevelopment, the city wanted to transfer power away from the Housing Authority, which had its hands full managing its rental units. In 1957, the city established a new city agency, the Boston Redevelopment Authority (BRA), through new state legislation.[5] Unfortunately, the creation of this new agency proved insufficient for revitalizing the city; the BRA was essentially an independent version of the former BHA's renewal department with the same staff and the same inability to get work done. The new agency needed new leadership to be effective.

In 1959, that new leadership arrived with John Collins, who upset John Powers in the mayoral election.[1] To move renewal along, Mayor Collins appointed Edward Logue as head of the BRA because the mayor wanted a strong leader to push redevelopment forward, and Logue promised action. Over the next eight years, Logue's control over redevelopment in Boston was nearly absolute as he had the backing of the mayor, downtown business interests, the Catholic Church hierarchy, and mainstream opinion leaders.[1] In the South End, the course of renewal would be steered solely by Logue's hand and guided by his vision of where he wanted to take the neighborhood. Logue had full power to implement his ideas of what cities should look like.

Born in Philadelphia in 1921, at an early age Logue developed what many in his time considered to be a progressive ideology. For example, he organized his fellow workers in Yale's cafeterias to fight for better wages. After flying as a bombardier over Italy in WWII, he graduated from Yale with a law degree and worked for Connecticut Governor Chester Bowles. When President Harry Truman appointed Bowles Ambassador to India, he took Logue with him. Logue intended to practice law when he returned to New Haven, but Mayor Richard Lee, a friend of Bowles, lured him into public service. Logue first worked in the city's law department and then was appointed head of redevelopment in 1954. Logue had no training or experience as an urban planner; it was his energy and forceful personality that impressed his backers.

Though it seemed successful in 1960, his plan's long-term effects have left many questioning Logue's New Haven legacy. Mayor Lee and Logue built highway connectors that demolished longstanding neighborhood commercial districts, promoted the construction of fortress-like developments that destroyed much of downtown, and devastated the city's Black community by Logue's focus on demolishing their homes. Nearly everyone was impressed by Logue's ability to secure redevelopment funds; but though it was one of the country's largest recipients of federal urban renewal money, New Haven was crippled by Logue's plans for decades.[6] Unfortunately, this reassessment of the New Haven experience would come long after Logue left Boston.

Hiring Logue was not a straightforward process, and many opposed his coming to Boston. Logue demanded a salary of $30,000, which was much higher than the pay of other city employees who had to work within the constraints of municipal austerity. In addition, his outsider status and high-class manners didn't help him win allies in a city dominated by tough-talking politicians whose power rested on generations-old connections. Despite the controversy surrounding Logue, however, Mayor Collins was determined to hire him. To help speed the process along, he gave Logue an initial ninety-day contract in an advisory capacity. Full of energy to transform the city, Logue began work at the BRA in March 1960. His first task was to create a citywide renewal plan.

Logue's proposal called for the dramatic rebuilding of the city. He wanted to incorporate almost twenty percent of Boston's land into ten urban renewal areas and six improvement districts. By 1972, he forecast that the city would spend more than $2 billion on reshaping its built environment. Mindful of the opposition to renewal that stemmed from the devastation of the West End and NYS, his press releases stressed that the plan promoted rehabilitation over demolition. He wanted to build new housing for middle class and wealthy households and rehabilitate existing substandard housing for the poor without large-scale displacement or neighborhood-wide demolition. At the completion of the plan, he promised, the city would have new roads, schools, parks, industrial areas, and a significant increase in jobs. Logue showcased the plan's benefits for everyone; no group would suffer any negative consequences from renewal, he promised. In November 1960, the federal government approved Logue's optimistic plan. It gave the city $2 million for detailed planning and pledged $28 million for capital expenditures.[7]

Logue's efforts to shake up redevelopment ran into problems with the existing BRA leadership, setting off a political dispute in 1961 between Logue and Board Chairman and Executive Director Kane Simonean who did not want to give up control of the agency. The conflict peaked when Mayor Collins moved to make Logue's position permanent. The initial legislation establishing the BRA stated that the current Executive Director, who had come over from the BHA, could not be demoted, and Simonean's opposition to Logue was based on this clause. To circumvent Simonean and this language, Mayor Collins inserted an amendment allowing him to appoint Logue Redevelopment Administrator into a bill before the legislature that would facilitate the development of the Prudential Center.

It wasn't simple, however; the BRA board still had to approve Logue's hiring. To win over the five men who oversaw the agency, Collins and Logue's used the intense sense of desperation that the city needed renewal to generate widespread public support for hiring the new Administrator. They knew Logue had two votes for him and two votes voraciously against him. The swing vote was Melvin Massucco, picture editor for the Boston Herald and the governor's appointee to the BRA, who was under intense pressure from both sides. Illustrative of how the South End establishment wanted renewal, there was almost unanimous support for Logue from the South End Planning Council, South End Business Association, and South End Neighborhood Rehabilitation and Conservation Commission (SEN-RAC). These three organizations—none of whom had more than a handful of low income or non-white members—issued a joint statement praising Logue.[8] Charles Fraggos, director of South End House, also backed Logue.[9] In a strange expression of political power, one of the most publicized demonstrations during the renewal era was not made up of residents opposing it but was a group of conservative men in suits supporting large-scale redevelopment and advocating for Logue's appointment. On January 25, the day of the vote, these business leaders, clergy members, and other prominent members of the downtown establishment staged a pro-Logue rally outside City Hall.

Massucco voted for Logue, and Simonean stayed on as the Authority's Executive Director and Board Chair. All these struggles resulted in a very weak BRA Board of Directors that focused on the minutia of management, leaving Logue as the unchallenged master of urban renewal. Rather than setting policies or evaluating programs, 1960s BRA board meetings were concerned with authorizing bill payments, ratifying contracts, appointing staff, and monitoring pay raises. At the September 30, 1966 meeting, for example, the BRA Board approved a payment to Adams, Howard & Oppermann for forty-five dollars, the eviction of George Bailey from 591 Warren Street, and a reduction of rent for the Edmands Coffee Company on India Wharf to $300 a month. During this meeting, which lasted one hour and forty-five minutes, thirty-two unanimous votes were taken.[10] There was clearly little discussion at these meetings.

It did not matter if a vote would have major impacts. At the October 13, 1966 meeting, the board voted to acquire all the land and buildings along the west side of Dover Street between Tremont Street and Shawmut Avenue. These thirty buildings would eventually be demolished for what was intended to be a widening of Berkeley Street but are now the Berkeley Community Garden. All takings were approved through twenty-seven unanimous votes held in less than ninety minutes.[10] If a neighborhood had a problem with any detail of renewal, the BRA board would not be of any assistance.

For the most part, those few South Enders who knew about renewal were more concerned that it was stalled than they were about any potential negative effects it might have. Unaware of the 1959 plan for the neighborhood's total destruction, South End organizations—including SENRAC and SEFCO (the South End Federation of Community Organizations)—continued to press the city for a comprehensive urban renewal plan.[11] These residents thought that other renewal projects were moving forward at a quicker pace, perhaps ultimately meaning there would be no funds and administrative capability to implement renewal in the South End. Their efforts created a sense of urgency among neighborhood individuals and institutions. Even many Black leaders supported renewal at the time.[1] The most prominent of these were Melnea Cass and Otto and Muriel Snowden, strong civil rights advocates, who saw renewal as the only chance to improve living conditions in the Black community.[12]

On the surface, it appeared that the neighborhood was highly organized in support of renewal. SENRAC, for example, had forty members from resident groups and representatives from the institutional, professional, and business communities. It held twenty-six meetings on renewal, two per sub-area, with one on physical planning needs and one on social needs.[13] But many of the resident groups were weak or existed only on paper. Most included only a fraction of the community, many of whom earned the highest incomes or were the most educated in an area. SEFCO's membership was comprised of the leaders of neighborhood social service organizations, but most of them did not even live in the neighborhood. Meanwhile, the great mass of South End residents was uninvolved in local institutions and had no idea renewal was coming.

Professionals from South End House and other agencies had long represented the neighborhood in its dealings with the city. But renewal came at a challenging time for the South End's settlement houses because most were merging into United South End Settlements (USES). The push for consolidation had come from downtown funders who sought to eliminate duplication of services and reduce overhead, garnering large support from outside the community even as there was little consultation with residents. USES's charter was written by McGeorge Bundy, then at Harvard University and soon to join President John F. Kennedy's administration, where he would play a central role in advocating for the escalation of the United States' involvement in Vietnam. The merger consumed much of the time and energy of settlement house staff and boards just as renewal was gaining momentum. The creation of USES occurred on December 31, 1959 with Hale House, the Harriet Tubman House, Lincoln House, the Children's Art Center, Ellis Memorial, and the South End House forming the new organization. Ellis Memorial would subsequently pull out of the new agency rather than give up its building. Especially important, these organizations lacked resident input or leadership. They were all run by outsiders.

Logue dramatically jumpstarted citywide renewal with the launch of the Prudential and Government Center developments, two projects that had been stalled for years. Soon, Boston rose to fourth among all cities in receipt of federal renewal funds. Logue's tenure saw the beginnings of private investment in the city as a new Boston began to emerge.

He was less successful in the neighborhoods, however. Though he was hired on the promise that he would work with residents, Logue controlled all decision making and only listened to people who supported his plans. His public outreach was no more than "a method for disseminating information and building the illusion of consensus."[1] The BRA sought to work with sympathetic residents and encouraged them to show their enthusiasm for renewal at public meetings and not question plans' assumptions and projections.

In New Haven, Logue had perfected a process to suppress opposition to his plans, and he used these anti-democratic methods in every Boston neighborhood he proposed to renew. To facilitate local support, the BRA would present multiple plans, and select participants were allowed to vote for their favorite. Those opposed to any renewal were ignored or silenced. Another way Logue dealt with conflict was by agreeing to provide what opponents were asking for regardless of his ability or intent to meet those commitments; Logue promised many things to many people. Business interests sought tax breaks and new amenities for their commercial properties, low-income residents looked forward to jobs and renovated housing, and good government advocates wanted honesty and transparency.[1] Some of these he easily delivered; others he swiftly ignored.

Despite his promises of cooperation, his motto was "Planning with the People," criticisms poured in from residents living in neighborhoods targeted for renewal.[14] Most complaints centered on issues of displacement, design, buildings and land takings, and the lack of detail.[4] Any opposition, no matter how trivial, enraged Logue, however, and "his reactions became increasingly dictatorial" as communities fought his proposals.[1] As a result of these conflicts, urban renewal in Boston degenerated into a battle between Logue, who was intent on forcing his ideas into reality with as little compromise as possible, and residents, believing in the overall health of their neighborhoods despite the need for rehabilitation, desperate to preserve their homes and way of life.

A critical failure of the citywide program was that Logue did not allow any analysis of how individual projects would impact the city as a whole. He purposely walled off each neighborhood undergoing planning from activities from all other renewal areas to avoid a unified, citywide opposition. Personnel working on each renewal area were physically separated as well.[1] This isolation caused planning to become uncoordinated, increasingly decoupled from reality. Staff managing each individual renewal project, for example, assumed that all citywide apartment vacancies would be allocated to their project alone—they had no alternative because otherwise they wouldn't be able to promise housing to displaced residents. Because of these assumptions, a given location—such as the new housing in Castle Square—became the relocation site for multiple projects. As a result, the number of families planning to move to that development far outnumbered available units. Regardless of Logue's repeated public announcements that everyone displaced by renewal would have adequate affordable replacement housing, his actions and policies made that promise impossible from the very beginning.

Urban renewal in the Castle Square area bridged the preliminary and main phases of renewal in the city. The area was one of the oldest parts of the South End and home to well over one thousand families, almost all of whom were displaced by renewal. One of Logue's first acts was to accelerate the existing, stalled renewal plan, having been told that the current state of the project was a "fiasco".[15] Another memo referred to "anxiety" and "bitterness" over Castle Square because property owners were still paying taxes even after their tenants had moved out to escape the deteriorating conditions. Logue was also told that the elderly were having problems finding alternative housing.[16] Logue and the BRA learned nothing from this experience; the problems of relocating businesses and residents here would go unheeded as large-scale renewal came to the remainder of the South End.

Logue's initial redevelopment program reflected the traumatic 1959 plan, calling for the entire Castle Square area to be converted from residential to industrial.[17] Residents throughout the South End opposed this proposal because it failed to create a proper gateway to the mostly residential neighborhoods to the west and did not provide enough housing for the site's current residents. Backing off, the BRA announced another plan that would have turned half of Castle Square into a manufacturing district with more than one million square feet of industrial space along with only 350 units of housing. Residents were still unhappy, arguing that the gateway from downtown should not be an industrial park. Opponents of the plan also pointed out that while the city might need the revenue from industrial land, residents' top priority was housing.[18]

Logue placated the opposition through a compromise that kept the area north of Shawmut Avenue residential.[18] He proposed to spend $5.2 million to fast track the clearance in the twenty-eight-acre area, which included a $90,000 contract with USES to help displaced tenants. Even under this plan, the area was to be completely demolished and its street network totally re-made; there would be no trace of the neighborhood that had been built in the first half of the nineteenth century.[19] Holy Trinity Church was spared, while Lincoln House—now part of USES—was demolished. The project replaced a fine-grained neighborhood of small tenements and apartment buildings with a large superblock of concrete buildings set among mediocre landscaping.[20] It was utilitarian, Modernist housing at best, though renovations over the years have softened its hard edges.

7.1 MORSE FISH IN 2014

Residents continued to oppose the plan even as they were being forced out, but the BRA prevailed in part because many left in advance of property takings. Almost half the original residents moved out early because the proposed acquisitions caused deteriorating housing conditions. In a pattern that would be repeated in Logue-administered urban renewal projects across the city, acquisition and demolition of buildings began well in advance of the establishment of a formal urban renewal plan.[21] Once the federal government approved the loan for Castle Square, condemnations were swift, giving the remaining 531 households and seventy elderly people just two weeks to relocate.[17] The Castle Square apartments were budgeted to cost $9.7 million for five hundred units on fifteen acres, and rents were projected to cost $88 to $132.[22] These were far too high for most residents. Businesses were just as vulnerable. Of the 174 businesses with 169 owners and 454 employees in Castle Square, 48 percent had been there for over ten years. Few survived the trauma; Morse Fish, Morgan Memorial, and Lincoln House (now part of USES) were the only identifiable establishments still in operation in 2015.[23] Morse, relocated to Washington Street, would shut down in 2020 to make way for a new luxury housing development.

Just about everyone knew early on that the city would judge renewal performance by how well the BRA managed relocation, and Logue was repeatedly told that he had to ensure that residents would not be displaced. After Charles Liddell, the head of USES, gave Logue a tour of the South End, for example, he reminded the administrator of the need to accommodate the eight thousand low-income elderly in the neighborhood.[24] Meanwhile, internal memos to Logue outlined the particular problem of finding replacement housing for low-income Black residents.[16] When Liddell moved on to lead Action for Boston Community Development (ABCD), he again told Logue that the BRA had a legal responsibility to help relocate all people displaced by urban renewal into decent affordable housing.[25] Unfortunately for South End residents, Logue ignored these warnings, and the BRA failed to address displacement.

In late 1963, the Boston Globe presented an analysis that found only a fraction of those moved out of Castle Square had been relocated into public housing. The BHA's inability to find homes for displaced families by BRA-referred projects was now public knowledge. In its defense, the BHA said that many tenants were not eligible for its housing or refused to move into the projects. But the BHA couldn't make housing for displaced families a priority because it used vacancies to either facilitate the movement of existing tenants to more appropriate units or for its very long waiting list, a direct consequence of the BRA's misplaced reliance on turnovers as a source for units.[26] Time and again, residents would find there was no BHA replacement housing.

Even though most residents of Castle Square wanted to stay in the South End, few actually did. A follow-up study found that of the 50 percent eligible for low-income housing, 23 percent applied and only 12 percent ultimately moved in.[27] The city's tight housing market made it difficult to assist those displaced, and dissatisfied former residents felt alienated and powerless. Among the poor, 22 percent thought their new housing was better, but 44 percent said it was worse. Even 28 percent of middle-class residents said they had been better off in Castle Square.[28] A reporter from The New Yorker interviewed former residents at a senior center in 1966 and found that "It was clear the slums had provided, along with rats and backed-up drains, a freedom in which these underprivileged but often resourceful people could work out for themselves a delicate balance in satisfying their emotional and material needs."[29] New housing in unfamiliar neighborhoods did not provide this support, but that did not matter to the city, the BRA, or Logue.

When Logue took over the BRA, the South End project was lagging behind the city's other urban renewal projects. In the absence of a plan for the entire neighborhood, the BRA was considering a variety of projects that were disjointed and uncoordinated, including actions in Castle Square, Northampton Street, Dover Street, and in the area around Boston City Hospital. There were also debates regarding funding, issues of finding money to help Boston University Hospital acquire the adjacent State Armory as an expansion site, and how to pay for the demolition of the old Girl's High School on West Newton Street to create a park.[30] While the BRA had received a $1.2 million loan for early land acquisition in the South End,[31] efforts were haphazard and poorly coordinated. Real estate uncertainties sparked a collapse in the housing market for the poor when many property owners stopped maintaining their buildings because of fears the city was about to condemn them.[32] Thus, while conditions were deteriorating, renewal began, adding to the panic among many residents.

Between pressure from inside the neighborhood and city hall, Logue knew he had to act. He needed a plan for the western 90 percent of the neighborhood—the easternmost 10 percent had already been cleared for the Castle Square and NYS projects. Communicating this urgency, Logue sent a memo to his staff calling for immediate action on February 13, 1962.[33] In response, South End Project Director Russell Traunstein said that the plan would not be complete until March 1963 at the earliest.[34] Logue deemed this unacceptable and gave his staff two weeks to develop a document that would decide the fate of the neighborhood, its buildings, and its people.[35] Developing the plan took five months and it was first presented in-house in November 1962.[36] By rushing this plan, Logue ultimately doomed it.

Logue's first proposal was based on the problematic plans for the South End that had been on the table since the 1940s.[27] Much of what Logue said he would do simply incorporated elements of the 1959 plan. To add to its drawbacks, it was developed by staff isolated from the South End. Its designer had not attended any of SENRAC's twenty-six community meetings and had only recently moved to Boston from South Africa.[14] He ignored resident concerns and never considered the thousands of hours of citizen participation.[37] Not even Logue thought the plan was good, particularly when he found significant inaccuracies in it.[1] Logue's South End allies, carefully selected to be most accepting of renewal, hated the proposal and turned out against it.

As he rushed the plan forward, Logue demanded it incorporate his own ideas about renewal. He believed that any neighborhood undergoing redevelopment must demolish 20 percent of its housing because this was what he considered to be the ideal balance between limiting the displacement of existing residents and demonstrating the city's commitment to change. There was no planning theory to support his ideas; there were no examples to suggest his assumptions were based on reality, but Logue autocratically decided on 20 percent none the less. To pressure a target community to accept 20 percent demolition, he put forward plans that included two alternatives: a 10 percent and a 40 percent demolition agenda.[14] He meant for the public to ignore the first and wanted to scare them into submission with the second. Unfortunately for Logue, the larger scale demolition plan spurred South End residents into open revolt.

The plan had many disruptive elements. The area where Villa Victoria now stands was to be redeveloped into midrise housing blocks offset from the grid. A large park filled most of the space currently occupied by the Center for the Arts, and public facilities were slated for where Rollins Square and Peters Park are today. There were scattered high-rise apartment buildings including one where Titus Sparrow Park is now, a pair of new buildings at the current site of Tent City, and another on Worcester Street. Washington and Tremont Streets were to have narrow green spaces running down their length, while new commercial buildings were planned for the corner of Washington and Berkeley Streets.[38] Most controversial, the plan called for a long linear park about where Shawmut Avenue is located, creating a buffer between rehabbed middle-class areas to the north and low-income and industrial areas to the south. To accommodate this park, large numbers of rowhouses would be demolished and the substantial Syrian population near Union Park evicted. Publicly, Logue was enthusiastically in favor of the greenway concept and arrogantly stated that without its large swath of demolitions, there would be no South End plan.[39] However, when opposition proved too great, he changed his mind.

This plan would have displaced almost everyone to the west of Massachusetts Avenue and south of Shawmut Avenue, moving out 8,300 people from 3,700 occupied housing units. Elsewhere in the neighborhood, 3,640 people living in lodging houses and 1,700 families would have been displaced. Altogether, 5,400 apartments were to be cleared. In the most extreme version of the plan, 40.4 percent of the population faced displacement, not counting those who would be evicted for renovations of private housing.[32] The BRA estimated that about half of those forced out would not be able to afford the new rehabbed or constructed housing without some sort of subsidy, but all were promised they could remain in the South End—there is no supporting documentation to show how the BRA would enable the evicted to stay.[32] On the contrary, background memoranda show that planners acknowledged the difficulty of addressing the needs of residents they called "problem people:" those in lodging houses, the poor on the southern edge of the neighborhood, low-income families between Shawmut Avenue and Tremont Street, and middle-income groups in the northern third of the area.[41] They struggled with the neighborhood's demographic diversity and saw the community as a very troubled place. BRA staff believed it was best to force these people to leave.[42]

Given that the BRA released multiple versions of its plan, we cannot know the exact details, but the mostly likely alternative called for $25 million of the citywide federal renewal grant of $90 million to go to the South End.[40]

Parts of the 1962 plan were racist. Its existing conditions report, for example, said Puerto Ricans did not like to work, had a hard time establishing permanent personal relationships, and spent too much money on food with poor nutritional value.[32] Thus, rather than address the needs of existing residents they despised and didn't know how to assist, planners focused on bringing new people into the South End.[32] In addition, the BRA promised to reduce the total number of units in the neighborhood because contemporary planning theory thought it was impossibly dense, an objective that was inconsistent with Logue's public promises to keep low-income residents from being displaced.

Another background report for the 1962 plan highlighted the many needs of the vulnerable people in the South End: social support, job training, help for troubled families, lack of open and recreation space, services for the non-English speaking, and so forth. To address these issues, Logue proposed creating a new independent agency dedicated to serving Boston's poorest and most at-risk residents. Thus, one of Logue's greatest contributions to Boston was his work to establish Action for Boston Community Development (ABCD), an important, non-profit social-service provider to this day. Logue's plan was to have ABCD attend to the social needs of the poor while he rebuilt the physical environment.

The middle-class planners made it a point to eliminate the South End's wide range of businesses, even though these small establishments served the needs of the poor. Finding these small businesses distasteful, the BRA's goal was to eliminate the ecosystem that supported the independently living poor in the neighborhood. The plan noted there were forty liquor stores, seven pool rooms, twenty-seven bars, and 119 eating places; almost all were to be shut down. The remaining South End jazz clubs were doomed.

Addressing the South End's residential infrastructure, the BRA discovered that looks can be deceiving: most buildings in the neighborhood were structurally sound even if they needed total interior rehabilitation, new roofs, and repointing. Using federal planning money, the BRA was finally able to conduct a comprehensive assessment of the South End's housing stock that included detailed inspections of every structure in the neighborhood. Most previous studies relied on the opinions of inspectors who never actually entered a building. The new study concluded that out of 3,986 residential buildings in the neighborhood, 2,756 had deficiencies and 1,089 should be demolished (27.31 percent).

This new survey had limited objectivity, however. The standard for demolition was two or more major defects or one major defect plus ten minor ones. There were three types of major defects: foundation walls that were deteriorated, sinking, or out of line; exterior walls that were out of plumb; and roofs that were deteriorated or sagging. The report said that most of the buildings that had rotting pilings or bad foundations had already been demolished, therefore few buildings had foundation problems, nor were there many buildings that had exterior walls out of plumb. For the vast majority of buildings, the roof was the only major defect, a problem that the owners could fix with a simple, if costly, roof replacement. The minor problems included serious deficiencies such as exposed wiring, sagging floors, and deteriorated chimneys—again, expensive but easy to remedy conditions. The list of forty-two items, however, also included many problems that were simply inconvenient or not up to modern standards such as bathrooms without adequate ventilation, rooms lacking at least two electrical outlets, and leaking faucets. Others reflected the type of construction common in the South End like basements that lacked impermeable flooring (as of 2024, many South End buildings still had dirt floors in their unoccupied subbasements) and shared bathrooms and cooking facilities—standard features of lodging houses.[43] Thus, the BRA used a metric for housing quality under which every lodging house and most tenement buildings were deemed to need demolition regardless of the quality of the structure. Experience over the next several decades demonstrated that the South End's buildings simply needed to be renovated, not demolished. Fifty years later it is impossible to know how many demolished South End buildings could have been saved, but it is likely that all but a handful were unnecessarily condemned. It didn't matter to Logue; he demanded that 20 percent of a neighborhood should be demolished as part of a quality urban renewal plan.

The BRA released the plan to community members in December 1962 and held a series of neighborhood meetings in January 1963. Residents quickly attacked it and forced Logue to temporarily retreat. Changing tactics, he hired a new person to oversee the project, Ellis Ash. But by April, even Ash was publicly backing away from his predecessor's proposal.[36] Faced with overwhelming opposition and the reality that the plan was flawed and un-workable, the BRA withdrew it in the summer of 1963 and began to develop a new one. Without giving notice to the neighborhood, however, the BRA launched a large-scale property acquisition program at this time.[37]

7.2 ABANDONED ROW HOUSE, 1974

While the 1962 plan was being debated, market conditions in the South End suddenly changed. After nearly a century of disinvestment, properties started to increase in value. The area experienced substantial development pressure even though banks were still reluctant to lend, and despite the lack of access to capital, investors began to acquire large numbers of buildings.[44]

First to move into the neighborhood were gays and lesbians, followed quickly by others who were intrigued by the old buildings and found the cost of housing affordable. By 1963, several hundred middle-class households had moved into the neighborhood.[45] The movement of gays and lesbians into the South End marked the beginning of an era when the neighborhood would play a key role for this emerging population.

Given that its lodging houses provided a cloak of anonymity for large numbers of unmarried people, there must have always been a substantial gay, lesbian, and gender nonconforming population in the neighborhood, though the period's horrific repression makes it impossible to find much evidence in written records. In the late nineteenth century, to name one man, Ralph Adams Cram, a noted architect and member of Boston's substantial gay underground, lived in the South End for several years prior to finding better accommodations elsewhere.[47] There are other small hints that gay men lived in the South End in the twentieth century. The Boston Globe, for example, published a 1931 article on South End lodging houses that quoted a landlady as saying, "Most people nowadays want their own room. But if chums come to me looking for a room together, I'm glad to have them double up. It's a little cheaper for them and means a little more income for me." This was quickly followed by. "[A landlady] must be sympathetic and friendly, but she must not butt into her roomers' affairs."[48]

Part of the lack of documentation on gay life in the neighborhood pre-1970 is due to the reluctance of scholars to discuss gay men. One early analysis of urban renewal in the South End, for example, dismisses gay people, along with drug addicts and prostitutes, as unworthy of study in its first several pages.[14] Even a 1975 report on changes in the neighborhood went to great lengths not to identify men as gay, instead saying "[T]he first arrivals came as individual households tended to settle in a fairly small area; were nearly all single men of slightly below median income...and characterized by a special type of eccentricity."[49] Despite the invisibility of gay men in public discussion, the foundations for the blossoming of the South End as a gay neighborhood in the 1970s and 1980s were set at this time.

In 1963, the rehabilitation movement picked up steam as new owners and their architects declared buildings structurally sound but in need of substantial renovations.[50] The BRA arranged realtor tours and opened a center to help property owners access architectural and financial assistance. On Union Park alone, nine rooming houses were converted to upscale residences between 1960 and 1963, three into single family homes, the rest into apartment buildings.[51]

These new residents were vastly different from the poor and working-class people who had been living in the neighborhood since 1870. In 1963, people moving into the South End included "a couple of architects, a couple of sculptors, artists, a bio-chemist, several salesmen, and a social worker. New residents also include educators, a contractor, a physicist, two engineers, a newspaper copy editor, [and] a social worker for a South End settlement house." Some came for the architecture, others arrived to make money by promoting further gentrification.[52]

With a new project director and the promise of an alternative way of approaching renewal, Logue released another plan in late 1964 at a community meeting with more than forty-five representatives from various constituencies in the neighborhood though again, there were few low-income or high-risk elderly allowed to attend.[53] Projected to take five to ten years to complete, Harrison Avenue would become the boundary between residential and non-residential uses with Tremont Street as the main commercial artery. There were to be four new elementary schools and one intermediate school, seven playgrounds (and the elimination of the Rotch playground), three indoor recreation areas, and a library. One way Logue jumpstarted renewal was by using the city's ongoing capital improvement budget (which he controlled) to satisfy the federal requirement for a local match to its funds. The city was going to build new schools, libraries, and other facilities regardless of renewal, but this way they secured substantial additional resources. HUD would disallow this practice in the early 1970s, derailing the project's finances, but Logue would be gone by then.

A vestige of the 1959 plan was to develop a proposed Blackstone Field at West Canton and Shawmut Avenue. "The residential community would be further strengthened by the creation near the heart of the district of a new community center. In addition to new and rehabilitated housing and commercial facilities, existing churches, and institutions, this would provide new recreation space including a proposed year-round indoor-outdoor swimming pool, and a community school." [54] It was also to have a library and a skating rink. Another community recreation area was proposed for Massachusetts Avenue next to the Carter playground.

7.3 DOVER STATION C. 1978

Transportation improvements were to include the widening of Dover Street, the construction of new roads along the railroad tracks, and the dead-ending of Columbus Avenue at a park. The 1964 plan called for the construction of the South End Bypass, the development of a new service road along the Turnpike, the relocation of Albany Street, and the building of a 1,500-space garage at City Hospital.

To increase neighborhood support, Logue promised displacement out of the South End would be minimized and stressed rehabilitation over demolition.[53] The 1964 plan called for the construction of 2,200 units of housing, the rehab of three hundred more for use by the BHA, and a new financing mechanism for moderate income households—the 221(d)3 low interest loan program— to create 1,100 units. Again, Logue was lying: the number of replacement units included Castle Square even though these had long been promised to thousands of other evictees. There were to be 2,990 units demolished resulting in a net reduction of 490 units in the neighborhood.[55] The plan also called for spending $88 million to renovate the other 75 percent of the 3,500 residential buildings that were not part of the formal federal project. This renovation represented private market investment.[53] The plan did not mention that while most of these units were currently occupied by low-income residents, post renovation they would be unaffordable and thus they would contribute to displacement. In addition to the stretches of land to be cleared, the BRA revealed it owned 352 units in sixty-six buildings in non-clearance areas, which were taken for nonpayment of taxes. The fate of these buildings was not specified.[56]

The plan called for substantial non-residential investment, including new industry along the Inner Belt and the expansion of the neighborhood's two hospitals, which would lead to an increase in neighborhood jobs—from 17,000 to 20,200.[53] The area desperately needed a new hospital for Boston University. By 1962, the majority of the facility's physical plant was in poor condition. Boston University also looked to expand eastward to include the blocks as far as East Canton and the parcels across Albany Street in its medical center complex, and the university wanted to build new facilities across East Newton Street.[57] Nearby, the Roxbury Canal and the remnants of South Bay were called an "industrial sewer." The city planned on filling them to use for new development and an access road. After more than 150 years of fill and expansion, the South End would reach its final size.

The BRA incorporated a proposal to turn the flower market into the Center for the Arts, relocating the market to Albany Street. These employment expansions would be offset by losses in other areas, and clearance would eliminate 572 businesses employing 4,620 people.[58] Many of these were the small businesses lining the major arterials.

Though the BRA suggested that the new plan was well received, the Boston Globe reported the reaction of the neighborhood was mixed, colored by experience with delays and displacement in the Castle Square area, ongoing issues with trash and code enforcement, and the continued increase in liquor licenses in the neighborhood. Many were also concerned with the social impacts of redevelopment and the effects on the poor and troubled in the neighborhood. Responsibility to service this portion of the community was given over to ABCD and USES, but these plans were yet to be finalized.[59]

The BRA's network of support represented about 5 percent of the neighborhood. Most were elite homeowners or higher-income tenants who wanted to "upgrade" the South End and who could afford to live in a more expensive neighborhood.[4] Langley Keyes, the respected urban scholar, noted in his analysis of the South End project approval process that the BRA had focused on the small segment of the population deemed essential for the public approval of the plan.[14] Others were not invited to speak out on the renewal program.

Despite the Snowdens, Melnea Cass, and other Boston Black leaders' favorable stance regarding renewal, plans would go forward with little or no input from Black or Latino stakeholders. Part of the disconnect between the BRA and minority communities was inevitable because in the early 1960s, neither the BRA nor the City had any high-level Black or Latino employees. Instead, Mayor Collins relied on the Snowdens and State Representative Royal Bolling to be his connections to the Black community. There were also competing issues just as vital to Boston Blacks. Many—including Cass, the Snowdens, and the Boston branch of the NAACP—were more focused on problems in the city's schools, which were deteriorating even as they were growing increasingly segregated. As a result, when the Black public turned violently against renewal a few years later, this mid-twentieth century group of activists would be pushed aside by more radical leaders. Meanwhile, Mayor Collins saw no political reason to change his methods or to consult with others. Fresh off his re-election in 1963, he promised to push urban renewal forward with vigor. Mayor Collins claimed his re-election was evidence the community supported renewal.[60]

Logue told the press that the community supported the proposed urban renewal plan. But he was not taking any chances. After public opposition scuttled his plans for renewal in Charlestown and Allston, he laid down a number of rules to limit the potential for protest at the community meeting for the plan at the Mackey School. Most residents were kept out of the main auditorium, potential protesters were threatened with arrest, and 125 policemen were engaged to maintain order.[61-63] This tight control over the process explains the lack of opposition at this and other hearings. In any case, the plan survived its lengthy review process, which culminated in HUD approval in June 1966. Urban renewal began in full force that summer.

1. Rose TF. Civic War: *People, Politics, and the Battle of New Boston, 1945-1967*. Berkeley, California: University of California, Berkeley; 2006.

2. Kennedy L. *Planning the City upon a Hill: Boston since 1630*. Boston: University of Massachusetts Press; 1994.

3. Dentler RA. Boston School Desegregation: The Fallowness of Common Ground. *New England Journal of Public Policy* 1986; 2.

4. Mollenkopf JH. *The Contested City*. Princeton, New Jersey: Princeton University Press; 1983.

5. Boston Revelopment Authority. *History*. 2014. (Accessed March 18, 2014, at http://www.bostonredevelopmentauthority.org/about-us/bra-history.)

6. Jackson MI. *Model City Blues: Urban Space and Organized Resistance in New Haven*. Philadelphia PA: Temple University Press; 2008.

7. Hanron R. U.S. Pledges $30 Million to Hub Renewal. *Boston Globe*; 1960 November 11.

8. Hanron R. Massive Support for Logue: They Want Logue! Business, Industry Insist He Be Kept Showdown Due Tomorrow On Boston Renewal Expert. *Boston Globe*; 1961 January 24.

9. Hanron R. More Citizens Back Logue: Compromise Today Seen Giving Logue Top Renewal Spot. *Boston Globe*; 1961 January 25; Sect. 1.

10. Boston Redevelopment Authority. Board of Directors Meeting Minutes. 1966.

11. Urban Renewal Coordinating Committee. *Meeting Minutes* December 17. 1959.

12. Carden L. Witness: *An Oral History of Black Politics in Boston 1920 - 1960*. Chestnut Hill, Massachusetts: Boston College; 1989.

13. United South End Settlements. Urban Renewal. Focus – *USES Newsletter*. 1963 6.

14. Keyes L. *The Rehabilitation Planning Game: A Study in the Diversity of Neighborhood*. Cambridge MA: MIT Press; 1969.

15. Green D. *Memorandum* to Logue E. 1960.

16. Green D. *Memorandum* to: Logue E. 1961.

17. Castle Sq. Renewal. Castle Sq. Renewal Gets $5 Million Federal Loan. *Boston Globe*; 1962 November 28.

18. Yudis A. So. End Upset by BRA Plan. *Boston Globe*; 1963 July 18; Sect. 13.

19. Next. Next: New Castle Sq. *Boston Globe*; 1962 March 22.

20. Yudis A. B.R.A. Seeks Assistance Of Settlement Houses. *Boston Globe*; 1962 April 1.

21. Urban Renewal Coordinating Committee. *Meeting Minutes* October 1959.

22. Yudis A. $88-$132 Monthly Rentals for So. End Project. *Boston Globe*; 1965 March 21.

23. Business Relocation Department – Castle Square. *Report on the Castle Square Business Community*. 1962.

24. Liddell C. *Letter* to Logue E. 1960.

25. Liddell C. *Memorandum* to Logue E. 1962.

26. Yudis A. Do Displaced Get Housing? *Boston Globe*; 1963 November 18.

27. SEPAC. *Report on Urban Renewal* 1974.

28. Muchnick DM. *Family Relocation in Urban Renewal: An Agent of Social Change*. Dartmouth College; 1968.

29. Colebrook J. The Renewal. *The New Yorker*; 1966 January 1.

30. Urban Renewal Coordinating Committee. *Meeting Minutes* June 4. 1959.

31. Boston Redevelopment Authority. Board of Directors *Meeting Minutes*. 1962.

32. Boston Redevelopment Authority. South End Report 1962.

33. Logue E. *Memorandum* to Traunstein R. 1962.

34. Traunstein R. *Memorándum* to Logue E. 1962.

35. Crane D. *Memorandum* to Traunstein R. 1962.

36. Ash E. *Memorandum* to Logue E. 1963.

37. Downs A, Bolon L. *Urban Renewal Land Disposition Study*. Real Estate Research Corporation. Washington1974.

38. Boston Redevelopment Authority. *Illustrative Site Plan: South End Urban Renewal Area Massachusetts R.56*. 1964.

39. Drought J. *Memorandum* to Logue E. 1963.

40. Keblinsky J. South Enders Will Aid In $25 Million Renewal. *Boston Globe;* 1961 July 9.

41. Pikielek F. *Boston's South End Past and Present*. Research Department BRA. 1974.

42. Boston Redevelopment Authority. *Preliminary Plan for Urban Renewal* 1962.

43. Boston Redevelopment Authority. *South End Urban Renewal Project: Final Project Report - Application for Loan and Grant, Part 1*. 1965.

44. Kneeland P. Owners Set to Modernize 2000 Units in Hub. *Boston Globe;* 1962 February 18.

45. Lukas A. *Common Ground: A Turbulent Decade in the Lives of Three American Families*. New York: Vintage Books; 1986.

46. The History Project. *Improper Bostonians: Lesbian and Gay History from the Puritans to Playland*. Boston: The Beacon Press; 1998.

47. Shand-Tucci D. *Boston Bohemia*. Amherst, Massachusetts: University of Massachusetts Press; 1995.

CHAPTER 8

Protest and Community in Conflict: 1966-1968

The period of peace after HUD approved the South End urban renewal plan in the summer of 1966 lasted only months. By 1967, tensions in the neighborhood were rising once again. The changing housing market and the BRA's land takings had emotions running high. The neighborhood's three thousand residential buildings were being rapidly sold and renovated; by the end of the 1970s, private individuals will have rehabilitated most of the South End's buildings, almost always displacing previous tenants. This high level of turnover made the neighborhood's private housing market completely unaffordable to low-income residents as their middle-class counterparts converted lodging houses and tenements to apartments and single-family homes.[1] In combination with the BRA's extensive use of eminent domain, the incoming middle class made affordable housing for low-income residents difficult to find.

Using millions of dollars of federal assistance, the BRA hired dozens of planners, administrators, and support staff to manage subcontracts, write proposals for property disposition, and work with tenants and businesses. But though the BRA would be heavily involved in redevelopment for the next decade, the agency was unable to manage the renewal process. Its administrative structure disconnected acquisition and demolition from rehabilitation and redevelopment, for example, which depended on additional funding sources with each individual project requiring a new application to HUD. Employee turnover and fiscal mismanagement exacerbated the BRA's difficulties. Money taken from the South End program was used for other purposes, severely limiting the ability of the agency to meet expenses. Administrative costs rose to 25 percent of the total budget by 1970 with interest payments on borrowed money representing an additional 19 percent.[2] As planned, the program was underfunded; as implemented, there was an even greater shortfall.

Residents grew frustrated. The agency repeatedly solicited neighborhood organizations for recommendations regarding a specific project but would then disregard them because of pre-established budget and project parameters. Neighbors would meet with BRA staff but then find familiar personnel suddenly replaced with newcomers who were ignorant of a project's history and resident concerns.[3] Most distressing was the BRA's lack of communication regarding demolitions. Though it promised to consult with neighbors in advance, the BRA regularly razed buildings without notice, saying the structures were so unsafe that immediate action needed to be taken though by then it was clear to all that most buildings were sound.[4] The BRA would also withhold information, and it was reluctant to release details on its staging plan, even to allies in SENRAC.[5]

Tenement dwellers and lodging-house residents were most vulnerable to the displacement and chaos redevelopment was causing. USES and the BRA conducted a 1966 study of five hundred residents in areas marked for demolition and found they were overwhelmingly low-income earners, minorities, people in poor health, and predominantly detached from community institutions. Only 11 percent paid more than one hundred dollars a month in rent; 10.4 percent paid less than fifty dollars. Housing conditions were substandard with 18 percent having shared baths, 57 percent lacking central heating, and 41 percent without hot water. A significant two-thirds of those to be displaced wanted to stay in the South End.[6] Unfortunately, their social and economic resources were extremely limited. To stay in the neighborhood, these tenants would have needed substantial economic assistance and social support.

Relocation was not an easy process for residents. First there was an initial home visit and interview. After residents completed a ten-page intake form—a particular challenge because many had limited English skills or were illiterate—and were declared eligible for assistance, the BRA would schedule another meeting to develop a plan for that household. Counselors next assessed whether the family needed social services and subsequently arranged permissions and program assistance. It was only after all this work that the process of finding an apartment began, perhaps months or even years after the BRA notified a household that it needed to relocate. At this point, a family would usually be told there was no affordable unit for them in the South End and they were going to be relocated outside the neighborhood or even outside of the city. Many were told that no one had any idea of where to place them. Most dropped out of the program, and 80 percent of affected residents found alternative housing on their own, which the BRA considered to be a voluntary move.[7] Even with this attrition, so many families were pleading with USES for assistance that its staff was overwhelmed.[8] Residents felt betrayed and abandoned, and oftentimes their new housing was just as bad or worse than what they had left but at higher rents.

The BRA plan called for rehabilitation of the majority of South End buildings, mostly through private investment.[9] This stance may have seemed ambitious in 1964, but the housing market for the middle-class exploded, and private and public money poured into the neighborhood. Demand was most likely driven by workers in the new Prudential Center and other developments as Boston's downtown woke up from its long period of decay. There was also a new appreciation for urban living and a reborn affection for the South End row house. On its own, the renewal program would not have been sufficient to change private investment in the South End. Nearby Washington Park, for example, which had a similarly large-scale program, saw no market revival.[1] Private rehabilitation in the South End began in the area between Tremont Street, Dartmouth Street, and the railroad tracks, as well as in the area near Boston City Hospital. From those centers, it began to spread, skirting the main arterials where the BRA had already targeted much of the housing for acquisition and demolition. Some developers purchased as many as one hundred buildings during this modern-day gold rush.[10]

For nearly a century, banks had refused to provide mortgages in the neighborhood.[11] But suddenly, lending institutions competed to finance new development. By the early 1970s, private loan activity ranged from $2.5 to $11.4 million per year with the median loan amount per building reaching $37,000 in 1974.[1] At one point, Suffolk Franklin Bank extended so many loans to newcomers in the South End—many of them gay men—its competitors started calling it the "fag bank." In contrast to this outside bigotry, the neighborhood welcomed everyone.[10]

The pace of renovation amazed residents. As longtime Holyoke Street resident and author Lynne Potts described the era, "dumpsters appeared on the street daily, with enormous gray chutes jerry-rigged from connected garbage cans coming from windows on upper floors to bring slabs of old plaster, woodwork, doors, flooring, bathtubs, toilets, and abandoned furnishings to dumpsters below. A huge bin would fill in a few days, get hauled away, and a new one appeared immediately in its place. A host of panel trucks (plumbers, electricians, carpenters, and floor sanders) lined the curbs or double-parked in the alley."[12]

As some made fortunes, many more lost their homes because the new units were priced too high for low-income residents. Overall, average sales prices of buildings more than doubled between 1961 and 1967, from $7,400 to $15,800, while blocks such as Rutland Square and Dartmouth Place saw prices jump from $4,000 to $20,000.[13]

The BRA had limited tools to help finance private-market housing rehabilitation, but it used what it had to foster higher-end development. One of the most important of these tools was the Section 312 loan program, which was created by the Housing Act of 1964. Intended to help homeowners, it provided twenty-year loans at 3 percent interest. There was also the 115 program, which provided direct loans and grants for households too poor to afford a new mortgage. These programs used federal money with the BRA's and acted as HUD's local agent. The BRA awarded its funds on a first-come-first-serve basis, so the loans went to developers who had greater experience, higher incomes, and better access to capital. In the years up to April 1970, the program funded about 37 percent of the rehabilitation activity in the neighborhood, with 1,365 units in 472 buildings rehabilitated at a cost of $10,889,000.[14]

Though publicly subsidized loans went to developers, existing residents could not afford this new housing, and the city—which wanted to attract higher-income households—refused to attach rent control to rehabbed units. In the South End, there was tension from the start over how to recruit low-income households for the program while still making enough loans to impact the community. In addition to this push and pull, the minimum level of rehabilitation for financing eligibility also steadily rose. Over time, the maximum grant increased to $3,500 per structure and the maximum loan per unit to $17,400, indicative of the realities of the expense of renovations. Together these factors transformed the rental market.

8.1 BOSTON CENTER FOR THE ARTS

In addition to missing out on subsidized loans, existing residents—especially lower-income and elderly homeowners—did not have the technical skills and financial capabilities to meet program requirements. HUD programs also excluded lodging houses unless they were going to be converted to apartments, because it could not aid projects that produced less than full-service units. Another rule required that any project costing more than fifty dollars per unit must be brought up to full compliance with all building codes, substantially raising the level of rehabilitation and dramatically increasing costs. One problem with this, for example, was that the code now prohibited horsehair plaster, standard nineteenth century construction, because it was not sufficiently fire resistant. Thus, rehabilitation required owners to completely gut interiors, adding to the overall cost of rehabilitation. Altogether, rather than helping prevent displacement, the programs accelerated it.[14]

In April 1974, HUD put income restrictions on the program, effectively ending it,[1] but it was too late for many tenants. Along with non-subsidized rehabilitation, the program resulted in the displacement of thousands by raising rents and property values. "Minority families living in rented town houses were pushed south toward Roxbury to make way for music rooms, skylights, and roof decks."[10] The very first loan went to a couple who used it to convert a rooming house into a four-family apartment building.[17] The fate of the building's former tenants is unknown.

For many low-income tenants, displacement was not a gentle movement benignly stemming from friendly suggestions that they find more affordable accommodation in alternative locations. On the contrary, many were brutally evicted from the neighborhood. Speculators bought and quickly emptied buildings because new owners usually required prior owners to deliver vacant buildings—otherwise they'd feel guilty for the displacement they caused. These abrupt evictions allowed newcomers to deny responsibility for what had happened to former tenants. Some developers and new owners were merciless; they didn't renew leases, cut off services, and threatened tenants to move. Some landlords even cleared their buildings with arson.[18] Many tenants gave up and fled the chaos, as it seemed that every month, more were forced from their homes.[19] The BRA did not help those who lost their housing to rehabilitation—even if the 312 program financed the improvements—because its staff claimed the organization was not legally responsible for private market displacement. Therefore, when these residents applied to the city's relocation program, they were denied assistance.[14] The neighborhood's buildings may have been saved by the defeat of Logue's 1962 plan, but the South End's people would be just as mercilessly displaced by his 1964 alternative.

As redevelopment escalated, the consequences of the city's deliberate miscalculation of available replacement units became clear to residents, relocation staff, and the BRA. The BHA had no units for displaced residents; Castle Square was quickly rented, and other housing was still years away. Of the five hundred South End families relocated by the BRA and USES between 1966 and 1968, only twenty-five were rehoused within the neighborhood.[18] Across the city, the poor had few options for other housing. No new public housing had been built in Boston since 1954, and the suburbs proved to be very resistant to low-income housing.[13] The BRA reported that only 9,500 low-income units were even planned for the entire city between 1960 and 1972, and of these, only 5,800 units actually broke ground by the end of that period.[20] For the city housing market as a whole, the 1960s saw a net loss of six thousand units even though twenty thousand new units were constructed. The city was disappointed in the number of new units built and it blamed rent control for the shortfall.[2] This flawed reasoning ignored the fact that the city had exempted new units from rent control, and without it, units were unaffordable. Desperation turned to anger as people were forced out.

The BRA had hoped to use units in Washington Park for the relocation of families from the South End, but delays in that project, displacement in Roxbury, and the desire of South End residents to remain in their neighborhood made that option problematic[21] Not that relocation to Washington Park was even feasible. Indicative of the lack of coordination and communication within the BRA, other BRA staff members were simultaneously planning to use newly constructed South End units for displaced Washington Park residents.[22] Thus Logue's compartmentalization of urban renewal staff and programming produced disastrous results.

The effects of displacement can be seen in the neighborhood's shifting demographics. The total population of the South End dropped from 27,439 in 1960 to 18,820 in 1970, a 31.4 percent loss. Over a two-decade period—when the city's Black population had increased by more than 160 percent—the South End's Black population declined by 38 percent. These numbers do not reflect the overall level of displacement because they include new, mostly well-to-do residents who came in to replace the poor. Many low-income residents left the South End because the BRA or private developers pushed them out.

These changes can be seen more acutely at the block level. Union Park is representative of the neighborhood's most expensive real estate; Northampton Street from Tremont Street to Columbus Avenue reflects its poorest blocks; and Greenwich Park is a middle-income street (for the South End).

Every year, cities and towns in Massachusetts are required to conduct a census of residents that includes occupations, which provides a near continuous portrait of residents' socio-economic positions. In 1958, just before renewal began, on all three blocks combined there were just three officers and managers and thirty-eight professionals, almost all of whom were living on Union Park with a significant number living in South End House. At the same time, there were 314 laborers, helpers, and service workers on the three blocks. In 1970, as the first wave of gentrification crested, the combined total of officers, managers, and professionals for the three blocks was fifty-nine (up 55 percent) while the number of laborers, helpers, and service workers had dropped to 207 (down 34 percent). While there had been no increase in the number of officers, managers, and professionals on Northampton Street or Greenwich Park, in Union Park the number went up from twenty-five to forty-seven (an 88 percent increase). A new economic class of people was moving into the neighborhood.

Desperate to save their homes and frightened by evictions and displacement, South End residents challenged the city. Mel King and others, working with low-income and minority residents, organized CAUSE (Community Alliance for a Unified South End) in April 1967. CAUSE's goals centered on the needs of long-term residents, and the emerging problems with the implementation of renewal led CAUSE to focus its energies on fighting the BRA and private developers.

To advance an alternative agenda, two hundred residents participated in a meeting at the J.J. Williams Building on October 27, 1967. Their most important demand was that the city establish an elected neighborhood organization to oversee renewal. This organization had to include low-income residents, and the city had to grant the maximum amount of local control to residents. CAUSE wanted the BRA to agree that no major action would take place without this local committee's approval. To advance their argument, residents submitted a legal brief that held there was no statutory problem with this arrangement as the final responsibility for urban renewal was still in the hands of the BRA. These recommendations were then discussed at a series of neighborhood meetings, and on December 15, 1967, a seven-hundred-person gathering was held at the Union United Methodist Church, where these principles were enthusiastically adopted.[18] The recommendations went to the city council, which would take months to act.

Up to early 1968, CAUSE used legal methods of protest, including letters to elected officials and presentations at public hearings, but a lack of response prompted CAUSE to embark on a more militant strategy.[18] The inability of the BRA to keep its promises fueled this opposition. Over the next several years, CAUSE would organize large public protests, block development sites, occupy BRA offices, and openly challenge the mayor and the legitimacy of renewal.

As it moved forward, however, CAUSE had an internal dispute on its hands. Its mostly Black leadership saw urban renewal as a struggle of class and race between tenants and the city.[19] But its membership also included large numbers of home-owning whites who were also members of SEFCO, a much more conservative group. Many of these members viewed urban renewal as something that could be negotiated or modified to make it less harmful rather than a disastrous program that had to be stopped at all costs. This difference in viewpoints created tensions around goals and tactics. The conflict increased when the Black United Front offered the group $10,000 if CAUSE agreed to become an all-Black organization. This offer created a split along racial lines with the white group quickly falling apart and the Black group taking over the Steering Committee. Charles Grisby became CAUSE's executive director with the mandate of stopping renewal by any means possible.[26]

In 1967, Mayor Collins' decision not to run for reelection set off a scramble for the open office. Among those who jumped into the race was Logue, who resigned from the BRA on July 27, 1967, scarcely a year after the South End urban renewal project had begun. His electoral experience reflected the popularity of his tenure at the BRA. Logue failed to win any South End precincts and came in fourth overall in the primary. Stung by the rejection, Logue left Boston, first moving to Philadelphia, then New York. He was never involved in the South End again.

Logue's departure had negative impacts on renewal. Without his strong vision and forceful advocacy, conflicts arose between the site office and the central staff over who had authority over disposition and developer selection. With no one in charge, individual projects stalled just as community groups grew angrier as the projects' impacts began to emerge.[21]

Kevin White's mayoral win ushered in a new era in Boston politics and began with important implications for renewal. Rather than appointing a strong BRA administrator to replace Logue, Mayor White turned to a number of weak directors who stayed on the job for only a short time. There would be four between 1967 and 1973, and they had limited powers; Mayor White preferred to manage redevelopment himself. Over his four terms, Mayor White devoted substantial amounts of personal attention to projects downtown where political opposition was weak and the ability of the city to influence development was strong. Suddenly, downtown and Back Bay were filled with construction, and the Boston comeback was in full swing.[27]

In the South End, Mayor White tried to be conciliatory at first. When seven hundred people showed up to a tense gathering at the Mackey School on a snowy night in 1968, Hale Champion, in his first community meeting as BRA Director, promised to increase the percentage of low-income units in 221(d)3 developments to 30 percent and increase the pace of construction.[28] The city also proposed to increase the number of leased units for low-income households from 800 to 1,475.[8] But residents knew these units would not be available for years; the promises failed to dampen the anger in the community.

In addition to opposing the overall renewal plan, CAUSE began to turn its attention to individual projects. The city had a longstanding plan for the Back Bay/South End border called the "High Spine," initially proposed by the Boston Society of Architects. Adding to the Prudential and John Hancock towers, the "High Spine" plan called for the construction of a series of tall buildings outward from downtown to as far west as possible. The plan was conceived as a way to promote development without disrupting the architectural unity of the two historic neighborhoods it separated, but development would prove difficult. Issues related to traffic, density, and shadows delayed projects.

One prominent development site was the block bordered by the Massachusetts Turnpike, Dartmouth Street, Columbus Avenue, and Yarmouth Street. It was targeted for a multistory parking garage, which many deemed inappropriate given the value of the parcel and its eminent position at the intersection of the Back Bay and South End. People also objected to the garage because the site had once been residential. As with other parcels, there was a long-time lag between land taking and redevelopment, and the lot was used as a surface parking lot. Though the BRA owned part of the block, it leased its parcels to the owner of the remainder, the Fitzgerald family, whose members included the city's former fire commissioner, Mayor Hynes' brother-in-law.[29]

When a building on the site was demolished for more surface parking, CAUSE realized that the BRA needed to be challenged on a building-by-building, lot-by-lot basis. On April 27, 1968, one of the most important community protests of the era occurred when a group of demonstrators associated with CAUSE occupied a parking lot to demand affordable housing. The loss of low-income housing for market-rate units and non-residential development had radicalized residents.

Protestors included Mel King, Marty Gopen, and other prominent South Enders. By camping out on the lot, they dramatically—but peacefully—demonstrated the seriousness of the problem. Despite their calm approach, the demonstration provoked a violent reaction. Mel King would later recall: "We had a big truck and a bus, and we put it on one side because it took up a city block. Put it on one side and then formed a human chain around the rest of the lot. One person who was in a car, who did not like that he could not get in, drove into a group of us and knocked me down and people reacted by going after him and his windshield got smashed and in the long run they arrested some us and in the long run we went to jail."[30] Through this action, the neighborhood was able to stop the development of a parking garage and force the BRA to retreat on much of its renewal agenda. The protest also inspired residents across the city to take up direct action to save their homes, but it would take nearly twenty years to realize their housing goals.

8.2 TENT CITY

The issue of neighborhood renewal oversight grew in importance and controversy increased, even as business groups, upper-income homeowners, and social service organizations wanted to quicken redevelopment.[1] These conflicting goals came at a time when new HUD regulations required the city to establish a local project advisory committee (PAC).[26]

BRA Administrator Hale Champion was adamant that no veto powers be granted to the PAC, but the BRA had granted this power to downtown business groups, and South Enders wanted these same rights.[26] So CAUSE tried working with the city council to achieve its aims. Under the leadership of Thomas Atkins, chair of the urban renewal committee and the only Black person on the council, it voted on May 13, 1968 to establish an elected citizen's advisory committee representing the entire South End. Atkins laid out a bottom-up, resident-driven approach for the organization of the renewal advisory committee: local groups would be formed, issues aired, local votes taken, and recommendations submitted to the council for action. The council would then transmit a program to the BRA and—after approval by the mayor—the city would follow through with elections. Preparing for their takeover of the process, six resident committees were formed: powers, districts, communications, public hearings, business, and institutions. All but the last met through the summer of 1968.[26]

Though there were deep divides over many aspects of renewal, the neighborhood was united regarding the PAC's powers. For example, realtor John Sprogis, vice president of SEFCO and a frequent critic of CAUSE, demanded, "We either obtain total power for the elected Urban Renewal Committee or we throw the Boston Redevelopment Authority out of the South End."[26]

In the face of neighborhood demands, the mayor overruled Champion's opposition, and the PAC was given veto power over changes in the renewal plan and developer selection. It could also veto demolition unless the building was an imminent hazard or the demolition was in accordance with previously approved projects.[1] But Mayor White refused to alter the election procedures because he did not want to create a political power base he could not control. CAUSE was not satisfied, even after the BRA declared a moratorium on further land takings.

The city council recommended that residents elect the PAC in an official city election, with each of the fourteen districts electing two representatives and seven at-large representatives. Atkins also tried to get the BRA to set forth the powers of the PAC before the election was held, but the council refused to support him. Frustrated, CAUSE rejected this compromise and decided to go forward with its own elections under the mandate of the December 1967 meeting resolutions, which called for elections regardless of how the city proceeded.[26] CAUSE boycotted the official elections, though some of its members ran for the seats anyway. In June, the community elected representatives to its alternative People's Urban Renewal Committee (PERC) with thirty-five tenants, seven homeowners, twenty-three Black, fifteen white, and four Latino representatives, while in the city elections, five PERC representatives (out of thirty-five total) were elected. In August, Mayor White declared he would only recognize the official organization, now called the South End Project Action Committee (SEPAC), not the community alternative.[1] To their credit, the first SEPAC boards did not veto any low-income housing proposals. Instead, they focused on what would today be called quality-of-life issues: abandoned cars, liquor licenses, policing, trash pickup, and so forth.[1] But it did not try to stop or slow renewal.

The BRA's unquestioning acceptance of certain elements of the 1959 plan caused problems in the 1960s, particularly in the area known as Parcel 19. Consisting of the blocks between West Newton and Upton Streets and Tremont Street and Shawmut Avenue that had few rowhouses, but many non-residential uses, it was one of the most neglected parts of the South End. By the 1960s, the area was a jumble of tenements, garages, lumber yards, and warehouses.

It was also the center of Boston's Puerto Rican community. Ignoring the growing vitality of the area, the BRA's 1964 plan called for the clearance of Parcel 19 with the complete demolition of its buildings. By now, the various replacement ideas included a shopping plaza, market-rate housing, a school, swimming pool, and hockey rink. In all scenarios, most of the 1,500 people and five hundred jobs in the area would be relocated out of the South End.

Though the planned demolition and clearance was still three years away, the area was becoming abandoned, and tenants were displaced as the legal process of takings began. Alarmed, resident Helen Morton and St. Stephens Church's William Dwyer began meeting with neighbors. Together with Carmelo Iglesias, a community organizer hired by the Catholic Church, and two seminarians from the Episcopal Theological School in Cambridge, they worked to mobilize the neighborhood. By knocking on doors and through a series of labor-intensive house meetings, the group organized public meetings and bus trips to other developments in the city. Slowly, other individuals and institutions joined in the effort to save the neighborhood, eventually resulting in Villa Victoria, the award-winning Puerto Rican run development in the heart of the South End.

This activism helped create a new model of community planning and resident housing that differed drastically from the BRA's traditional renewal methods. The tenants in the area worked with their consultants to produce a superior alternative to the outdated BRA plan and used their political organizing skills to convince Mayor White to grant them development rights. Ultimately, they built a community owned and managed by residents who inspired similar efforts across the country. That these successes were accomplished by Puerto Rican residents, one of the city's most marginalized populations, is a testament to their organization skills, vision, and competency. At the height of their activism, sixty to eighty people would attend a regular meeting and well over five hundred people would go to a special meeting. By 1968, the large numbers necessitated the creation of a formal organization, the Emergency Tenants Council (ETC); eight of the ten signers of the articles of incorporation were Puerto Rican.[26]

With the help of architects and volunteers, ETC began to work with the community to prepare its own plan for redevelopment. Slowly, ETC's plan was approved by the many layers of bureaucracy—from SEPAC to the BRA to the City Council. In 1969, ETC made a slide presentation to Mayor White and received the support of BRA and the city government. BRA's director ordered a joint planning effort to accommodate the group's ideas for development.

Throughout this community-based process, ETC received technical assistance from Urban Planning Aid, a Cambridge group based at Harvard and MIT, and developmental assistance from the Greater Boston Community Development Corporation, which would also assist with the development of other affordable housing projects in the South End. In December of 1969, ETC was formally granted development rights for Parcel 19. Most of the features of what became Villa Victoria were proposed by the residents working with their architect John Sharratt such as the large numbers of rehabilitated buildings, the central plaza, and the distinctive architecture of its new housing.[33] Sharratt traveled to the hometown of Israel Feliciano, ETC's director, to gather design ideas and shoot photographs to enable him to produce a slide show that was used to solicit input from residents. He and Feliciano collaborated, not only working to involve residents in the plan, but also creating a strategy for turning Parcel 19 into a neighborhood full of homes.[34]

Villa Victoria was a major achievement of the renewal era. It has a variety of housing types, including a high rise built by the BHA for elderly tenants, rehabilitated row houses along West Newton Street, and a core of two- and three-story walkups painted in multiple colors. Centered on Plaza Betances, the community is home to more than nine hundred households, most of which are Puerto Rican. Since its completion, it has operated a day care center, elder programing, and even a television station. This award-winning development served as a model for other areas confronted by redevelopment and gentrification. Most important, it preserved a community.

ETC formally became IBA, Inquilinos Boricuas en Acción (Puerto Rican Tenants in Action) in 1974. This name change marked a process of coming to terms with an increasingly professional staff that was becoming distant from the community. The new name reflected a number of activities that occurred to ensure that the residents were firmly in charge of the organization even as it reaffirmed the Puerto Rican nature of the area.[31]

Villa Victoria, 2011. The bra wanted to build a park and sports complex on this site. The activism of Puerto Ricans created this award-winning community in the heart of the South End.

8.3 VILLA VICTORIA

The Villa Victoria project directly helped spark the rescue and renovation of the South Ends' TDC buildings. The South End Tenants Council (SETC), the forerunner of the Tenants' Development Corporation (TDC), was an organization of primarily Black tenants from across the neighborhood. There had been previous unsuccessful efforts to organize renters, but in 1968 a group of residents, along with Ted Parrish of USES, began fighting landlords who were letting their buildings deteriorate.

Inspired by Mel King's actions in April of 1968, the group decided to confront the Mindick brothers, who owned forty-four buildings in the neighborhood. The tenants were aided by a group of progressive Jewish clergy, who had been working on civil rights issues in the South and were horrified to find Jews involved in injustices back home.[10] One of the Mindicks led services at his synagogue, and the brothers had used a Hebrew Psalm as a mnemonic device to track their shell corporations, creating an opening for their tenants to take their dispute to the Beit Dein, a rabbinic court. An adverse ruling could have resulted in the loss of Mindick's ability to lead services, and the repercussions would be serious even though the court lacked formal legal standing.[35] Attempting to mediate a settlement, the Beit Dein oversaw the signing of an arbitration contract calling for the Mindicks to address the housing conditions and the tenants to help maintain the buildings. But conditions failed to improve, and the court fined the Mindicks $48,000 for conditions in twenty buildings.[36] Eventually, it helped broker the deal in which the BRA purchased the buildings from the Mindicks and then arranged for tenant management and redevelopment.[37]

SETC then took aim at another landlord, Saul Larner, and picketed his apartment at Charles River Park, which promptly terminated his lease. He also agreed to submit to the Beit Dien. Again, the court ordered negotiations, and in August 1968, tenants reached an agreement with the landlord encompassing fifty-eight buildings and 1,200 tenants. The tenants agreed to pay their rents on time, and the landlord would not evict the tenants and would bring the buildings up to code. The agreement also established a court-monitored grievance process.

Larner failed to comply with the agreement, resulting in a rent strike in October 1968. The arbitration board sided with the tenants and gave administration of six of Larner's eleven buildings to the SETC. Now without rental income, Larner encountered financial problems, and in November, the buildings went to public auction. SETC secured a $19,000 loan from the Black United Front to purchase two of them, but speculators bought the other nine.

Collecting rents on substandard units they did not own and thus could not renovate put SETC in an awkward position. The rents were insufficient to cover necessary repairs, even with volunteer labor, and tenants began to blame SETC for problems. There were two ways out of this: SETC could acquire titles to the buildings and secure funds for their rehabilitation or only become involved in buildings that were already up to code. The sale of some of Larner's buildings to speculators also demonstrated that the SETC's tactics could backfire and displace tenants. Therefore, in November 1969, SETC began to explore the creation of a development corporation that could acquire, rehab, and manage housing. In December, the BRA agreed to apply to HUD for funds for SETC to rehab one hundred buildings.[1] The next step was for SETC to form a development subsidiary, TDC, to bring the buildings up to code.[26]

The BRA assumed control of twenty of these buildings and made plans for the acquisition of eighty more. Having secured funds, the first one hundred units were rehabbed in 1971. But the next thirty-six buildings were not even scheduled to break ground until 1974. Because they were so badly deteriorated, it was not clear if HUD would even let them be rehabbed. To add to TDC's problems, a group of upper-income South End residents opposing more low-income housing began to work against TDC, even filing suit to stop the project. The process of creating affordable housing in these units would take years.

Perhaps the South End institution that renewal changed the most was USES. It had worked closely with the city's redevelopment planners, organized neighborhood associations with the goal of promoting renewal, and managed relocation under contracts with the BHA and BRA, first in Castle Square and then elsewhere in the neighborhood. It was also in the process of receiving city assistance to build new facilities for itself at the corner of Massachusetts and Columbus Avenues.[18] When it initially agreed to oversee relocation, USES had substantial institutional backing for its involvement in renewal with support from the South End ministers organization, SEFCO, and the Inter-Agency group.[5] But now that the community had turned on renewal, USES found itself alone. How could it reconcile this advocacy for redevelopment with its client base that was being displaced by it?

At one point, USES employed more than twenty-five people to assist with relocation, and these staffers saw firsthand the consequences of displacement and the failure of the city to help those affected. One USES employee, Al Boer, spoke out against the relocation program at a staff meeting in 1966, provoking a rebuke from Executive Director Charles Liddell and resulting in Boer's resignation.[38] USES did not realize this incident was a warning of what was to come.

As a South End resident, Mel King was angered by the destruction of his neighborhood and the loss of longtime tenants, who were evicted by the BRA and private developers.[19] As a USES employee, King was distressed that the organization was being compromised by its participation in a program pushing out the residents it was supposed to assist. So King began to speak out against renewal and USES's involvement in relocation, causing conflict with USES's management. Board President Douglas Cochrane became so angry with King's behavior— particularly his public criticisms of USES policies—that King's status was discussed at an Executive Committee meeting on January 30, 1967. Though there were some board members who wanted to fire King, others were sympathetic to his concerns and cautioned that there were no specific grounds to let him go.[39] Seeking a middle ground, USES continued to support King and his efforts while still working with the BRA.

Meanwhile, CAUSE turned on USES, trying to prevent any further participation in renewal.[41] Motivated by the need to stop displacement, King and others met with Cochrane to present three demands: USES must fund CAUSE, stop participating in relocation, and open its board meetings to the public. Cochrane conceded that USES went into the latest relocation contract with the BRA despite serious concerns, but he was not yet willing to terminate the relationship. Trying to compromise, Cochrane agreed to look into USES's right to exercise a clause allowing it to pull out of the contract. At this point, USES did not believe the threats of King's allies that they would picket the agency.[42] But a few weeks later, as its 1967 annual meeting approached, USES became very concerned that King and his supporters would attempt to disrupt the gathering.[43]

Pressing forward with a detailed proposal, CAUSE asked USES to fund a community-controlled organization that would develop a neighborhood-wide constituency. CAUSE estimated that it needed funding for at least seven positions (with a total budget of $34,200) and office space at the USES offices at 48 Rutland Street.[44] After much debate, USES rejected the proposal on the grounds that as a charitable organization, it was not consistent with its mission to support protests, and legally, it could not attempt to influence legislation or lobby government. But USES had organized neighborhood associations to support renewal, so CAUSE didn't see a problem organizing local associations to oppose it. Rejecting this argument, Cochrane grew angry with CAUSE, accusing it of only wanting USES to terminate its relocation contract because it would then be free to confront the BRA more aggressively. Furthermore, he argued, to terminate the contract would mean abandoning services to the families being displaced.[45]

Stepping up the pressure, King and other relocation workers protested any USES involvement in the increasingly chaotic and destructive urban renewal program, and an angry Charles Liddel tried to fire King in early 1968, publicly citing a difference in opinion. Now questioning the legitimacy of the organization, King and other critics charged that USES was run by suburban interests that were not adequately representing the community. Liddell, for example, lived in Natick. As King would discuss in his retrospective analysis of the events of the late 1960s, the Black community in general—and the South End in particular—was moving away from a model of dependence on the support and leadership of outsiders towards building, owning, and operating its own institutions.[46] Now it was time for South End residents to take control of USES and shift its focus toward supporting their interests, not working to help displace them. This newfound outlook created an existential crisis for the agency. If it wasn't community based, what right did USES have to even be in the South End? Searching for consensus in an increasingly polarized environment, the USES board struggled with issues related to the extent to which the organization could fund or foster political advocacy. Was it legal? Did it fit within the agency's mission?[47] Though many board members supported King, USES still refused CAUSE's demands, insisting that relocation and renewal might not be working out as planned but that it had committed to the program.[48]

USES had run out of options, however. Having boldly confronted the BRA and the mayor, King, South End residents, and USES employees took over USES's offices at 20 Union Park on May 6, 1968. The action began when eleven staff members met with Kenneth Brown (who had replaced Liddell as executive director when he was appointed to head ABCD) to raise the issue that USES's involvement with relocation was making it impossible to continue to work with residents. They voiced this concern at a staff meeting at 9 a.m. where Brown asked for a week in order to consult the board, but the staff members told Brown to expect immediate action. At 1 p.m., the staff moved into Brown's office accompanied by several members of CAUSE.

Board President Edwin Abrams called an emergency meeting of the Board the next day at the Hotel Bradford with twenty board members and five staff members present. In a two-hour meeting, the board agreed to review the agency's involvement with the relocation program and to explore legal action to evict the protesters.[49] Some conservative board members were very angry with CAUSE, and one called King dangerous.[50] But overall, the board considered the issues CAUSE raised to be legitimate, and they struggled to address the problems the protestors had brought to their attention.[51]

Three days later, the Board met again and voted to seek a court order to evict the protestors, filing a suit against CAUSE and twenty-six individuals, including Mel King, Carmelo Iglesias, Marty Gopin, Ted Parish, Kay Gibbs, and Chuck Turner. Even though the court would side with USES and issue a restraining order, USES' board still heard a representative of the protestors outlining the problems with the relocation contract. Searching for a compromise, it voted to continue providing services, but it would enter into negotiations with the BRA regarding the problems with relocation and would ask the newly elected SEPAC to get involved in the issue as well.[52]

The board knew this was an insufficient response; it was becoming clear that it would have to meet the protestors' demands. Critical to the solution to the crisis was Melnea Cass, whose support for the demonstrators jolted other board members.[53] Once they considered a change of direction, the agency's action was swift, and USES quickly realigned itself with the forces against renewal. On May 13, 1968, Brown issued a memorandum stating that while the agency would continue to provide services to the more than one hundred households currently in the relocation process, it would end its participation in relocation after these households were resettled.[54] Now committed to a new course of action, on May 20, 1968, Brown released a statement castigating the BRA and the urban renewal program. "To low-income families, renewal has meant the further contraction of their already inadequate supply of housing, it has displaced poor Blacks and created a climate for speculation in the South End, which, coupled with the alarmingly high cost of rehabilitation, has encouraged the conversion of many areas to middle and upper income occupancy."[55] USES would no longer be part of renewal.

USES also realized it was no longer legitimately representing the neighborhood. There were increasing concerns that only ten of the thirty-six board members came from the South End with another six from Roxbury. Eventually, USES elected a new board that was more reflective of the community it served. USES would continue to work in the neighborhood, and it would be a major resource for the people of the South End nearly fifty years after this crisis ended.

Renewal, displacement, and gentrification were creating chaos in the neighborhood and low-income residents were desperate. For the most part, the target of their anger was the BRA and its allies. But the rapid growth of middle-class newcomers was creating a new force in the South End. Soon, residents would begin to fight with each other.

1. SEPAC. *Report on Urban Renewal.* 1974.

2. Real Estate Research Corporation. *Urban Renewal Land Disposition Study - Boston, MA.* 1974.

3. Sprogis DC. *Proposal for the South End Urban Renewal Committee.* 1964.

4. South End Urban Renewal Committee *Minutes.* 1966.

5. South End Urban Renewal Committee. *Minutes.* 1966.

6. Boston Redevelopment Authority. *Diagnostic Report: Residents of the South End Urban Renewal Project.* 1967.

7. Boston Redevelopment Authority. *Family Relocation - 1967 Annual Report.* 1968.

8. Truce. Truce in the South End. *Boston Globe*; 1968 April 30.

9. Boston Redevelopment Authority *Housing in the South End: A Report on the Current Status of Urban Renewal.* 1974.

10. Levine H, Harmon L. *The Death of an American Jewish Community. A Tragedy of Good Intentions.* New York: The Free Press; 1992.

11. Boston Redevelopment Authority. *South End Environmental Assessment.* 1979.

12. Potts L. *A Block in Time: A History of Boston's South End From a Window on Holyoke Street.* New York: Local History Publishers; 2012.

13. Urban Planning Aid. *Report on the South End Urban Renewal Plan for Boston City Council Hearing*. 1968.

14. Achtenberg EJ. *Rehabilitation Loans and Grants in Boston*: Massachusetts Institute of Technology; 1970.

15. Boston Redevelopment Authority. *Subsidized Housing in the South End*. 1978.

16. Mollenkopf JH. *The Contested City*. Princeton, New Jersey: Princeton Universit Press; 1983.

17. Boston Redevelopment Authority. *Press Release*. 1965.

18. Maxwell AH. *The anthropology of poverty In black communities: A critique and systems alternative*. *Urban Anthropology and Studies of Cultural Systems and World Economic Development* 1988; 19:171-91.

19. King M. *Chain of Change: Struggles for Black Community Development*. Boston MA: South End Press; 1981.

20. Boston Redevelopment Authority. *Project Selection Rating Report – Franklin Square House Community Center*. 1972.

21. Downs A, Bolon L. Urban Renewal Land Disposition Study. In: *Real Estate Research Corporation*, ed. Washington. 1974.

22. Boston Redevelopment Authority. *Family Relocation Development Report 1968-1969*, 1970.

23. Florists. Florists Plan Center In So. End. *Boston Globe*; 1964 January 1.

24. Cardoso W. Artists thrive in South End. *Boston Globe*; 1971 June 7.

25. Kelly K. Arts Center--Progress Amid Controversy. *Boston Globe;* 1972 October 22.

26. Womble PB. *The Neighborhood Autonomy Movement: A Study of Opposition to Urban Renewal's South End:* Harvard University; 1970.

27. Kennedy L. *Planning the City upon a Hill: Boston since 1630*. Boston: University of Massachusetts Press; 1994.

28. Economy Units. More Economy Units Set for South End. *Boston Globe*; 1968 January 26; Sect. 1.

29. Sasaski Associates. *Draft Environmental Impact Statement, Tent City*. Cambridge, Massachusetts. 1985.

30. Turner D. *Interview with Mel King*. 1990.

31. Uriarte-Gaston M. *Organizing for Survival: The Emergence of a Puerto Rican Community:* Boston University; 1988.

32. Shannon HJ. *Legendary Locals of Boston's South End*. Charleston, South Carolina: Arcadia Publishing; 2014.

33. Brown J. South End Puerto Ricans Join in Planning of B.R.A.'s 'Parcel 19'. *Boston Globe*; 1969 June 22.

34. National Endowment for the Arts. *La Comunidad, Design, Development and Self-Determination*

in Hispanic Communities. 1982.

35. Rabbinical Court of Justice (Beth-Din Zedeck). *Official Decree.* 1968.

36. Coaxum A. Rabbinic Court's Rare Move Settles So. End Dispute. *Boston Globe*; 1968 August 6 Sect. 34.

37. Osgood V. Tenants Win Owners Rights in BRA Accord. *Boston Globe*; 1969 August 12 Sect. 18.

38. Knight L. *Interview with Al Boer.* 1991.

CHAPTER 9

The End of Renewal: 1968 – 1974

During the renewal years—1964 to 1974—the exteriors of buildings were spared; passersby would see unchanged facades. Inside, in contrast, there were dramatic upgrading of finishes and building systems so that every modern-day convenience could be had: heat in each room, state of the art plumbing, well-applianced kitchens, and upgraded electrical service. Also within these newly renovated row houses and apartment buildings, there was a profound demographic shift from poor to middle class and Black to white. During this upheaval, the neighborhood went through its first wave of gentrification, and the South End became a middle-class neighborhood. These residents pushed out most of the poor as property values increased by 250 percent between 1959 and 1972.[1,2] By the end of this period, South End townhouses were rivaling Beacon Hill in luxury, and the neighborhood was attracting professionals from the suburbs and socialites from the Back Bay.[3]

Developers accumulated large groups of buildings, sometimes more than they could manage. One speculator, for example, amassed twenty-four row houses on West Newton Street along with scattered buildings elsewhere in the neighborhood, but the units were so rundown that tenants held rent strikes and staged protests. The developer gave up, and in 1970, the BRA brokered the sale of the West Newton Street buildings to the BHA. Today, they are part of Villa Victoria and managed by ETC, IBA's property management subsidiary.

Other developers were more successful. Mark Goldweitz moved into an apartment in 1969 and immediately saw the potential for real estate profits. Goldweitz's father provided capital for a real estate company, and the Harvard Business School graduate eventually bought forty-five buildings, which he renovated into 279 luxury apartments.[4]

These apartments represented a new style of living that was vastly different from that of the rooming houses and tenements they had replaced. "The college professors, lawyers, and admen who rented his apartments—many of them gays, young singles, and couples without children—brought with them all the accouterments of urban chic: hanging ferns, butcher block furniture, Marimekko fabrics, Cuisinart food processors, and KLH sound systems. The curbs outside were lined with Volvos, Saabs, and BMWs."[5] The poor were gone.

Neighborhood activists opposing gentrification protested the venture, arguing that Goldweitz was displacing tenants. Goldweitz countered that he only bought empty buildings, but the activists contended that he made vacant buildings a condition of purchase, encouraging sellers to evict tenants.[5] In one action, more than three hundred protestors showed up at the Victorian Ball, a fundraiser for the South End Historical Society held at the BCA in January 1974, to protest Goldweitz and the continued destruction of low-income housing. Demonstrators linked the individuals profiting from the gentrification of the neighborhood to the hardships the lower-income residents were enduring.[4]

A study of Goldweitz's activities found extensive displacement. In 1969, Goldweitz owned thirty occupied and fifteen vacant buildings. By 1974, these were transformed into forty-two occupied buildings and three vacant ones. After Goldweitz assumed ownership, the percentage of unskilled workers dropped from 52 percent to 21 percent, while the percentage of professionals rose from 4 percent to 33 percent. Of the 204 people in Goldweitz's buildings prior to acquisition, only forty-seven were there post-acquisition.[6]

The extent of turnover across the neighborhood was staggering; an estimated thirty thousand people were displaced between 1965 and 1978.[7] The displacement of small businesses was even greater. In 1963, a decade after clearings began, a BRA retail survey found forty-seven businesses on Massachusetts Avenue, 118 on Columbus Avenue, seventy-six on Shawmut Avenue, 249 on Tremont Street, and 184 on Washington Street.[8] Over the next fifteen years, almost every one of these businesses would disappear, most never replaced by other establishments because the BRA wanted to shrink the neighborhood's retail footprint.

Boston's annual census for Union Park, Greenwich Park, and Northampton Street show the depth of gentrification by 1980. Almost 52 percent of Union Park's working residents were now in professional or managerial occupations; in Greenwich Park, they made up 41 percent of residents. Even on Northampton Street, the percentage had increased to more than 8 percent. At the same time, the percentage of laborers and service workers declined. On Union Park, they now made up only 22 percent of employed residents; on Greenwich Park, they were 25 percent; and on Northampton Street they were 35 percent, a decrease of about one-third. These new residents were not the very wealthy; they were middle class. They were, however, vastly more affluent than those they replaced.[9]

At this time, almost all of the South End was comprised of rental units.

In 1980, there were only 936 owner-occupied units, down slightly from 1,091 in 1950, and the BRA reported only a handful of condominiums. What remained of the private rental market that had once served low-income residents was rapidly falling apart. Poor tenants were paying more for units that were growing ever more decayed, and they knew whom to blame for the increases and displacement. While the newcomers may have been welcomed in the early 1960s, by the end of the decade, resentment against the middle class was high, and the conflict between newcomers and older residents often turned ugly. There were "raucous shouting matches, litigation, picketing and inflammatory press releases and exposes in the continuous skirmishing between racial and class factions."[10]

The experience of the Diver family provides an insight into the minds of some coming into the neighborhood. Before moving to the South End, "what [Colin Diver] noticed first was the varied colors of the children— black, white, brown, even a scattering of yellow."[5] This diversity may have been desirable, but the reality of living near people who were so different could be jarring.[1] Some newcomers became aggressive, publicly disdaining previous residents[9] while others were more progressive, committed to diversity and accepting of previous residents. Some of the first opponents of the more upscale newcomers were the social workers, themselves newly arrived in the neighborhood, who saw the effects of rising housing prices and displacement.[5]

Many newcomers failed to adjust to urban living. Some, including the Divers, became disillusioned with the South End; life there, with its crime, grit, and diversity, could be overwhelming. For example, one night Colin Diver snapped and went after a mugger with a baseball bat. "Colin hesitated for a moment. Tremont was a significant boundary to his world, the southern border of the gentrified South End. Beyond it stretched a row of tenements, occupied principally by Puerto Ricans, and Cubans. The O'Day Playground halfway down the block was the center of the South End's heroin trade, a dangerous place day or night. On other chases in months past, Colin had always stopped at Tremont, unwilling to carry his pursuit into alien territory." The Divers later moved to Newton.

Over time, many of the newcomers became committed residents and greatly contributed to the quality of life in the community. One well-known newcomer was Betty Gibson, who was born in Jamaica Plain in 1907. A lieutenant in the Women Accepted for Voluntary Emergency Service program in World War II, she tried working in retail positions after the war but found them stifling. Looking for a field where sexism would not hold her back, she turned to real estate in 1962, and her firm became one of the most successful in the neighborhood. For decades before her death in 1991, she was noted for her charitable work in the neighborhood. Another contributor to the South End's betterment was Royal Cloyd, originally from Illinois. A resident of Union Park, he was central to launching the BCA, serving as its first president. Previously, Cloyd had worked for the Unitarian Universalist Association and had been head of SEFCO. Doe and David Sprogis also began contributing to the neighborhood when they moved into the South End in 1963. They helped establish both the BCA and the South End Historical Society and were known for their patronage of neighborhood institutions.[11] As decades passed, the line between newcomers and old timers has faded for many, but not all.

Low-income residents were still frustrated and enraged by the fact that the renewal program had made little-to-no progress in creating new housing, even as evictions and land takings continued. Acquisition initially proceeded rapidly, and by the summer of 1968, the BRA owned almost half the land they targeted. Then work stalled. By 1974, they had acquired less than 65 percent of the original scheduled list of properties. Disposition was even slower. Of 167 parcels, only seventy had passed completely through the program, most in the Castle Square area. The majority of parcels to be acquired were in a legal and management limbo with property owners unwilling to make repairs and tenants living in squalor. The rehabilitation projects for low- and moderate-income residents were the slowest of all; only 32 percent were complete by the summer of 1973.[12]

In light of the plan to demolish 3,500 units, it was critical that the BRA build replacement units quickly. The program, however, had limitations, and builders had to make construction compromises to meet budgets and deadlines. Even after tenants moved in, buildings and units often needed multiple rounds of rehabilitation to make the units habitable. Developing permanent housing would take years longer than planned, disrupting lives, displacing people, and ultimately contributing to the fight against renewal.

The main vehicle available to fund low-income housing was the federal 221(d)3 program, which provided thirty-year loans at 3 percent interest to developers. The BRA, and the federal government, incorrectly assumed that these low-cost loans would make a project affordable for moderate-income households. Prior to 1960, local public housing authorities, such as the BHA, owned most government-funded housing for low-income households. But issues with corruption, faulty designs, high costs, limited funds, and the general prioritization of private- over public-sector management prompted a new model of housing: one that was privately owned but publicly funded.

These ideas were the rationale for the 221(d)3 program.

Non-government owners quickly found that developing and running low-income housing, which was expensive to build and manage, was difficult. By design, they could not use renewal funds or 221(d)3 money to directly meet the total costs of development. The program called for additional capital to make the projects. These funds came from developers and the syndication of housing depreciation expenses. After construction was complete, rental income was expected to pay mortgages, taxes, operating expenses, reserves for capital expenses, and profits to investors. For the most part, builders aimed these developments at moderate-income families since low-income households would need additional subsidies. In the end, however, much of the middle-income housing was repurposed for low-income families because resulting rents were too high to be afforded by their target demographic.

As with any untried program, no one knew what to expect from this new model of housing development, and neither the BRA nor developers had experience building low-income housing. No one except housing authorities did, and these were barred from the program. Developing plans, producing construction drawings, selecting contractors, working with neighbors, evaluating bids, and completing other development activities were long, slow, and expensive tasks. Even after all this was complete, the developers still had to secure HUD approvals and 221(d)3 commitments. Inexperienced and overwhelmed, developers floundered as some projects took ten or more years to complete.[1]

Budgetary constraints led to inferior construction, and inexperienced developers only exacerbated these problems. Union United Methodist Church's experience in low-income housing development highlights how good intentions were insufficient to build affordable housing. The church agreed to participate in the housing program in 1965 because it saw it as an extension of its mission to assist the poor. But three years later, the project still had not broken ground. After rounds of reworking plans to meet budget constraints, the bleak design for its Columbus Avenue buildings was jarring and inappropriate. By 1968, those who wanted to preserve the architectural heritage of the South End thought the new housing was drastically alien to the Victorian sensibility of the neighborhood. Unfortunately, the new development sponsors lacked the financial resources to emulate the look of the old buildings, and HUD had neither sympathy for the neighborhood's architectural uniqueness nor additional funding for complementary designs. A new round of conflict regarding the development of housing ensued, and Methunion Manor did not break ground until April 1970, five years after the project officially began.[5]

The complex suffered from poor design, inferior construction, and inadequate management. To make the project affordable, the church had to cut every corner and downgrade every possible amenity to reduce costs. The results included overflowing toilets, overheated apartments, cracked plaster, flooded basements, and wobbly shower heads. As they moved into the already failing buildings, tenants fought the management company, the managers pointed at the tenants, and both blamed the contractors. At the same time, HUD accused the developers of incompetence, and everyone singled out the BRA for its role in the fiasco. Methunion Manor's first-year expenses were double what had been budgeted.[5]

In another example, St. Cyprian's Roxse Homes had problems with DCA, a for-profit developer the church hired to build its new housing. DCA's founder had constructed several public housing developments; there was no reason to question the company's expertise. Sadly, the aging founder had been replaced by inexperienced successors, and the project almost failed before it was completed.

Roxse Homes' construction was particularly bad. "The heating system and the hot water didn't always work well. When it rained or snow melted, water poured into the apartments and hallways. In some cases, waste materials from the toilets flooded apartments when they were flushed." Unable to make repairs or pay its mortgage, the church increased rent from $25 to $30 in July 1972, and tenants organized to take over the development. Estimates to repair the units suggested rents might have to rise to $90, well beyond the tenants' incomes.[17] St. Cyprian's was overwhelmed, and the church gave up on the project, leaving it adrift. The BRA had to work with the tenants to keep the development from closing.

Though these developments were supposed to be reserved for South End residents displaced by renewal, the long lead times caused most former tenants to be lost to relocation consultants or settled into new living arrangements from which they could not or would not move. When new units were completed, five years or more behind schedule, developers desperate for any cash flow would rent to any qualified tenant rather than turn units over to the BRA relocation office and face delays. When Grant Manor opened, for example, the BRA only relocated seven South End displaced families into the development.[12]

One casualty of the 221(d)3 program's failure was the South End's moderate-income housing. At the beginning of urban renewal, the BRA had allocated most new units to moderate-income households and planned to use a different program that enabled the BHA to lease units and then rent them to low-income tenants at a markdown. But as the number of qualified moderate-income eligible tenants fell short and the desperation of low-income families grew, the BRA and property managers turned to a new subsidy program known as Section 8. Under this program, HUD paid the difference between what a tenant could afford—first 25 percent and then later 30 percent of a household's total income—and an agreed-upon rent. Section 8 allowed developments to raise rents without losing tenants and bought time for many troubled buildings. But the new Section 8 program was only available to low-income households. So as time went on, what were once moderate-income units were restricted to low-income families.

Less than 2,100 of 3,300 planned units were completed by 1978, over fifteen years after the demolitions had begun, and most of these projects were in trouble.[19] By the late 1970s, seventy-three 221(d)3 housing projects in the South End, Roxbury, and North Dorchester were on the brink of financial disaster.[20] Four South End developments—Methunion Manor, Interfaith-West Concord, Grant Manor, and Rutland Housing—were experiencing major financial difficulty, and three additional developments—Roxse Homes, Camfield Gardens, and Tuckerman Homes—were in default. Even Castle Square's units needed a substantial rent increase to meet its higher-than-anticipated costs.[7]

Tenants in poorly maintained buildings responded by withholding rent and mounting public demonstrations. The remaining moderate-income tenants who could find better housing left, further contributing to financial problems. Defaulting on these mortgages potentially meant that HUD would foreclose on projects, properties could be sold to for-profit developers, and tenants put out on the street. Though the churches were shielded from legal responsibility for defaults by the subsidiaries they set up to manage development, they were embarrassed and enraged by the general incompetence of the program. Most withdrew from further involvement in redevelopment.

The city used Section 8 contracts to recapitalize failed projects and fix the worst problems in the most troubled developments, but these efforts were time consuming and further eroded the BRA's ability to manage renewal. In addition, some developments needed more money than this fiscal bailout could provide. By itself, converting 221(d)3 projects into new Section 8-based projects would not solve all the issues in the South End's affordable housing stock.

Conflict over renewal in the South End shifted after the BRA's 1968 moratorium on demolition. Now, rather than just fighting the BRA, residents turned on each other as well.[20] Some newcomers used the prolonged delays in affordable housing construction to form the Committee for a Balanced

South End (CBSE), which advocated for less low-income housing. Louise Day Hicks, an ally of the group, introduced legislation in the city council that called for a moratorium on new low-income housing in the neighborhood. CBSE and Hicks also fought low-income housing by claiming that the South End was receiving too large a share of the city's funds for assisted housing. Those opposed to low-income housing made up only one quarter of the South End's population at most, but they were very influential through their money and political connections.

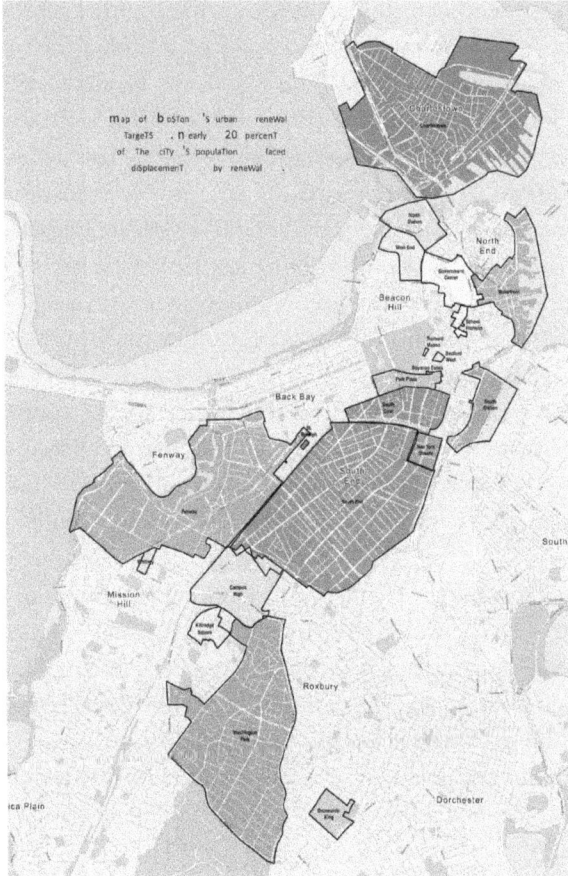

9.1 BOSTON URBAN RENEWAL DISTRICTS

Kevin White succeeded in insulat ing himself from the reaction against renewal. In the 1971 mayoral election, White carried most of the South End in the primary, losing only three precincts to Thomas Atkins, the first Black to run for mayor of Boston. Atkins came in fourth citywide, and White would go on to win every neighborhood precinct in his rematch against Louise Day

Hicks. His victory reflects the dilemma that South End progressives would find themselves in the four mayoral elections after the launching of renewal: no matter how angry they might be with the program, they had no viable alternative to Kevin White in the final election. They felt obligated to support White in his two elections against Hicks and in his two campaigns against a less racist, but no friend of people of color, Joe Timilty.

The BRA tried in vain to mollify the neighborhood by emphasizing market-rate rehabilitation to the middle class and affordable housing to the poor. By 1973, there were three groups in the South End vying to influence the course of renewal. The progressives included the poor and their middle-class allies and advocates. Their goal was to increase the supply of low-income housing and stop the conversion of affordable rental units into more expensive housing. The conservatives were determined to protect their investments, afraid of crime, distrustful of poor long-term residents, and forcefully demanding to keep any additional low-income housing and social services out of the neighborhood. The moderates were politically torn. For the most part, these progressive-leaning newcomers and long-term residents were sympathetic to the poor but hesitant to slow renewal.[21]

Radicalized by displacement, the progressives had few alternatives to militancy. Conservatives felt ignored and turned to the courts. Moderates, wanting stability, were willing to use conventional practices of negotiation and bargaining but were drowned out by the more radical and conservative residents. Sadly, one of renewal's major legacies in the South End was acrimony.[21]

The growing number of conservative newcomers began to flex their political muscles. CBSE claimed that low-income housing goals had been met and therefore all remaining parcels owned by the BRA should be exclusively for market-rate housing. CBSE counted 5,522 subsidized housing units, but this included homeowners who had received loans to produce market-rate units.[2] In truth, no one, including the BRA, knew how many units were being developed or rehabilitated because the agency lacked the ability to track the program's progress.

The CBSE proposed the city build low-income housing for South End residents in other neighborhoods and the suburbs, but this was impossible. The busing crisis was about to explode. The same neighborhoods opposing integrated schools would have risen to fight low-income family developments for South Enders in their neighborhoods. Integration of Blacks in their communities would have been met with the same, if not more, hostility. Nor was the suburban alternative feasible; Boston lacked the jurisdiction to build outside the cities.

The effort against low-income housing grew increasingly bitter when, in February 1974, CBSE sued to stop TDC's second phase of housing based on environmental concerns, overconcentration of low-income units, and noise. Others associated with CBSE filed suit to stop part of Villa Victoria and Concord Towers.[7] These fights continued for most of the decade as Union Park and West Concord Street residents opposed the Salvation Army opening the Harbor Lights Center on Shawmut Avenue. Others fought housing for teenagers on Dwight Street in 1977, calling them "misfits" and complaining that the South End had more than its share of facilities.[22]

After several years of boycotting SEPAC, progressives shifted tactics and campaigned for a slate in the 1974 election, winning a majority of seats. But they continued to face opposition from conservatives in the neighborhood. While lawsuits failed to stop any project, they forced the BRA to devote considerable staff time anticipating challenges. These setbacks further slowed down the already much-delayed redevelopment process, and the BRA became reluctant to go forward with new projects that would serve the low-income residents of the neighborhood. Coupled with demands from other neighborhoods for scarce federal and state housing dollars, the conservative backlash convinced the city to build assisted housing and fund social services outside the South End. Subsequently, the entire urban renewal program ground to a halt, leaving a number of large parcels empty.[21] It would take a decade or more to build on some of the cleared land.

The progressives felt empowered by their SEPAC board victory and stepped up their militancy. These actions, however, alienated their moderate allies. Though the moderates generally agreed with the progressives' goals, the strategy of confrontation and vilification made many moderates uncomfortable. They deeply cared about what was happening in the South End, but some of their values put them on the wrong side of the progressives, whose radicalization sometimes made it difficult for them to work with anyone who did not share their entire vision. This conflict had already boiled over regarding the issue of preserving the neighborhood's distinctive architecture. When the progressive Ad Hoc Committee for a South End for South Enders picketed the Victorian Ball and disrupted the South End Historic Society's annual house tour,[20] it generated important publicity for the plight of low-income tenants. It also, however, alienated a growing constituency in the neighborhood and left the protestors open to the charge that they didn't care about the South End's architectural heritage. In addition, some moderates opposed the anger directed towards the BRA. Many were city employees or were of similar background, and they were sympathetic to the complexity of implementing renewal in the neighborhood.[21]

A final progressive miscalculation was underestimating how City Hall might react to protests. Though he had a liberal reputation, Kevin White was not a mayor who tolerated the militancy of the progressives, and he responded to their attacks on his administration by eliminating SEPAC's budget. The progressives thought that the strength of their coalition politics would gain them victory in this funding dispute, but their tactics had disillusioned the moderates, limiting their political power. By this time, a growing middle group of residents simply wanted an urban renewal program that would finish ongoing projects and not generate further controversy. They yearned for neighborhood leadership that could work with everyone.[21] What they were getting was a complete halt to all projects and programs.[20]

Despite the rancor, newcomers and longtime residents slowly learned to work together. One positive outcome of this era was the preservation of the South End's architectural legacy. Though the South End's row houses had been maligned for decades, newcomers loved the neighborhood's architecture, which resulted in an organization dedicated to preserving the streets' unique design. As Richard Card noted in a personal journal entry on February 13, 1966, "Tonight I went with Jim and Joan Fitzgerald to Roger Vogtmen's. We decided to organize a South End Historical Society." Within two weeks, fourteen people had signed up. On the night of March 23, 1966, the group met at the League of Women for Community Service on Massachusetts Avenue to formally establish itself.[23]

The group became a strong proponent of preserving and rehabilitating the South End's unique architecture. The Historical Society thought the South End could "best be preserved not as something embalmed and dead, but as thing still full of life and peopled with real people."[24] The Historical Society continues to be a major asset to the community fifty years later, sponsoring events, conducting tours, educating the community, and aggressively challenging any threat to the neighborhood's architectural heritage.

Despite some opposition, the neighborhood continued to be a place where people devoted their lives to helping others. The South End Community Health Center, for example, was established in 1969. Originally a pediatric clinic, it eventually expanded to provide services to the entire community. Today, it is affiliated with most of the major hospitals in the city, serving twenty thousand patients per year.[25] Part of the reason for the center's success was the long-term stability of its leadership. It was founded by Dr. Gerald Hass in response to South End residents' concerns that they had no place to access medical care. After seeing the need for a place where people would be treated with dignity and respect, he devoted his career to helping the neighborhood.[26] Hass was the Center's chief physician for forty-one years.

He was assisted by Tristam Blake, who served as the Center's resourceful executive director for thirty-eight years before retiring in 2009. Another important contributor was the indefatigable Jovita Fontanez, a Dartmouth Street resident who helped found the Center in 1969 and continued to serve as an honorary board member forty-five years later. Fontanez had a career of community activism ranging from work at Casa Esperanza to serving as a delegate to the Democratic National Committee.[11]

Problems with urban renewal were not limited to Boston. In many cities, the program had become increasingly unpopular with low-income and minority residents, who were bearing the brunt of its impacts—so much so that some thought urban renewal should really be called negro removal.[27] At the same time, conservatives objected to the broad powers urban renewal gave local government and had issues with eminent domain and the forced sale of properties. They did not want public sponsorship of housing, either.[7] With support for urban renewal vanishing, on August 22, 1974, President Gerald Ford signed legislation phasing out federal funding for urban renewal over the next three years. The new law rolled the program into block grant funding, and all federal urban renewal programs had to formally end.[7] Across the country, redevelopment agencies retrenched, and the BRA laid off a sizable portion of its staff. HUD told the BRA to submit a plan for the completion of the South End project; the era of federal urban renewal in the South End was over.[28]

A blossoming Boston went from being one of the most troubled cities in the country to one of its most prosperous. But the successful renewal projects were mostly downtown; low-income residents did not benefit from them for a variety of reasons. First, downtown projects relied on large tax breaks, which increased pressure on residential property rates. Second, renewal did not create lower-wage jobs, which is what many residents wanted. For the most part, redevelopment created jobs that required skills beyond the abilities of working-class residents.[29] Finally, the BRA's policy of planning for each neighborhood in isolation caused another problem: the South End now had to compete with other neighborhoods for scarce housing funds. The ability of the BRA to fund any additional projects was limited, and the supply of affordable units never met the demand.[28]

As the urban renewal program drew to a close, HUD commissioned an analysis of urban renewal in Boston and the South End in particular. The review was scathing and declared that the South End plan was simply not feasible insofar as it covered an area too big and complex, and despite its large budget, there were insufficient funds for its ambitious program. The plan greatly underestimated the costs of housing rehabilitation; its projections of project improvements were unrealistic."[30] Defensive, the BRA countered cost increases, plan changes, delays, and outside pressures had blocked its ability to complete the South End and other renewal projects.

As early as 1969, the South End project experienced financial difficulties due to cost overruns and diverted funds. As a result, acquisition and disposition became haphazard, and as conditions changed, chaos further increased. Overall, there was a shortage of money to keep the promises that were made in 1964.

Community complaints regarding urban renewal included inadequate relocation assistance, rampant real estate speculation, lagging city services, and the overconcentration of low-income residents in the outer parts of the South End. Blacks and Hispanics found their housing options severely constrained by the refusal of whites to let them into their neighborhoods and by the limited supply of affordable housing. Ultimately, the cumulative effect of urban renewal across the city was entrenched segregation.[31] For many Boston Blacks, the legacy of urban renewal is one of displacement and destruction. They saw "the South End as a social disaster: a predominantly poor Black neighborhood usurped by white middleclass home buyers."[32] By confining most of the assisted housing to new construction and leaving most of the renovation of row houses to the private market, the BRA helped create stark segregation within the South End.[33] Even inside the BRA, there would soon be concerns that the plan encouraged the "ghettoization" of Lower Roxbury and displaced far too many people.[34] One mid-1970s analysis concluded, "In a sense, the easiest way to characterize the plan is by the term containment."[9] Other reviews were more critical. Sociologist John Mollenkopf, for example, called the plan "highly regressive social engineering."[35] The scars persist. Decades later, Black community leaders invoke the experience of the South End when considering new development proposals.[36]

The BRA tried to implement an impossibly flawed plan with inadequate tools and an inexperienced, disjointed staff. The BRA's goal of bringing in higher-income residents also contributed to the crisis. Every new upper-income household meant at least one, if not more, lower-income household had to leave. As gentrification ran its course, almost every poor resident was pushed out of the private housing market. Furthermore, many of the new upper-income residents were not happy to be living near poor neighbors. Due to their political and social power, upper-income residents actively organized to force out lower-income residents and limit replacement housing. In hindsight, it is difficult to see how the conflicts accompanying urban renewal could have been avoided, as the central aims of urban renewal itself are now disputed. Was the goal to bring in new, higher-income residents as Logue, Collins, and the downtown establishment wanted? Or should its aim have been to improve the lives of existing residents, which TDC, CAUSE, IBA, and other groups called for?

As the busing crisis descended on Boston and HUD phased out funding for renewal, development in the South End stalled. But the neighborhood continued to change as many projects were finally completed and demographic forces reshaped the community. As the 1980s approached, residents were confronted by the need to complete the agenda laid out in the 1960s without a secure funding source. It would take a great amount of work to heal the scars created by renewal, but residents were up for the challenge.

1. Maxwell AH. The anthropology of poverty in black communities: A critique and systems alternative. Urban Anthropology and Studies of Cultural Systems and *World Economic Development* 1988; 19:171-91.

2. Kirchheimer A. Haves, have-nots fight over S. End. *Boston Globe*, 1974 April 30.

3. Sherman M. South End glows as suburbanites move in. *Boston Globe*, 1971 October 17.

4. Ad Hoc Committee for a South End for South Enders. *Special South End News*, 1974.

5. Lukas A. *Common Ground: A Turbulent Decade in the Lives of Three American Families*. New York: Vintage Books; 1986.

6. Ad Hoc South End Committee. *A Statistical Analysis: Occupancy and Displacement History in Buildings of the South End Now Owned by Developer Mark R. Goldweitz*. 1974.

7. SEPAC. *Report on Urban Renewal*. 1974.

8. Pellini S, McMahon J. *South End Retail Store Listing*. 1963.

9. Rappaport AH. *From Skid Row to Brownstown Chic*. Harvard University; 1975.

10. LeGates RT, Hartman C. Gentrification-caused displacement. *The Urban Lawyer* 1982; 14:31-55.

11. Shannon HJ. *Legendary Locals of Boston's South End*. Charleston, South Carolina: Arcadia Publishing; 2014.

12. Downs A, Bolon L. *Urban Renewal Land Disposition Study*. Real Estate Research Corporation. Washington; 1974.

13. Yudis A. 3 Churches Develop Housing. *Boston Globe*, 1966 December 17.

14. Pikielek F. *Boston's South End Past and Present*. Research Department BRA. 1974.

15. Yudis A. Asks B.R.A. Permission to Overcome Blight. *Boston Globe*, 1966 April 23.

16. Yudis A. Bill Russell, 6 Businessmen Consider South End Project. *Boston Globe*; 1966 April 19.

17. SEPAC. Roxse: "The place to live better?". *SEPAC Newsletter*. 1972 December.

18. Howe A. *Letter* to Warner J. 1970.

19. Boston Redevelopment Authority. *Subsidized Housing in the South End*. 1978.

20. Boston Redevelopment Authority. *South End Environmental Assessment*. 1979.

21. Auger DA. The politics of revitalization in a gentrifying neighborhood: The case of Boston's South End. *Journal of the American Planning Association* 1979; 45:515-22.

22. Osgood V. Halfway house plan stirs quiet South End street. *Boston Globe*; 1977 September 25.

23. Card RO. *The Beginning. South End Historical Society.* 1967.

24. South End Historical Society. *Untitled flyer.* 1978.

25. *About us.* 2014. (Accessed October 9, 2014, at http://www.sechc.org/en/?page_id=2.)

26. King B. South End Community Health Center saying goodbye to two pillars. *South End News*; 2009 June 3.

27. Goodman R. *After the Planners.* New York: Simon and Schuster; 1972.

28. Boston Redevelopment Authority *Housing in the South End: A Report on the Current Status of Urban Renewal.* 1974.

29. Rose TF. *Civic War: People, Politics, and the Battle of New Boston, 1945-1967.* Berkeley, California: University of California, Berkeley; 2006.

30. Real Estate Research Corporation. U*rban Renewal Land Disposition Study* - Boston, MA. 1974.

31. Chancy J, Franklin B. Report from Boston: The struggle for desegregation. *The Black Scholar* 1975; 7:19-27.

32. Stocker C. Highland Park: A Dream Come True Neighborhood Residents Want To Keep: The Mix Of Black, White, Rich, Poor. *Boston Globe*; 1980 December 7.

33. Smith MS. *Between City and Suburb: Architecture and Planning in Boston's South End* Providence, Rhode Island: Brown University; 1977. 34. Stainton J. Memorandum re South End Plan to Crane D. 1968.

35. Mollenkopf JH. *The Contested City.* Princeton, New Jersey: Princeton University Press; 1983.

36. Medoff P, Sklar H. Streets of Hope. Boston MA: *South End Press;* 1994.

CHAPTER 10

Consolidation: 1974-1983

After the closeout of the federally financed renewal program in 1974—it continues without HUD funds, and fifty years later the South End urban renewal project was still somewhat active— the BRA struggled to complete its infrastructure and housing projects. Many parcels had been cleared, but the city had no ability or inclination to develop them. Despite the ongoing delays, however, the neighborhood continued to change, and the full effects of renewal finally became visible.

Boston's dramatic economic gains continued during the late 1970s even as recession and inflation exacerbated urban problems across the country. Boston shed its reputation as one of the country's most troubled cities; by the 1970s, it had become one of its most prosperous, attracting eager investors despite its strict and capricious development process.[1] By the end of the Kevin White era in 1983, the mayor was able to pick and choose developers, and because virtually every project needed zoning relief or tax agreements, the mayor's power became extreme.[2]

As a result of the rebirth of the city's economy, Boston-based companies began to play a major national and international role in finance and consulting. The rapid rise of federally funded medical research programs, new technologies, and investments in education also boosted area colleges and universities. Between 1960 and 1985, more than 20 million square feet of office space were constructed in the city, doubling the supply. Employment in the finance, insurance, and real estate industries also doubled; other service employment tripled.[1]

Unfortunately, the new prosperity did not help the city's budget. In 1980, a statewide property tax limitation initiative along with Reagan-era budget cuts resulted in a financial crisis, and the city had to lay off almost 20 percent of its workforce.[3] Between the mid-1970s busing crisis and the early 1980s budget crunch, it appeared that Boston might once again descend into poverty. Most of the related violence, arson, and other lawlessness bypassed the South End, however, as it transitioned into one of the city's most desirable neighborhoods.

Unfortunately, the area still faced other battles. The planned construction of highways along the northern and western periphery of the neighborhood proved to be a threat almost as destructive as renewal. The state had already cut off the South End from Fort Point Channel with the Southeast Expressway and from most of downtown and a portion of Back Bay with the Massachusetts Turnpike Extension. Now other proposed major roads would create similar barriers on the remaining edges of the neighborhood. Formal planning for a new highway into Boston from the southwest began in 1948. Though the project was not officially initiated until 1964, property acquisition had been underway for decades.[4] It was a massive project, projected to cost $160 million, 90 percent of which was to come from federal funds.[5]

At Ruggles Street, just to the west of the neighborhood, the highway would have split into north and south segments with the northern part connecting to Interstate 93 after cutting through Cambridge and Somerville. The southern branch would have traveled along the western edge of the South End, connecting to the Southeast Expressway at the present-day location of the Massachusetts Avenue off-ramp. The southern branch also would have walled off the South End from Roxbury. By the 1960s, land takings for this highway had claimed large areas along the South End's western border.[6] Since neither branch would have connected incoming traffic with the Back Bay, the South End Bypass was proposed along the northern edge of the neighborhood between Columbus Avenue and St. Botolph Street. Whether constructed as a trench or elevated structure, it would have devastated the area north of Columbus Avenue because the bypass would have needed a 150-foot-wide corridor of land to accommodate forty thousand cars per day.[7] These plans were the result of a national philosophy that prioritized cars over pedestrians, public transit, or any other obstacle, including neighborhoods. As a result of this autocentric ideology, urban expressways tore apart cities across the country.[8]

The roads seemed inevitable. Highway engineers enjoyed extensive federal funding and the backing of a powerful coalition of construction companies and car manufacturers. Few places had been able to stop freeways, but opposition in the Boston area grew as plans became public and the scale of displacement began to impact neighborhoods from Jamaica Plain to Cambridge and Somerville. Desperate to save their homes, residents rallied against land takings and right-of-way clearings, ultimately finding logistical problems with the project. The Inner Belt could not be built without the Bypass, because cars could not otherwise access the Back Bay. But that stretch was not eligible for the federal 90 percent matching funds because technically it was a local road. Lacking funds to pay for it, state planners assumed the city would pay for its construction.

In the South End, opposition to the Inner Belt and Bypass was led by a group of residents who initially called themselves the Tubman Area Planning Council. Its executive committee included Barry Adams, William Glennon, Ann Hershfang, Ken Kruckmeyer, and David Scott. The group organized neighbors, sponsored community meetings, and created alternatives to the state plan. At first, the city administration was hesitant to oppose the project. At a 1969 community meeting attended by one hundred residents, for example, then-Mayoral Aide Barney Frank said the mayor opposed the project in general but needed more information before reaching a final position.[9] Mayor White finally came out against the project in December.[10] Along with State Representative Michael Dukakis, who filed legislation against the project, Mayor White asked the governor to halt the entire project including the Inner Belt and the Bypass.[11]

10.1 SITE OF PROPOSSED BOSTON BYPASS, C1970

Mayor White made it clear that the city would not build or fund the project. Therefore, the state would either have to fund the road itself or face the prospect of a major highway ending on city streets that could not possibly accommodate the traffic. Without the Bypass, the Inner Belt was technically impossible because its six lanes would merge to three and then dump their traffic on Tremont Street and Huntington Avenue, creating gridlocks that would back up onto the highway.[12]

In 1970, Governor Francis Sargent bowed to growing opposition and declared a moratorium on new highway construction within Route 128 pending a re-evaluation of current plans. While the state reassessed, highway proponents put pressure on the governor, saying that the federal highway money might not be available at a later date and that delaying the project would only add to its cost.[13] At the same time, anti-highway activists were concerned because parcels taken or earmarked for condemnation continued to deteriorate. They noted that "the right of way is littered with junk, boarded-up buildings and abandoned autos."[14] These activists continued to mobilize efforts to stop the highway.

Governor Sargent canceled the entire project on November 30, 1972, calling instead for $2 billion in transit and road improvements.[15] Though he killed the project for political reasons, the governor used the work of South End residents as justification for his decision. Without their strategic attack on the plan, the project might have continued. Many of Governor Sargent's proposed alternatives—including a trolley line from Dudley to Mattapan, a circumferential link from Boston City Hospital to Cambridge, and an extension of the Orange Line to Canton and Needham—never came to be. But other projects, such as the relocation of the Orange Line to the Southwest Corridor and the construction of a third harbor tunnel, would dominate transportation infrastructure improvements over the next several decades.[16]

The work of the Tubman Area Planning Council was far from complete as state and city transportation planners continued to press for more roads in and around the neighborhood. The planners saw the South End as an obstacle. Engineers wanted higher speeds on Columbus Avenue and Tremont Street, for example, as a way of helping commuters get through the neighborhood, even though the residents wanted pedestrian improvements. As it opposed car-centric proposals, the Tubman Area Planning Council committee eventually came under the umbrella of SEPAC, creating the South End Committee on Transportation (SECOT).

SECOT fought the various problematic proposals. In keeping with what was becoming the standard South End way of confronting outside plans, residents collected data, analyzed problems, and developed alternatives that better addressed community needs. They entered into extensive negotiations with city and state transportation planners, eventually reaching an agreement with the city in 1974. SECOT's plan called for keeping traffic on the peripheral arterial roads, addressing the needs of commuters while restricting isolating interior roads. The plan also emphasized safer pedestrian circulation and called for better public transit inside the neighborhood. SECOT's proposals included narrowing Columbus Avenue and Tremont Street by creating wide sidewalks and pedestrian amenities, rerouting one-way streets, cancelling plans to widen Berkeley and Dartmouth Streets, building frontage roads along the Expressway, planting trees along streets, and constructing a dedicated transit lane along Washington Street to replace the Elevated when it was demolished.[17] To varying degrees, most of this vision has been implemented over the years.

The principles behind these plans were part of a transportation alternative that is now called "complete streets." They aim to give pedestrians, bicyclists, and public transit vehicles equal priority to cars, humanize the landscape, and enable motorists and pedestrians alike to have access to the goods and services they need. In the 1970s, these ideas were revolutionary. Today, they are the gold standard for how to create walkable, high-functioning urban neighborhoods.

10.2 TREMONT STREET, 2014

Implementing these innovative proposals was not easy. Just reconstructing Tremont Street and Columbus Avenue involved satisfying a number of diverse actors. The Federal Highway Administration required that the design meet American Association of State Highway Officials standards; the city and the neighborhood wanted brick sidewalks; residents demanded relief from traffic; and the state insisted the project remain within budget. Design development dragged on through the 1980s; construction on Phase I didn't begin until 1984.

Eventually, residents came to believe that these redesigns didn't go far enough and in 2020, a new planning process was initiated to further slow traffic on Columbus and Tremont. Tremont Street was again narrowed with new protected bike lanes and pedestrian islands created. The design process for Columbus Avenue was ongoing in 2024.

Some of the South Enders involved in these transportation disputes went on to careers in public service. Herbert and Ann Hershfang, for example, had purchased their house on West Rutland Square sight unseen at an auction in 1965. Herbert was a lawyer who worked with the NAACP and was the campaign manager for Thomas Atkins' two city council campaigns. He drafted the state's racial imbalance law, which would become the legal basis for desegregating Boston schools in the 1970s. He later became a judge.[18] Ann Hershfang, a graduate of Radcliffe, was appointed to the board of the Massachusetts Port Authority by Governor Sargent in 1974. She was the first woman to serve on its board.[19] Later, Hershfang helped launch WalkBoston, one of the premier pedestrian advocacy groups in the country, and she was instrumental in the maintenance of the Southwest Corridor Park, picking up trash and working with other volunteers and public officials to keep the park clean. Despite her lifetime of community work, she was modest. "Don't make me sound like a goody goody or a drip," she once told a reporter.[20] Ken Kruckemeyer, another longtime neighborhood transportation advocate, eventually taught at the Massachusetts Institute of Technology (MIT) and served as coordinator for the Southwest Corridor Project during its long approval and implementation process.

Advocates for the South End were instrumental in protecting the neighborhood and bringing its problems into the public eye. The neighborhood produced staunch champions with no better example than Mel King. He was born in 1928 and raised in the NYS neighborhood, where his childhood experiences shaped his uncanny ability to create diverse and effective coalitions. King attended the Church of All Nations, and his political speeches reflected the cadence and rhythm of the liberal Protestant evangelical activism he heard there. King's political work was an outgrowth of his experiences as a youth worker for South End House, and his relationships with the people displaced by renewal shaped his outlook and commitment to social justice. His strong belief in education—taking root at Claflin University and Boston Teacher's College—resulted in his founding of the Community Scholars Program at MIT in 1971, where he taught until 1996.[18] King's contributions to the neighborhood were not just political; they were intellectual. King and his wife, Joyce, hosted a Sunday brunch at their home for decades; it was famous as a salon of ideas and a venue for deep discussion. "People come to nourish their bodies as well as their souls, feasting on the free-flowing ideas that permeate the room between bites of fruit cocktail, swordfish ceviche, and curry rice. Nothing is off limits: Adoption. Foster care. Bees and honey. Neoconservatism. The Nation of Islam. Media sensationalism."[26] He was loved and respected by nearly everyone in the neighborhood for decades, and when he died in 2023, there was an overflow crowd at his funeral.

King ran for office several times, winning his first election to the state legislature in 1973 when reforms created a South End district. King's first mayoral candidacy was in 1979. He based his platform on the idea that "we are all interrelated and interdependent; either everyone owns everything or nobody owns anything. This means we all have a responsibility to the physical and psychological resources and profits in our society."[27] Though he was unsuccessful, he raised important issues regarding the revitalization of Boston.[28] His stance was that the city had to accommodate everyone's needs, which led to a call to decentralize government and send decision-making power down to the neighborhoods. This approach was the opposite of centralized bureaucracy, which was the preferred style of downtown businesses and guiding philosophy of the BRA.[29] At the core of King's progressive values was a religious and moral fervor. When asked if he had a model for an ideal political world, King responded, "Sometimes I refer to the Book of Revelations, when they talk about the heavenly city where all the tribes are welcomed."[30]

King won eight precincts in the South End in the 1979 primary with 2,192 votes to White's 1,779. This was insufficient; King finished a distant third citywide, and in the final election. Mayor White led Joseph Timilty in every South End precinct to win his fourth term. King's loss was a disappointment, but it set the stage for another mayoral bid four years later.

In 1983, Mayor White surprised many by announcing he would not run for another term, and King again ran for mayor. Despite the open office, however, few expected that King would have any more success than he had in the last outing. Surprisingly, the primary produced Ray Flynn and King as the contenders for the final election, with King topping the ballot in every South End precinct. His total margin of victory over Flynn in the neighborhood was 3,567 to 586. Citywide, the two were very close: 47,549 for King to 48,118 for Flynn. In the final, King again won every neighborhood precinct with a total of 6,468 votes to Flynn's 2,218, even as Flynn beat King citywide 128,578 to 69,013. Thereafter, Mayor Flynn would win all South End precincts in every mayoral primary and final election until 1993, when he announced his resignation after President Bill Clinton appointed him Ambassador to the Vatican.

Though King lost, he transformed Boston politics. After this election, mayors used a liberal base to achieve citywide victories while the more conservative candidates would lose every final election. This shift led to the election of the next two mayors, Mayors Flynn and Thomas Menino. They consciously adopted progressive positions on issues like housing, education, and policing. Then their successors, Marty Walsh and Michelle Wu, both represented further steps to the left. Never again would a reactionary such as Louise Day Hicks push city policy making to the right. The national Democratic Party would also adopt King's coalition-building strategy. Jesse Jackson called it the Rainbow Coalition—just like King— and used it to describe his broad base of support. Later Presidents Bill Clinton and Barrack Obama incorporated this strategy into their platforms.

The neighborhood continued its demographic shifts as a new group— gay men—rose to prominence. The Irish in the 1880s and Blacks in the 1930s were the demographic face of the South End despite not being a majority. Similarly, gay men were now the very visible main demographic group in the community. Part of their new visibility was due to the sudden arrival of commercial establishments. A wave of gay bars had opened in the 1970s in the Back Bay, but it was not until the 1980s that gay and lesbian establishments began to move into the South End.

These bars included Club Café on Columbus Avenue, Fritz on Berkeley Street (first named Uncle Charlie's Rustler), and the Eagle on Tremont Street (originally the House of Quagmire). These bars were not the only gay- and lesbian-oriented businesses; by the 1980s, there were bookstores, shops selling a variety of specialized goods, and other establishments catering to gay and lesbian people throughout the South End.

The great flowering of gay life in the neighborhood was the result of new attitudes in society as a whole and among gay men themselves. This new generation celebrated their sexuality rather than suppress it, and they clustered in neighborhoods like the South End and lived as openly and freely as they wanted. Frank Ribaudo and Caleb Davis, for example, opened Café Calypso on Tremont Street in the early 1980s, and their restaurant became a center for gay men in the neighborhood. These entrepreneurial gay men found other successful market niches, driven in part by the homophobia of other establishments. The partners also opened up the Metropolitan Fitness Club on Columbus Avenue, for example, when a nearby gym began expelling gay men. As a result of this new openness, gay men seeking support and excitement flocked to the neighborhood. "It was like a big frat house," recalled one partner. "You had all these twenty-somethings acting like college kids. For the first time they were free and easy. It was a wild place."[31]

10.3 CLUB CAFE, 2015

This personal freedom was accompanied by strong advocacy for civil rights. Also at this time, a new political organization, the Boston Lesbian and Gay Political Alliance (BLGPA), was strongly rooted in the South End. Its chair was Eric Rofes, a Chester Square resident. Progressive politicians solicited support from the community through BLGPA, seeing it as a powerful group that offered campaign donations and votes. Despite his strong ties to the LGBT community, King did not win BLGPA's endorsement in the 1983 mayoral preliminary election, however. He lost to former city council president Larry DiCara, who had a substantial number of gay people in his campaign including press secretaries and major fundraisers.[32] In the 1983 mayoral final election, King easily beat Flynn for the BLGPA endorsement, winning 73 percent of the more than 150 votes cast.[33] After the election, Flynn worked to secure progressive support and he continued Mayor White's policy of having a liaison to the gay and lesbian community. At one point, the liaison was a South End resident, John Menuier.

Despite the neighborhood's new prosperity, old issues continued to vex residents. Crime and vice had been major factors in the South End since the 1870s, but assessing their magnitude has been difficult. Crime statistics are very unreliable, particularly on the neighborhood level, and the science of accurately using location to gauge crime hot spots only emerged in the 1990s. Even arrest numbers aren't reliable. Black and Latino youth, for example, are more likely to be arrested for a given incident than young white people, and a crime committed in the South End might result in an arrest whereas in Dorchester or South Boston the offender might be let off with a warning. Most interpretations of the South End's crime patterns are anecdotal.

The reality and perceptions of crime often influenced whether a given person or household stayed in the South End or moved out. Again, some of those perceptions might have been related to prejudice. Some new affluent white residents might see every young person of color as a potential criminal. Residents' stories, particularly in the early decades of the neighborhood's gentrification, describe a community that was rife with muggings, burglaries, and street crime. In one unverified account, a couple reported that there were eight muggings on their block in one week in 1976.[34] Residents found the crimes impossible to ignore and victims were traumatized.[35]

It wasn't only whites who complained about the crime; it was also a problem for Black South Enders, who also suffered from muggings and burglaries.[36] Prostitution and drug use were major issues, and though they may not have directly impacted the gentry, they often were associated with other crimes that did. There were also reports that the neighborhood was the city's center for heroin.[37] Whether this was true is irrelevant as most believed it to be the reality of life in the South End.[38] Another common complaint was that women walking to work would be accosted by men looking for sex.[39] The areas around the intersections of Massachusetts Avenue and Tremont Street, Columbus and Shawmut Avenues, and along Washington Street were major locations of prostitution, but women could be propositioned anywhere in the neighborhood.

South Enders fought back by pressuring the police for better enforcement and by organizing crime watches. Chris Hayes, a native South Ender, was named citywide head of neighborhood crime watches in recognition of his work on the issue in the South End.[18] Others found the crime overwhelming and ultimately moved out of the neighborhood.

There was a dramatic change in crime in the South End and Boston after the mid-1990s. Prior to that time, crime was a top issue for everyone with ubiquitous street muggings, home burglaries, and car break-ns. After the mid-1990s, however, crime became concentrated among youth of color and was often associated with young men who were both the perpetuators and victims of the violence. This allowed the middle-class South Enders to ignore the issue, even as Villa Victoria, Tent City, and other communities were rocked by tragedy.

Years after the BRA promised South End residents parks, new or rebuilt green spaces began to appear across the South End, many on the sites of

194   Boston's South End

former schools and social service institutions. What was once the Franklin School became Ringgold Park, Girl's Latin was torn down for the O'Day Playground, Warren Avenue Baptist was bulldozed for James Hayes Park, and the former Home for Little Wanderers was eliminated for Titus Sparrow Park. Rotch Playground, a frequent target for destruction by planners, was saved and renovated, as was Carter Field in Lower Roxbury. The neighborhood greatly benefited from these new open spaces.

10.4 HAYES PARK

Another positive South End tradition that continued in this era was its strong commitment to hosting social services. This included the Pine Street Inn (PSI), founded in the South Cove area in 1916, which moved to the former Boston Fire Department headquarters. Originally built for $84,000, the old building's primary feature was a 156-foot high tower modeled on the Palazzo Vecchio in Florence. The Department used the tower, ornamented with marble and copper, for ladder practice and as a lookout for fires.[41] PSI preserved this landmark when it renovated the building into a shelter and service center.

Not everyone welcomed the move. Some opposed PSI because the area was "a family neighborhood."[42, 43] One resident protesting at the zoning board hearing on the move declared, "Our neighborhood will be overrun by drunks and derelicts."[44] Some opponents became quite emotional. One letter writer to the Boston Globe declared that the Inn would result in glass shards covering the area, rendering Rotch Playground unusable, and that the homeless would cause an epidemic of tuberculosis in the community.[45] Another resident laid down a theme that would be repeated for the next thirty-five years: while the neighborhood used to have problems, it was improving, and it was imperative to keep it from falling back into chaos by opposing the establishment or growth of any additional social service organizations.[46]

Other residents supported the move with the nearby Eight Streets Neighborhood Association voted in favor of it. One letter writer chastised opponents saying that the neighborhood should not turn its back on people in need.[47] As with low-income housing, the issue polarized the neighborhood. Those against the move said the South End had more than its fair share of social services, and those in favor noted that these institutions were morally imperative and helped to address problems in the neighborhood, not exacerbate them.[48]

PSI benefited from strong leadership with Paul Sullivan guiding it into the modern era. He was a reformed alcoholic known for his compassion and dedication. "He was always there for anyone who needed him, whether they needed a ride or sandwich or a cigarette or a cup of coffee or someone to listen to them or getting out of the cold at night or getting to a detox center." Sullivan was born in Boston in 1935 and attended Northeastern University and Boston State College. A veteran, he had also worked as a truck driver and a construction worker until a stint as a social worker led him to PSI. When Sullivan died of a heart attack in 1983, Bristol Street was renamed Paul Sullivan Way to honor him.[49]

After eight years of planning and construction, the new PSI renovation was completed at the cost of $3 million and included beds for three hundred men and fifty women.[50] The shelter took in everyone, no questions asked. "Tramps and scamps barred from other refuges were admitted, fed, bathed and bedded down. They did not have to be sober to get in. They were not preached at, analyzed, interviewed or categorized."[51]

Its diverse population was indicative of the pervasiveness of homelessness in a city where housing costs are unaffordable to many. A 2001 survey of PSI residents found that 29 percent were employed, some earning almost ten dollars per hour. In Boston's expensive real estate market, however, this was not sufficient to secure housing, and it sometimes took eighteen months or more to find housing for those eligible for assistance.[52] By 2003, PSI was serving more than 2,100 people at twenty-seven locations across the city.[53]

Another great South End institution that dates back to this time is Rosie's Place, which opened on Columbus Avenue in 1974 as the city's first shelter for homeless women. In the forty years since, it has grown into a network of shelters, programs, and housing in the South End and other parts of Boston. It was founded by Kip Tiernan, who was born in Connecticut in 1927 and moved to Boston in the 1940s. Her work with the homeless through her volunteer work at St. Philip's inspired her to found Rosie's Place.[18] Similarly, Casa Myrna Vazquez, a shelter for Latinas, was established in the South End in 1977. Named after a Puerto Rican actress renowned for her charity, it remains the largest organization helping the Spanish-speaking population in the state.

Despite the turmoil caused by renewal and the BRA's relentless campaign against small businesses, a few well-loved businesses survived past 1970. One was Harry the Greek's, owned by the Kamenides family. It opened in 1950 at the corner of Dover and Washington Streets and was managed by Milton Kamenides, known to everyone as Munchie. It closed in 2001. Nearby was the neighborhood's oldest bar, JJ Foley's. Opened in 1909 and run today by the family of its founder, it survived renewal and gentrification with a loyal clientele—everyone from Herald reporters to neighborhood residents can be found there. Another long-lasting business was Olympia Flowers. It was originally in Dudley Square and then moved to a building next door to its present location at the corner of Massachusetts Avenue and Washington Street. It has been in operation for more than 110 years and is still owned by the Bornstein family, descendants of Louis and Mamie who came to the United States from Russia. On Massachusetts Avenue, Walcott's daughter, Elynor, runs Walley's with her sons, Paul, Frank, and Lloyd Poindexter.[18]

Newer businesses that have served the needs of the community were founded in this era, as well. Skip Rosenthal and Alison Barnet, for example, started the South End News in 1980, producing the paper out of Barnet's apartment on East Springfield Street. Jim Hoover bought the paper in 1985 and sold it to Sue O'Connell and Jeff Coakley in 2002. The paper became famous for its contributors, including John Sacco, who was known for his witty crime descriptions. Barnet returned to the paper as a columnist, chronicling past and current residents and their special talents and eccentricities. A book of her columns was published in 2013.

The battles over renewal and busing made the public angry at the city's political structure. Many remained dissatisfied with how the Boston City Council was elected, and in the early 1980s there was an effort to reform its composition. This led to a system of four at-large councilors and nine district-elected representatives aimed to balance neighborhood and citywide interests. The new system set off a struggle over how to draw the districts.

Boston's growing Black, Latino, and Asian communities felt that their numbers justified at least three districts where minorities had a substantial chance of being elected. But the city's high level of segregation made it easy for the all-white city council to minimize the number of minority-dominated districts.[54] Advocates for greater minority representation, including many South End residents, faced an uphill battle to create an alternative map.

This effort was led by the Black Political Task Force, which used analyses by James Jennings, an academic and well-known Latino community activist, to demonstrate the feasibility of creating better representation for minorities. The South End played a key geographic position in the debate between a multicultural coalition of progressives and conservative politicians. For a variety of reasons—such as age, immigrant status, and income—its population was less likely to vote, reducing its potential political influence. The South End's strategic position next to right leaning South Boston was perfect for conservative politicians. On its own, South Boston didn't have a large enough population for an entire district. So conservatives on the council used the South End to pad a South Boston-centered district's numbers knowing that the South End didn't have enough voters to challenge the conservative candidates this would produce. Despite the best efforts of South End advocates, the neighborhood was split into multiple districts with most of the neighborhood grouped with South Boston,[55] and the two would be linked together going forward.

South End and minority advocates tried to break the link between the two neighborhoods each time there was redistricting, but boundaries have been only modestly modified to adjust for population changes. There was a flare up of controversy for the post-2000 redistricting, when South Boston councilor William Linehan tried to shed several precincts where he had been outvoted by Chinatown-based rival Suzanne Lee in the previous election.[56] A public outcry defeated that map, but the South End continues to lack district representation. The 2022 redistricting was equally disappointing for the South End. With some neighborhood precincts incorporated into a Dorchester-based district, again conservative leaning, which stretches nearly five miles to the southern border of the city.

The South End seemed to pause and collect its breath as projects initiated in the 1960s finally opened, easing some of the pressures on neighborhood residents. But Boston was changing, becoming upscale, even though many people in the city failed to benefit from the new economy. These outside forces would cause new battles in the neighborhood in the next decade.

1. Bluestone B, Stevenson MH. *The Boston renaissance: Race, Space, and economic change in an American metropolis.* New York: The Russell Sage Foundation; 2000.

2. Kennedy L. *Planning the City upon a Hill: Boston since 1630.* Boston: University of Massachusetts Press; 1994.

3. Drier P, Ehrlich B. Downtown development and urban reform: The politics of Boston's linkage policy. *Urban Affairs Quarterly* 1991; 26:354-75.

4. Bicks M. Evolution of the Southwest Corridor project. *Environmental Impact Assessment Review* 1981; 2:388-97.

5. System Design Concepts Inc. *Memorandum Southwest Corridor Issue Paper.* 1971.

6. System Design Concepts Inc. *Study Design for a Balanced Transportation Development Program for the Boston Metropolitan Region.* 1970.

7. Tubman Area Planning Council. *Fact Sheet.* 1969.

8. Kay JH. Asphalt nation: *How the automobile took over America, and how we can take it back.* Berkeley CA: University of California Press; 1998.

9. Lupo A. 100 in So. End Resist Bypass. *Boston Globe;* 1969 July 27.

10. Ellis D. White asks Sargent: Halt Hub road jobs. *Boston Globe;* 1969 December 18.

11. Nyhan D, Plotkin AS. Sargent Expected to Reject Moratorium on Highways. *Boston Globe;* 1970 February 11;Sect. 1.

12. Altshuler A. *Memorandum to Joint Committee on Transportation Re The Southwest Expressway.* 1971.

13. Carr RB. Inner Belt 'must be built eventually". *Boston Globe;* 1971 July 13.

14. Nyhan D. Nearly everyone seems dead set against Southwest corridor moratorium. *Boston Globe;* 1971 May 31.

15. Campbell K, Fuerberger J. Governor's $2 billion transportation program meets delight, anger, formidable opposition. *Boston Globe;* 1972 December 1.

16. Thomas J. Transportation plan is proposed by Sargent. *Boston Globe;* 1972 December 1.

17. McMillan G. $5 million plan revealed to redirect commuter cars around South End. *Boston Globe;* 1974 September 19.

18. Shannon HJ. *Legendary Locals of Boston's South End.* Charleston, South Carolina: Arcadia Publishing; 2014.

19. Pillsbury F. A Massport activist looks back. *Boston Globe;* 1981 June 30.

20. Lupo A. Crosstown Express Leaked memo department. *Boston Globe;* 1993 November 14.

21. Land Taking. Land Taking for South Bay Incinerator OKd. *Boston Globe;* 1955 October 4.

22. Incinerator. Farewell, old incinerator. *Boston Globe;* 1975 September 1.

23. Kindleberger RS. The Environment. *Boston Globe;* 1972 July 23.

24. Mayor's Office of Energy Conservation. *The Incinerator at South Bay, Its History and Future.*

1978.

25. Johnson A. Mel King arrested at eviction demonstration. *Boston Globe;* 2013 October 4.

26. Johnson A. After decades of activism, Mel King looks only ahead: At

84, former mayoral contender focuses on community. *Boston Globe;* 2013 July 8.

27. King MH. *A Professional and Personal Agenda.* Department of Urban Studies and Planning, MIT. 1976.

28. King M. *Press Release* - January 15. 1979.

29. Vlasic J. King: I'm the alternative. *Boston Ledger;* 1979 May 25.

30. Editor. Editorial. *The New Common Good* 1983 November.

31. The Beat Goes On. *The Boston Spirit,* 2013. (Accessed February 5, 2014, at http://boston-spiritmagazine.com/2013/09/the-beat-goes-on/.)

32. Robinson WV. Dicara Aide Quits Key Campaign Post. *Boston Globe;* 1983 August 20.

33. BLGPA. Alliance News – *News from the Boston Lesbian and Gay Political Alliance.* 1983.

34. Lockman N. They find happiness, headaches in S. End. *Boston Globe;* 1976 Mach 21.

35. Coleman S. Crime watch fosters trust. *Boston Globe;* 1993 March 28.

36. Wallace C. Control over own life isn't easy in So. End. *Boston Globe;* 1971 July 30.

37. Osgood V. South End: Moving along the road back. *Boston Globe;* 1971 August 25.

38. Jones A. Reputations as heroin centers painful to South End, Roxbury. *Boston Globe;* 1971 August 3.

39. Osgood V. South End residents, police seek end to prostitution in the area. *Boston Globe;* 1971 September 1.

40. First D. Boston Restaurant Awards. *Boston Globe;* 2014 December 31.

41. New Home. A new home for homeless. *Boston Globe;* 1977 July 17.

42. Zaborowski D. Pine Street Inn 'enough'. *Boston Globe;* 1977 September 9.

43. Kirchheimer A. Pine St. task force chairman resigns. *Boston Globe;* 1975 June 19.

44. Rogers D. Debate over Pine Street Inn renewed. *Boston Globe;* 1976 May 5;Sect. 12.

45. Herbert J. No place to play. *Boston Globe;* 1975 March 30.

46. Hajjar J. Can the South End Community 'afford' new Pine Street Inn? *Boston Globe;* 1975 March 24.

47. Curran J. Can the community turn its back? *Boston Globe;* 1975 March 24.

48. Hutson R. White picks S. End for Pine Street Inn; foes promise battle. *Boston Globe;* 1975 June 9.

49. Obituary. Paul D. Sullivan, 48, director of Pine Street Inn. *Boston Globe;* 1983 July 21.

50. Rivas M. New pine street inn opens its refuge doors. *Boston Globe;* 1980 April 15.

51. Wilson D. Pine Street Inn's Dilemma. *Boston Globe* 1986; December 23.

52. Raschke D. For working poor, home too often is only a shelter pine street inn refuge for many. *Boston Globe*; 2001 June 7.

53. Abraham Y. Pine street inn lays off 41 workers rising costs, cuts in aid hit shelter. *Boston Globe;* 2003 March 8.

54. Radin CA. Boston district debate begins with sparring over South End. *Boston Globe*; 1981 December 9.

55. Jordan RA. Council ok's 9 districts. *Boston Globe*; 1982 February 25.

56. Irons ME. Linehan stands by his council redistricting plan. *Boston Globe*; 2011 November 29.

CHAPTER 11

Conflicts Old and New: 1984 to 1993

The first wave of gentrification saw the South End's elderly, poor, minority, and female-headed households pushed out of the neighborhood entirely. The South End's population continued to evolve as a second pulse of gentrification began to transform the neighborhood's demographics once again. The victims of the first wave had been replaced by a variety of new residents. While some newcomers were families, many more were single or childless service workers in the hotel, hospital, or retail industries that served the needs of the new Boston economy. Though higher than before, rents were within the financial reach for waiters, lab technicians, hairdressers, and others, who—while living with a roommate or two—could easily access jobs in Back Bay, downtown, the Longwood Medical Area, or the hospitals around the South End periphery. Besides a handful of single-family homes and a few instances of landlord-occupied, multi-unit row houses, most residents were middle-class renters.

But now a second round of gentrification swept over the neighborhood. This time, the change pushed out lower-middle-class and working-class renters, replacing them with middle- to upper-middle-class condominium owners and renters. Condominium development had already begun to change the market in Back Bay and Beacon Hill, but in 1980 there were fewer than fifty condos in the South End. Then conversions sped up. In 1985, there were 1,319 condominiums.[1] By 1990, there were 2,223.[2] Altogether, about a quarter of the neighborhood's market housing was converted from rental units to condominiums during the 1980s. The pace of conversions would slow during a downturn in the Boston area real estate market in the early 1990s but would accelerate again after 1992.

In certain respects, this renewed investment was valuable because some units needed another round of rehabilitation. Apartments that had been renovated in the 1960s were reaching the end of their useful lives, and changing tastes in interior design made some units look tired. What was once the height of home fashion—exposed brick, track lighting, and Formica countertops—was now dated. Developers now covered up walls with sheetrock, introduced recessed lighting, and installed Corian countertops.

These newly refurbished condos were beyond the reach of most waiters, store clerks, and service workers, but they were affordable for middle-class families, dual-income households without children, professionals, and sufficiently well-off singles. Many condos initially sold for between $70,000 and $120,000 and required an annual income of $30,000 to $50,000 at a time when the median household income in the United States was $28,000. What was once a community with a wide range of middle-class renters was now split between upper-middle-income owners (those with the resources to secure mortgages and afford the prices in the neighborhood) and low-income renters in assisted housing. This process was also disruptive as many renters found themselves chased around the neighborhood by conversion, repeatedly forced to move as their rentals were slated for conversion or rents became unaffordable. Many were forced out of the neighborhood altogether, joining the very poor that had been previously displaced.

This second wave of gentrification can be seen in the employment composition of Union Park, Greenwich Park, and Northampton Street, blocks without new construction or assisted housing developments. From 1970 to 1990, when this wave crested, the number of professionals, managers, and owners on the three blocks combined went from fifty-nine to 319, with substantial increases on each block. The number of laborers and service workers on Union and Greenwich Parks had already declined, and their numbers held steady over these two decades. But the decline now extended to Northampton Street, where the number fell from thirty-five to twenty-nine. There was an increase in sales and administrative workers over this period as well, from forty-eight to 121, across all three blocks.

This second wave also produced tremendous profits for developers who renovated units in ways that maximized their income. One change in the housing stock was the conversion of heating systems from building-wide gas-, oil-, or hot water-fired systems to separate unit systems that used electric baseboard heaters. These were cheaper to install, but they were much less energy efficient and increased the cost of homeownership. They also burdened the entire electrical delivery system of the neighborhood. The rate of change to condominiums using electric heating was so great that the local utility, Boston Edison, struggled to keep up with demand, resulting in thirty-three blackouts in the South End between 1983 and 1986.

For too many gay men, the good times of the 1970s morphed into tragedy in the 1980s. As of May 1983, the Center for Disease Control (CDC) had reported twenty-two cases of HIV/AIDS within Route 128, including six deaths, but those working with people with the disease feared that the actual number of infections was much higher. The onset of the AIDS epidemic in the South End came on as a slow-moving tsunami that the community and advocates could see approaching but could not prevent. The AIDS Action Committee (AAC), which would have a leading role in support services and advocacy in Boston and Massachusetts, had been organized in 1982 at the Fenway Community Health Center. By necessity, AAC involved South End residents. In July 1985, four out of twenty-one members of its steering committee were from the South End.[4] By the beginning of the next year, twelve of fifty-six AAC volunteers were South End residents.[5]

The statistics on HIV/AIDS, representing personal suffering and the grief of family and friends, would get much worse. Even though the data for the South End must be interpreted with caution—cases included Chinatown, downtown, and many homeless victims—no one can doubt the number's severity. From 1989 to 1991, for example, the AIDS age-adjusted death rate was 94.1 per 100,000 people in the South End compared to 31.5 for the city overall. It was the third leading cause of death in both the neighborhood and the city at the time.[6] By the time drug therapies became available (to some), about ten percent of Boston's gay male population would die of the disease.

The South End's 1990 gay population also had to confront the neighborhood's crime problem. Some of the crimes against them were motivated by anti-gay bigotry; police reported fifteen cases of anti-gay violence in the South End in the first six months of 1990 compared to two in all of 1989. The numbers of anti-gay attacks were thought to be underreported as many gays and lesbians feared going to the police. Others suggested the attacks were motivated by race rather than by sexual orientation.[7] Whatever the exact nature of the crimes, the community rallied against the violence with straight and gay residents speaking out together.[8] Despite the grave issues challenging the South End, it continued to be the center of the city's increasin gly visible LGBT community, however. Reflecting the movement of gay and lesbian people to the South End, the city's annual gay pride parade route was shifted so that it went through the heart of the neighborhood. Though its route varied from year to year, it had generally gone from Copley Square to Charles and Cambridge Streets on Beacon Hill. But in 1992, the parade route was changed to go down Clarendon Street to Tremont Street and then back down Berkeley Street.

By now, people were recognizing the special architectural heritage of the neighborhood, and there were increased efforts to protect it from incompatible development. Through the work of the South End Historical Society and others, the city established the South End Landmark District Commission in 1984. It took years to create, beginning with a study commission appointed in 1978 that drew on a large-scale project in which the historical society photographed every building in the neighborhood.[11] The South End was added to the National Registry of Historic Places in 1973, which meant that instead of having to document each building, all structures in the neighborhood were shielded from alterations that would detract from its special architecture. As provided in 1973 state legislation, exterior renovations must be approved by the Landmarks District Commission.[12] The protection district includes most of the neighborhood, generally stretching from Camden to Berkeley Streets and the Southwest Corridor to Harrison Avenue. Design guidelines and development restrictions have been mostly well received, though they add a layer of approvals and can mean additional costs for renovations. There have been occasional challenges over the years, but the designation has helped preserve the neighborhood's architectural unity.

Fifteen years after the 1968 CAUSE sit-in, widely known as the Tent City demonstration, no housing had been built on the site. But though it was still a parking lot, large-scale development was underway next door. Most of the area just to the north had been an expansive, below-grade interchange for the Massachusetts Turnpike Extension. Since its construction in 1964 just over the Back Bay side of the railroad tracks, the Turnpike was an open trench separating the Back Bay from the South End. There were a few bridges and the very poorly designed Prudential Center, but otherwise it was a linear scar from South Station to Brighton.

Back Bay, always more fashionable than the South End, was changing too, becoming even more upscale and attracting high-end, international retailers and office tenants. Developer interest resulted in Copley Place, a complex with department stores, movie theaters, two hotels, a parking garage, residences, and office buildings. Though the design is fortresslike, reflecting 1970s ideas regarding crime and safety, the development helped knit the South End and Back Bay together and fueled more gentrification south of Columbus Avenue.

The Copley Place developers wanted the Tent City site for parking, raising the possibility of a new round of protests. But Mayor Flynn, deeply aware of the emotional history of the location, continued to target the site for housing to prove his commitment to prioritizing residents over developers. The building of affordable housing was a priority in his campaign, and the

Tent City site was across the street from Mel King's house, increasing its visibility and adding another incentive for creating housing there. By now, the city could turn to a large number of successful models of affordable, community-based, housing development. Creating publicly assisted housing had grown into a sophisticated industry since the late 1960s when most South End groups had failed in similar endeavors. Now there was a cadre of experienced developers, architects, contractors, and property managers, and the city relied on them to make the new project work. Residents had never stopped pushing for housing. First under the leadership of SEPAC and then the Tent City Corporation (TCC), they never lost sight of their goal. So the city sought to build housing on the site with TCC as the developer.

There were controversies. One was centered on who should be hired for its construction jobs. Most projects that received public support in the city used union labor, but the overwhelming majority of the building trades' membership was white, suburban men. The issue was how to leverage public funding to produce changes in the construction workforce, an industry that provided some of the highest paying jobs with the best benefits for those with limited education. Progressives argued for an ordinance mandating a percentage of jobs go to city residents, women, and minorities. Unions fought these requirements because they saw diversity as a threat to their livelihood.

Another dispute was over what the percentage of affordable units should be. Planning theory now maintained that having all units in a development devoted to low-income families led to a concentration of poverty and an increased likelihood of development failure. Mixing incomes was thought to be better for the poor and increase projects' financial stability, but assisted housing required subsidies to make the numbers work. There were also concerns that higher-income people would not want to live in these developments, perhaps threatening the marketing of units. Not surprisingly, there was a range of opinions on the ideal mix of incomes for new housing. There were still those who held out that all housing in every development assisted by the city should be affordable and those who said the neighborhood had far too much affordable housing and all new housing should be market rate. But most South Enders, as well as City Hall, wanted something in between.

The Flynn administration grappled with these issues as it found itself in the difficult position of needing to placate King supporters while preserving its own union-heavy coalition. Mayor Flynn went for a middle stance. In November 1984, the BRA submitted a federal grant application for a $10 million subsidy for Tent City that promised that 50 percent of jobs would go to city residents, 30 percent to minorities, and 10 percent to women. This funding would enable the construction of 270 housing units—25 percent of which were for low-income households, 50 percent for moderate-income households, and 25 percent for market rate. There were also 698 parking spaces and up to 10,000 square feet of retail space on the site's 3.3 acres. Goody Clancy was the architect, Greater Boston Community Builders was the development consultants, and Copley Place was involved in the development and management of parking. The project cost $47.5 million—including $7 million for land acquisition, $12.1 million for parking, $3.5 million in construction financing, and $7.1 million in professional fees.[14] Opponents on both sides of the issues complained, but the project went forward. The prominent gateway to the South End continues to thrive to this day.

Financing housing for low- and moderate-income families continued to be a problem. The federal government was curtailing its funding programs even as the lack of affordable housing was becoming a citywide concern. Those trying to develop more affordable units had to use as many different funding and financing programs as possible to meet development and operating costs. After 1980, the federal government moved to rely on two mechanisms to support low-income housing using its Section 8 program. The first was a direct subsidy to low-income households, who used a certificate to pay a portion of their rent to any property owner who would accept them. The other mechanism was to attach a Section 8 subsidy to a specific unit, owners had to rent it to a Section 8 eligible tenant. Both these programs provided stable, long-term subsidies, but Congress determined the number of certificates, and as years went by, the program became restricted by budgetary constraints and the competition for certificates was fierce.

The city had another way to fund housing: linkage, a method that relied on private development. In a strong real estate market like Boston, market-rate developers of housing and commercial buildings were willing to pay fees to the city in return for permits. The city started a program to create a pool of money for assisted development out of these fees. This was basically a tax on new development over a certain size; developers paid into a special fund administered by the city to subsidize affordable housing elsewhere or build affordable units on site, in essence linking the two types of development. Governments seized upon these programs as a way to enable lower-income residents to benefit from downtown development.

The city now had funds to restart development and a mechanism in place for preserving the South End's unique architecture. Along with a robust housing market, the environment was amenable for turning attention back to the shortcomings of renewal. The abrupt collapse of the South End renewal project in 1974 had left many vacant parcels, some quite large and in very prominent locations. Ten years later, nineteen major parcels and fifty smaller ones remained undeveloped, preserved as open space, or otherwise disposed of as the BRA, now under Mayor Flynn appointee Stephen Coyle, sought to restart development.

In June 1986, the Flynn administration announced the founding of the South End Neighborhood Housing Initiative (SENHI). Its goals were building housing development, enhancing commercial development, and preserving open spaces while promoting non-profit and minority developers.[18] With memories of renewal still fresh in their minds, many people in the neighborhood were skeptical of the city's promise to build assisted housing. In the extensive public review of the proposal, comments focused on whether its affordability guidelines were to be maximums or minimums for the number of units as well as the degree of affordability. Weighing these arguments, Mayor Flynn announced a standard of one-third low-income housing, one-third moderate-income housing, and a one-third market rate mix of units for SENHI projects in January 1987.[19]

After an extensive proposal process, SENHI created a number of the neighborhood's most distinctive post-nineteenth century developments. Their architecture reflects the depth of commitment of public funds, the substantial amounts of time devoted by neighborhood activists to review projects, and the growing sophistication of those involved in the development, design, and management of assisted housing. Many have won awards, and all have been financially successful.

Representative of this wave of new development was Langham Court, built on the site of the old Langham Hotel behind a large conventional elderly building owned by the BHA that dates back to the 1970s. The city selected the Four Corners Development Corporation for the project in October 1987. Four Corners then spent several years designing and constructing the complex of buildings that occupies most of its block. With its height, windows, and brick facades, Langham Court looks new, but complementary to the surrounding nineteenth century urban fabric. The complex has eighty-four units around a central courtyard with fifty-four underground parking spaces. One-third of its units are low income, one third moderate, and one third market rate. This ratio was made possible by linkage payments from the developers of 500 Boylston Street and Massachusetts Housing Finance Agency and State Housing Assistance for Rental Production (SHARP) funding. Its low-income units also received Section 8 contracts. Many Four Corners board members, such as Jeannette Boone, Pat Cusick, Myra McAdoo,

Victor Bynoe, and Thomas Plant, were longtime South End residents and advocates.[21] Through Langham Court, Parmalee Court, and other SENHI projects, the neighborhood's stock of low-income housing increased, though the number of market-rate units grew faster, and condominium conversions topped every other form of development.

Not all components of SENHI came to fruition. Mayor Flynn's tendency to rely on top-down solutions caused him to fail in another South End proposal: the Tree of Life project. It aimed to address homelessness, one of the most pressing issues of the decade. Stagnant incomes and a lack of affordable options were creating a housing crisis, and homeless families were being put in motels or in other problematic situations with women who were fleeing unsafe living arrangements facing a particular crisis of availability and affordability. Along with the feminization of poverty and the realization that struggling, single mothers often headed the poorest families, there was a demonstrated need for assistance.

Mayor Flynn, listening to advocates for victims of intimate partner violence, convened a panel to address the housing needs of homeless women and their children. The result was the Tree of Life project, a proposal to provide transitional (six months to two years) housing to be located at the West Concord-Washington-Rutland Streets block. It would have provided apartments for seventy-five to one hundred women and their children at the cost of $8.5 to $10 million. A special non-profit organization would have been set up to develop and manage the project as well as provide support services to the families.[22]

The development had a $7 million funding gap, which the BRA proposed to close using linkage dollars and by selling other parcels in the South End.[22] This monopolization of funds helped turn many potential supporters against the proposal. Others were in favor of providing housing for this vulnerable population but thought the project should be scaled down or perhaps have its units scattered across all SENHI parcels rather than concentrated at one place. Though some in the South End opposed the project in its entirety, others said they supported the programmatic aims of the project but not its proposed design.[23] Faced with this near-unanimous opposition, the proposal died, and the site became a mixed-income development with space for the South End Community Health Center.

Though he failed to launch his Tree of Life project, Mayor Flynn was successful in creating other important services in the neighborhood. The award winning Boston Health Care for the Homeless Program, for example, had its origins in the South End. It began when Mayor Flynn and Governor Michael Dukakis convened a group of eighty advocates and service providers to address the health care needs of the homeless. The city's efforts to address the unique needs of the homeless received a major boost in 1986 when the Robert Wood Johnson Foundation and the Pew Charitable Trust gave grants to Boston City Hospital and the Lemuel Shattuck Hospital in Jamaica Plain to fund teams of health care workers who brought their services to the area's shelters.[24] By 2010, the program had expanded to serve more than 11,000 people each year at more than eighty shelters and soup kitchens. It included mental health and dental services as well.[25]

11.1 RUTLAND/WASHINGTON STREET GARDEN

Neither the 1850s plans nor the 1964 urban renewal program adequately addressed the need for parks in the neighborhood. The South End had one of the lowest ratios of open space per thousand residents in the city with only 1.46 acres per thousand compared to 5.45 for the Back Bay, 7.42 for South Boston, and 2.19 for Charlestown. In the 1980s, much of the open space was poorly maintained, remained unimproved, or was plagued by criminal activity. There was a special need for tot lots and programming for children particularly in the larger, multiuse open spaces. By this point, the locked traditional squares were seen as inaccessible and almost an afterthought in a neighborhood that lacked parks and playgrounds. The neighborhood's schoolyards were mainly used for parking and were often covered by glass and other hazards, rendering them unsafe for children.

Concerned that the Flynn administration's push for affordable housing would result in the build out of every available parcel, open-space advocates—led by Betsy Johnson, Eleanor Strong, and others—began to work on an alternative community-based plan for creating open spaces and community gardens that would prioritize outdoor opportunities without jeopardizing the plan to create more housing. For more than thirty years, Betsy Johnson was one of the driving forces behind the South End's network of community gardens and open spaces. An advocate for the environment, she was president of the Boston Greenspace Alliance and worked with the Boston Collaborative for Food and Fitness. Perhaps her greatest achievement would be her work to establish the South End/Lower Roxbury Open Space Land Trust, the organization that would guide the development of new gardens and play spaces in the community.[26] By this time, South End residents were adept at developing plans that satisfied both the neighborhood and outside agencies. In this case, the residents' plan called for creating thirteen acres of open space across the South End along with ten gardens and three passive open spaces to be saved from development.[27]

Recognizing the broad support for this initiative, on June 29, 1989, the BRA voted to tentatively designate eight gardens to the Trust for Public Land, including the Lenox-Kendall, Worcester Street, Warren/Clarendon, West Springfield, and Rutland/Washington gardens and parcels at Columbus/Wellington, Dartmouth/Montgomery, and Northampton Streets. They hired Boston Urban Gardeners to facilitate a planning process that included organizing community meetings, assisting local garden coalitions, establishing a long-term maintenance plan, and developing a consensus for the future of the gardens. This labor-intensive process significantly enhanced the South End.[28]

Over the next decade, the gardens of the South End were transformed into visual assets for everyone in the neighborhood, not just the gardeners. Many gardens had iron fences and gazebos with lush plantings of flowers and vegetables. The gardeners included people from all parts of the South End's varied demographic groups and brought together diverse populations. To strengthen its long-term stability, the Land Trust merged with the Boston Natural Areas Network in 2012.

To support the gardens and other work, the Trustees of Reservations hosts the South End Garden Tour each June. This fundraising event helps bring the public into many of the community's hidden spaces. Residents have opened their private yards and rooftops, and in various years the tour has included the South End Burial Ground and Montgomery Park, two areas rarely accessible to the public.

11.2 SOUTHWEST CORRIDOR PARK

Fifteen years after Governor Sargent terminated the plans for the South End Bypass and Inner Belt, the city returned to his proposed alternative to build a new mass transit corridor along the Amtrak right of way. The result was the relocation of the Orange Line from Washington Street to the Southwest Corridor on May 2, 1987. The removal of the elevated tracks transformed the South End. Rebuilding the 4.7-mile-long corridor for a commuter rail, Amtrak service, a new subway, and a park cost $742 million. The construction was funded by the federal government, which allowed the state to use its highway dollars for transit.[29] The route replaced the Dover and Northampton Stations with new Back Bay and Massachusetts Avenue stops. These stations were handicapped accessible, cleaner, and quieter than the Elevated, but they shifted the axis of mass transit northward. The demolition of the Elevated proceeded quickly, and the state was caught unprepared for its promised replacement service. It would take fifteen years for another transportation option to be built, which would prove very disappointing to transit activists.

A related issue was the fate of the corridor between the South End and the Back Bay, the seam between St. Botolph Street and Columbus Avenue. The reconstruction of the corridor was to include a linear park knitting the South End and Back Bay together for the first time. Resident participation was critical for its success and "community members were involved in all aspects of the new park and transit corridor design, from the vertical alignment of the tracks and bridges to the flooring tiles and lighting fixtures in the stations."[31]

The park became a major asset for the neighborhood with a butterfly garden, bike paths, large specimen trees, tennis courts, basketball hoops, gardens, and play spaces for children. The corridor is what is now called multimodal, serving pedestrians, bicyclists, people in cars, and mass transit riders, and connecting the South End to distant parts of Jamaica Plain. Over time, the maintenance of the park has been mixed, however, and volunteers complete much of the work on the park now.[32]

In 1985, Boston struggled with a proposal to split the city into two. Its minority areas, including most of the South End, would be incorporated into a new city called Mandela in honor of the South African antiapartheid advocate. This was not a grassroots initiative. In an interesting parallel to Mayor Flynn's unpopular habit of proposing progressive and well-meaning—but top down—solutions to important problems, the idea for an independent city of Mandela was conceived in Cambridge at the Harvard Faculty Club by four men, only one of whom actually lived within the boundaries of the proposed municipality. "It was an imported academic notion." [35] Though it consumed a lot of energy and activism, it rested on unproved assumptions and relied on community support that did not exist.

The movement's two leaders, Andrew Jones and Curtis Davis, were convinced the new city would be economically viable. Others were less sure, and the economic feasibility of the new city would be a key issue in the debate that followed. For the most part, there was a strong agreement on both sides that Boston had failed its minority residents. From poor schools, the lack of jobs, and political powerlessness to the still-fresh scars of urban renewal and busing, many in Boston's communities of color were angry with the city government. The independence drive capitalized on this frustration over the lack of Black and Latino economic, political, and social progress.[36] Mandela advocates believed incorporation was a way to ensure community control of development; enable people of color to manage police, fire, and other services; and allow parents to take over control of the schools (in Massachusetts, schools are administered by city and town governments). Advocates held that all alternatives had been tried and had failed. "We must seize it, govern it, and pass it gracefully to our children, and our children's children, for the sake of our plural society, our heritage, our freedom."[37] These were the best of motives. But could a new city be financially viable?

Supporters of Mandela called the 7,600 acres "the most valuable piece of land in the United States" as they convinced themselves that the new city would be able to generate sufficient tax dollars to fund its services. However, the financial stability of the independent city would most likely have been rocky, as the experience of other majority minority communities has demonstrated. Unfortunately, Mandela's supporters ignored the effects of prejudice and racism on real estate markets (even in 2014, Roxbury's real estate values were below what they would be if properties were in equivalent white neighborhoods).[38] The constraints on the independent city's finances would have been crippling.

Mandela proponents gathered sufficient signatures to place the idea on the ballot, setting off a brief but intense public debate on the position of the Black community in the city. The boundaries would have split the South End, taking the precincts in the central, western, and southern sections but leaving those along the northern and eastern boundary of the neighborhood.[37] This division reflected the fact that gentrification had thoroughly displaced low-income and minority residents in the closer portions of the neighborhood.

The public face against the proposal was Reverend Charles Stith of Union United Methodist Church. Proponents made much of his alliance with downtown business interests, but the opposition spent less than $20,000 on the special referendum. This was more than twice as much as the pro-Mandela group spent, but it was hardly a major political money operation (even in the mid-1980s). The proposal was strongly defeated at the polls, losing two to one in every precinct regardless of demographics, as Boston's minority citizens decided they wanted to stay in the city. Stith maintained that the proposal failed because of a lack of support from the community, but he also said that proponents ran a bad campaign that had little grass-roots organization. In addition, they were weak at explaining the finances and advantages of the new city. Proponents maintained that though they were defeated, they had successfully changed the political environment by raising issues, and they vowed to keep on fighting for a new city.[35] However, within five years, the secession movement was forgotten. Its only legacy is the Mandela Apartments on Washington Street. The former Westminster-Willard development was renamed by its controversial owner who was in a dispute with City Hall at the time.

The Flynn years saw continued changes in the South End. The emotions of the 1970s had abated, but they continued to shape conflicts in the neighborhood, often providing the background to positions that had long hardened. Demographic change also continued. The neighborhood was on its trajectory toward becoming one of the most upscale in the city with implications for new development as the century ended.

1. Boston Redevelopment Authority. *South End Neighborhood Profile* 1988. 1988.

2. Boston Redevelopment Authority. *South End Planning District - 1990 Population and Housing Tables.* 1992.

3. Boston Redevelopment Authority. *Using the Zoning Code to Solve the South End Density Problem.* 1986.

4. Aids Action Committee. *Steering Committee Meeting Minutes.* 1985.

5. AIDS Action Committee. *Steering Committee Meeting Minutes* 1986.

6. Boston Department of Health and Hospitals. *Boston's Neighborhood Health Status Report: The Health of the South End.* 1994.

7. Garcia M. More Police Promised For S. End. *Boston Globe;* 1990 July 18.

8. park that is the muscle and bone of the city. *Boston Globe;* 2012 May 5.

9. Green J. The Making of Mel King's Rainbow Coalition: Political Changes in Boston: 1963-1983. In: Jennings J, King M, eds. *From Access to Power: Black Politics in Boston.* Cambridge, Massachusetts: Schenkman Books; 1986.

10. Canellos PS. The legacy of Boston's Sandinistas. *Boston Globe;* 2010 November 2.

11. Editorial. The South End as City Landmark. *Boston Globe;* 1983 October 20.

12. Boston Landmarks Commission. *South End Landmarks District - Standards and Criteria.* 1985.

13. *South End Landmarks District.* 2014. (Accessed October 9, 2014, at http://www.cityofboston.gov/landmarks/historic/southend.asp.)

14. Boston Redevelopment Authority. *Tent City Urban Development Action Grant Proposal.* 1984.

15. Ludgen MK. *The Politics of Urban Redevelopment in Boston, Chicago, San Francisco, and Denver: The structure of the private/public partnership:* Northwestern University; 1988.

16. Drier P, Ehrlich B. Downtown development and urban reform: The politics of Boston's linkage policy. *Urban Affairs Quarterly* 1991; 26:354-75.

17. Tenants' Development Corporation. *Neighborhood Housing Trust Proposal.* 1987.

18. Boston Redevelopment Authority. *Proposed Reuse for SENHI Parcels.* 1986.

19. City of Boston. *SENHI.* 1987.

20. City of Boston. *Langham Court: Neighborhood Housing Trust Proposal.* 1987.

21. Langham Court. *Neighborhood Housing Trust Proposal. Boston;* 1987.

22. Boston Redevelopment Authority. *Tree of Life: Transitional Housing for Women and Children.* 1986.

23. Boston Redevelopment Authority. *Community Comments, SENHI.* 1987.

24. City Hall Bureau. Boston's $1.4m share of grants to fund health care at shelters. *Boston Globe;* 1984 December 20.

25. O'Connell JJ, Oppenheimer SC, Judge CM, et al. The Boston Health Care for the Homeless Program: A Public Health Framework. *American Journal of Public Health* 2010; 100:1400-8.

26. Shannon HJ. *Legendary Locals of Boston's South End.* Charleston, South Carolina: Arcadia Publishing; 2014.

27. Boston Urban Gardeners. *South End Open Space Needs Assessment.* 1988.

28. Boston Urban Gardeners. *Report on Organizing, Maintenance, Physical Site Improvement and Fundraising Strategies for the South End-Lower Roxbury Neighborhood Open Space Land Trust.* 1990.

29. Bronner E. Southwest Corridor: Setting a new course. *Boston Globe;* 1986 November 2.

30. Minezzi JM. Down by Dover. *South End News;* 1987 April 30.

31. Mann RB. Boston's Southwest Corridor: From Urban Battleground to Paths of Peace. *Places* 1991; 7.

32. Harmon L. A park that is the muscle and bone of the city. *Boston Globe;* 2012 May 5.

33. Hyer L. At southwest corridor, from beauty to deceased. *Boston Globe;* 2002 August 25.

34. Crewe K. Linear Parks and Urban Neighbourhoods: A Study of the Crime Impact of the Boston South-west Corridor. *Journal of Urban Design* 2001; 6:245-364.

CHAPTER 12

Crossing the 150-Year Mark: 1994 to 2003

If the century prior to renewal was one of relentless decline in the South End, the fifty years since it began has seen nearly continuous economic growth (for those who could afford the neighborhood, at least). The South End's property value increases resumed after a brief pause in the early 1990s, which resulted from a national recession and a temporary oversupply of condominiums. Developers began to look south, and less-wealthy buyers were pushed out of the center of the South End toward peripheral streets. East Brookline Street, for example, was the neighborhood's most remote row house area, but by 1998 the tide of conversions had reached this area with 177 active building permits on the block.[1]

Development pressures produced a new kind of housing along Washington Street and Harrison Avenue. Most were multi-unit condominium buildings on larger parcels that had remained vacant after years of abandonment and urban renewal takings. These larger projects enabled developers to include underground parking and elevators, two innovations that were absent in most row house construction projects. They attracted a range of buyers and tenants.

Many of these developments were inspired by a key infill project called Atelier 505, one of the neighborhood's first luxury condominium buildings. Developed by the Druker Company on the eastern portion of the BCA campus, it incorporated high-value retail and restaurant space on its ground floor. With concierge service, high end finishes, and underground parking, it represented one of the most expensive developments in the neighborhood. Initial sales ranged from $600,000 to $3.3 million.[2]

Laconia Lofts on Washington Street, designed by South End architect David Hacin, aimed to provide living/work spaces for artists.[3] There was also a cluster of new developments along Harrison Avenue near BUMC, including the ArtBlock, a mixed-income project that featured gallery space and subsidized units for artists, and a large redevelopment of the old Boston College High School building along Father Gilday Street into high end condominiums.

One innovative project was Rollins Square, developed by the Archdiocese Planning Office. It cost $56 million and was supported by a variety of federal, state, and city subsidies. Rollins Square was a successful mix of low-income units funded in part by Section 8, limited equity moderate-income homeownership units, and market-rate condominiums that were well received by higher-income buyers. Rollins Square had affordable rental units costing $329-$982 per month and limited equity condominiums going for $90,000 to $172,000.[4] Indicative of both the success of this mixed-income development and the insatiable demand for real estate in the South End, market-rate units in 2014 sold for between $800,000 and well over $1 million. In contrast to similar projects in other cities, the various unit types are well integrated with each other, low-income residents are not separated from market rate owners.

The new developments reflected a radically different theory of urban design. Just as renewal was beginning in the early 1960s, Jane Jacobs published a book that rebuked then-conventional modernist designs proposed by Le Corbusier and others. Their architectural philosophy had preferred large-scale megablocks that separated businesses from housing and created large open spaces between streets and buildings. Jacobs called for a pro urban design. Her philosophy preferred fine-grained, mixed-use development that was up close to streets on small blocks. By the 1980s, her alternative had become mainstream; a number of innovative design theories—including new urbanism—relied heavily on these elements. Architecture advocates such as Andres Duaney and Elizabeth Plater-Zybek celebrated urban living and people-focused design, and their plans incorporated many of the best features of neighborhoods like the South End. In turn, these ideas strongly influenced post-1990 development in the neighborhood, particularly the larger projects along its east-west arterials.

As with past development, there continued to be controversies regarding the percentage of assisted housing in these new developments and how ever-higher sales prices were fostering gentrification. Though there were promises of affordable units in this new wave of housing, most were concentrated in Rollins Square with other developments' affordable units being located offsite (and out of the neighborhood). Some thought the city should make a greater effort to create units for poor and middle-class households in various locations. There were also accusations that the city was not getting a proper return on its investment, and that developers would pay higher linkage payments in return for project approvals. The land selected for the former Tree of Life proposal, for example, was sold to a developer who was allowed to commit to only seven affordable units because he included space for the South End Neighborhood Health Center. In another controversy, the BRA sold a property to a developer who had past felony convictions of which the BRA claimed to be unaware.[5]

12.1 WASHINGTON STREET

Making affordable units available to those who needed them was problematic. Many criticized the city's selection process for moderate-income households. In the case of Rollins Square, there were suggestions that some of the limited equity units went to purchasers who were too affluent. The city began to panic that interest in limited equity units would dip in the wake of the World Trade Center attack on September 11, 2001. Private sector development might have sufficient resources to weather a slow-buying market, but mixed-income, subsidized development did not. So in response to a potentially slow market, the city was willing to let households that had higher incomes and assets buy into the development.[6] In retrospect, demand remained robust, and the adjustments were unnecessary.

Non-residential development was also strong. BUMC constructed several high-rise buildings for laboratory space and medical uses, and the Boston Water and Sewer Commission relocated to Lower Roxbury.

Other commercial developments were less successful. For example, the once-mighty computer manufacturer, DEC, abandoned their site on the large block bordered by Massachusetts Avenue and Melnea Cass, and the empty buildings created a problematic entryway to the South End and Roxbury. Its redevelopment was a priority for the Menino Administration, and in 2004 developers Kirk Sykes and Corcoran, Jennison, Inc. opened Crosstown Development with the help of steep BRA subsidies provided to address the area. The office portion was viable thanks to high-cost leases with Boston University and Brigham and Women's Hospital, but the retail and hotel portion of the block lagged. Though the hotel generated almost $11 million in annual revenue, its net operating losses were almost $3 million per year. The hotel's debt had ballooned to more than $56 million by 2014, and its long-term stability is in danger.[7]

There was a feeling that the South End had peaked as a gay neighborhood by the end of the 1990s. As early as 1985, gays and lesbians were moving out of the South End, Back Bay, and Beacon Hill for other neighborhoods and the suburbs.[8] Some left because they no longer felt comfortable in the community. Some gay men disliked what the neighborhood lifestyle had become; its men were stereotyped as successful and intelligent but vacuous and afraid of commitment. A 1998 movie set in the neighborhood, All the Rage, captured this caricature of wealthy, well educated, good looking, shallow South End gay men. In the movie's depiction of South End gay culture, physical attraction trumped interpersonal relationships, and sexual conquests were preferred to human kindness. Roland Tec, the writer and director of the movie, was a neighborhood resident. His detailed observations made public what others had been thinking for years.[9]

The South End remains the primary center for Boston area gays, though the lack of demographic information makes it impossible to assess the community's stability. It could be that the numbers of gays dropped since the mid-1990s, or it could be that the residents are simply not as visible as they once were. The Boston Globe analyzed 2000 census data and found 543 gay couples in the South End out of 2,167 citywide.[10] Though there are issues of interpretation, the numbers for 2010 are similar, indicating that there was no change in the number of gay men in the neighborhood. There are suggestions that gay men living together in relationships make up about 25 percent of all gay men.[11] Applying this to the South End (a major assumption that is impossible to verify locally) suggests that the adult population of the neighborhood was about 20 percent gay men in 2010, still a substantial presence.

A maturing gay population may have become less visible due to the fact that many business that serve the gay community are now online and no longer need accessible storefronts.[11] Or it could be that the population is smaller than it once was, and gays have left the South End's culture of expensive row houses and stereotypical relationship-centric lifestyles. Some were pushed out by the increasing numbers of upper-income straight couples,[12] and others left due to the conversion of apartments into condominiums during the second wave of gentrification. Regardless, gays and lesbians have become more dispersed across the city and region.

Unfortunately, the South End's stock of low-income housing was still suffering the aftereffects of the failure of the urban renewal's 221(d)3 housing program. Twenty years after their construction in the 1970s, the financial collapse of many renewal-era low- and moderate-income housing developments created a crisis that threatened to leave thousands of low-income families homeless and the city riddled with vacant and decayed properties. This was a national problem, almost every 221(d)3 project in the country failed. As developments went bankrupt, HUD was forced to assume ownership, something that the various housing acts that had guided development since the 1930s never anticipated.

In response, Congress required HUD to dispose of these developments in what was called the Demonstration Disposition Program. HUD would partner with state housing finance agencies to renovate and sell failed developments from HUD's portfolio. In the early 1980s, the Massachusetts Housing Partnership used this program—nicknamed Demo-Dispo—to renovate 1,200 units in other parts of the city, preserving units for low-income housing. Its success prompted a new effort by HUD to expand the program. But in the meantime, another group of housing projects had been taken over by HUD.

Under the leadership of the Massachusetts Housing Finance Agency (MHFA), a coalition of organizations and agencies—including the Metropolitan Boston Housing Partnership, Community Development Assistance Corporation, the Boston-HUD Tenants Alliance, and the City of Boston Public Facilities Department—organized a bid for a package of developments in Boston, including several in the South End. Altogether, 1,900 units in Roxbury, the South End, and Dorchester would be part of the proposal. One of the most notable features of this new project was that it made tenant involvement a priority, ensuring that the various resident councils would be key participants in the development process. Tenant groups would work, with assistance, to create a management structure appropriate for each development, hire development teams, interact with management and architects, and participate in the relocation of tenants, if necessary. The result was a national model of tenant ownership.[13]

Three troubled South End developments—Camfield Gardens, Roxse Homes, and Grant Manor—were part of the project. Since its construction in 1970, Camfield Gardens had had three owners and multiple construction and financial issues with tenants facing eviction. Camfield Gardens had 134 residential units, a tenant mix that was one-third Latino and two-thirds Black, and a median family income of $19,200. Its residents had few resources and would have suffered greatly if the development were closed.[14] Roxse Homes and Grant Manor had similar issues.

The long development time led to difficulties; costs increased and funding commitments became shaky. In 1995, HUD estimated the project required about $7,300 per apartment each year for fifteen years while construction costs had doubled. Boston's proposal was in competition with 169 other troubled developments across the country, and HUD had only $250 million for all projects. Boston needed $200 million.[15] In the end, HUD and MHFA were able to come to an agreement to fund the project, but by the time construction was underway in 2000, costs had increased by another $30 million.[16]

In a major departure from 1960s renewal, the MHFA mandated that no relocation plan would be approved unless it had the support of a development's tenant council. Despite these safeguards, however, the magnitude of necessary rehabilitation created large-scale disruption and displacement. Fifteen hundred families had to face at least temporary relocation, and 881 moved permanently. There were insufficient units to relocate this many families in the city, and tenants faced moves as far as Lawrence and Lowell, over thirty miles from Boston. In this context, the relocation assistance specialists had to keep in close contact with families so they would not lose their rehousing rights and be ready to move into units once they were rehabbed. The scale of relocation was the largest in the city since urban renewal. Each family moved twice, once out and once back into its unit. Despite many reassurances, residents left reluctantly. "People are scared, but we know this is for our own good," said Maria Rivera, vice president of the Geneva Tenants Association. "Nothing could be worse than what we have now."[17] For the most part, relocation was a success.

Reflecting differing needs and priorities, the developments adopted a range of management structures. Camfield Gardens became wholly tenant owned, Grant Manor converted itself into a privately owned, non-profit development, and Roxse Homes opted for a blend of the two options. The entire project cost was $332 million, including $20 million for resident services, $17 million for security, $34 million for architectural and professional services, and $243 million for construction costs. Of total expenditures, $186 million went to certified minority-owned businesses and $25 million went to women-owned businesses.[18] The developments had been preserved for low-income residents, at least for the next few decades. Other failed developments in the region had similar restructuring of their ownership, and most have had substantial renovations to remedy their ongoing infrastructure problems.

Maintaining vital services was as difficult as preserving affordable housing. Nearly 150 years after it was founded, Boston City Hospital (BCH) was in a crisis caused by the high cost of providing care and the large numbers of poor, uninsured patients who relied on the facility for health care. BCH needed state and federal money to pay for its indigent clients., and any negative change in reimbursement rates, eligibility, or funding mechanisms would quickly drive the hospital into default.[19] Given its other budget obligations, this financial vulnerability threatened the fiscal stability of the city, which had been providing $30 million a year in subsidies to the hospital.[20] Because of these subsidies, BCH had a profit of $4 million in 1994 while its neighbor, University Hospital, had lost $1 million.[21]

Together, the two hospitals needed $40 million in capital improvements. BCH had $169 million of debt to cover its $171 million in assets, while University Hospital owed $105 million on its $106 million capital plant. BU had an $82 million endowment.[22] BCH had 356 beds after it opened its new hospital building in 1994. That year it treated 160,000 outpatients, 73,000 emergency patients, and 15,000 inpatients.[23] A block away, BU had 311 beds, 10,000 inpatient admissions, and 153,000 outpatient and emergency visits. It had 1,600 full-time employees and a budget of $158.5 million. It was also in precarious circumstances. Medicare paid for 47 percent of its costs, Medicaid provided 8 percent, and self-payments and insurance covered the remainder.[24]

Financing health care for the poor was a challenge in the 1990s. There was a federal program that provided money to states, which then distributed funds to hospitals, pharmacies, clinicians, and others. But health care costs were rising faster than federal and state appropriations, and the entire system of care for the poor was at risk. At the same time, other hospitals were competing for these poor patients, seeing federal and state programs as a way to fill beds and increase revenues. The state uncompensated care pool provided 45 percent of BCH revenues, while insured people were choosing other places to get care.[25]

To address these challenges, Mayor Menino appointed an advisory committee in 1994 made up of union members, community representatives and advocates, clinicians, and administrators from BCH and Boston University to study the possibility of merging BCH into BUMC. Opposition to the merger was spearheaded by the Coalition to Keep the Public in Health Care, a union-led group that was closely allied with Health Care for All, an advocacy group that would later play a key role in persuading Massachusetts to adopt the first in the nation universal health care law. Local 285 of the Service Employees International Union, with members at both hospitals, said it was not necessarily against a merger but worried that an independently run hospital would not have as much commitment to the people of Boston as a city-owned entity.[19] The role of the hospitals in providing services to those without insurance was a major priority for everyone involved in the merger.

Eventually, the city met the concerns of BCH unions and patient advocates, and the main unions announced their support of the merger on June 30, 1995. On September 27, 1995, the legislature approved the city's home rule petition, and a few weeks later Governor William Weld signed the merger law.[26] City Hospital ceased to exist and its medical functions, including extensive services to the poor, were assumed by BUMC. Its public health responsibilities were transferred to the Boston Public Health Commission.

The legacy of the South End's marshy beginnings has been causing problems ever since the city and BWPC used whatever materials were at hand as fill to raise the area above sea level. At the end of the twentieth century, a major threat to the South End's row houses was the problem of varying groundwater levels. For some buildings, water tables were too high, flooding basement units and causing sewer backups. On other blocks, water tables were too low, exposing wooden pilings to rot and threatening buildings with collapse.

The South End's fill consisted of dirt, gravel, dredged material, mud, and garbage submerged in groundwater, a substrate incapable of bearing the weight of its row houses. Barely above sea level, heavy brick buildings were supported on wooden pilings pounded into the soft muck. The piles were often whole trunks of pine and spruce, which were driven down to a layer of sand and clay twenty-five to thirty feet below the surface. They were typically two to three feet apart and cut off five feet above the "Boston base"—the mean low tide level. As long as they were submerged, pilings could last indefinitely. At least through the early 1900s, the water table was generally at eight feet, providing a three-foot margin of safety. If the water table dropped too far, exposing pilings to air, they could rot. Most buildings have more piles than they need and can withstand some loss without settling, but if too many pilings fail, the building could need substantial repairs, collapse, or need demolition. The length of time a pile can survive varies with the type of wood and what ultimately attacks it. Wood borers, termites, and winged beetles have been known to infest exposed pilings, but it is fungi, abetted by moist soil conditions, which are most problematic. Exposed pilings can disintegrate in three to twenty years.

The decay of wooden piles was noted as a problem as early as 1940,[27] and in 1957 a building collapsed on Harrison Avenue because its pilings had dried and rotted out.[28] But these were thought to be isolated occurrences and not an extensive crisis. That changed in the 1990s, when several structures in central Boston, including buildings in Chinatown and the flat of Beacon Hill, had so much damage caused by deteriorated pilings they had to be condemned. Other buildings required substantial renovations costing thousands of dollars. The full extent of the problem was unknown because it was difficult and expensive to determine if buildings were affected before there was costly structural damage. The only way to know for sure was to dig pits along the foundation to inspect pilings.

Complicating the search for a solution, no one understood why the water tables were dropping after more than a century of stability. In the South End, many thought the water table's falling levels were associated with the construction of the tunnel for the Orange Line, which required continuous pumping to keep it from flooding. As water seeped into the tunnel, it flowed out of the surrounding ground water, lowering the water table. Though there was one large aquifer underlying most of central Boston, groundwater movement was hampered by subways and other underground human-made features, and high amounts of impervious surfaces slowed replenishment. Still another legacy contributing to the problem was that the construction of the mill dam in the nineteenth century was watertight, preventing flows from the Charles River recharging groundwater in the Back Bay and South End.

In response to this threat to its architectural heritage, the city created the Boston Groundwater Trust in 1986 to monitor groundwater levels, educate the public, and make recommendations regarding how to remedy the problem of low groundwater. By 2000, there were more than eight hundred monitoring wells across the city including the South End. A survey of wells in 2006 found that 146 out of 571 monitoring wells had water levels below the crucial five-foot level.

In 2005, state and city agencies signed a memorandum of understanding to work together to solve the groundwater problem, pledging funding and cooperation. The city added a Groundwater Conservation Overlay District to its zoning code in 2006 that included the entire South End east of Massachusetts Avenue. In practice, this meant that for all new construction, renovation, or paving projects developers had to determine if they would impact groundwater and provide onsite mitigation and recharging of groundwater if necessary.[29] The goal was to prevent further damage to the city's historic neighborhoods.

While some buildings in the neighborhood suffered from a lack of water, others were threatened by too much. The South End and Back Bay are barely above sea level. Because the neighborhoods are so low and flat, it is impossible to build storm and sewer drains with sufficient pitch to provide adequate flows, creating drainage problems. By the 1990s, most of the South End's sewerage had been connected to drain lines, but heavy rains would overwhelm the system and result in the dumping of raw sewage into the harbor, a violation of the Clean Water Act. If the downpours were particularly heavy or occurred during extra high tides, the drainage system could back up, flooding basements and first floors in the heart of the South End.

With its low elevation, poorly sized drains, combined sewer and storm system, and below-grade first floors and basements, the area between Dedham, Tremont, and Northampton Streets and the railroad right of way, "could hardly have been planned more effectively to produce trouble if it had been done intentionally."[30] Chesbrough and Parrott built a sewer line down Tremont Street to Dover Street, where it turned to empty into South Bay in an attempt to prevent sewage from fouling the lower receiving basin created by the Mill Dam. The filling of Back Bay overwhelmed this solution, and storage drains were added to Union Park, East Dedham, and East Concord Streets in the late 1850s and early 1860s. The plan was to hold effluent during high tides in the drains and then release it into South Bay during low tides. This proved insufficient, and the city constructed the Union Park pumping station with a capacity of one hundred thousand gallons per minute. Even this would not be enough to protect the neighborhood in the decades to come.

On August 28, 1976, many homes on the north side of Upton Street were flooded. This flooding was traced to jammed tide gates and faulty operation of the pumping station. Another round of major flooding occurred on October 20, 1976.[31] Although some repairs were made in response to the floods, the system continued to deteriorate. The resulting periodic flooding, occurring with increasing frequency, became a crisis on the night of September 10, 1999, when the Union Park Pumping Station failed.[32]

As water and sewage flooded much of the neighborhood, the Boston Ballet lost the use of two dance studios, Jesuits at the Immaculate Conception Church were left scrambling to find sleeping spaces for guests coming for a meeting, and hundreds of other households and businesses were affected.[33] BWSC blamed an electrical short circuit for the "three feet of black, murky sewer water" that filled some houses, destroying carpets, furniture, and appliances and making units temporarily uninhabitable.[34] The flooding affected 350 properties across twenty-seven blocks and left many traumatized.[35] The eventual solution was to upgrade the Union Park Pumping Station and turn it over to a private company for maintenance and operation. Floods have eased, but the entire system may have to be revisited if rising sea levels overwhelm the current drains and pumps.

The neighborhood has had to contend with development proposals rejected by other communities. The South Bay or Newmarket district, located at the intersection of South Boston, Roxbury, Dorchester, and the South End, had been a neglected area for decades. It included some of the last acres in the city to be filled and was mostly occupied by food wholesalers, warehouses, and a jumble of support services vital for any modern economy. The location of this land made it attractive to developers, just like the South End's back in the 1960s. Beginning in the late 1980s, there would be a series of development proposals that South End residents were forced to confront.

One of the few projects actually constructed was the South Bay House of Corrections, which opened in 1991 at the cost of $115 million. The facility had been on Deer Island in Winthrop, but that site was needed for a new sewage plant to meet the state's obligation to clean up Boston Harbor. The new facility initially had about nine hundred beds but was eventually expanded to accommodate over 1,900 non-violent inmates.[36] When Governor Dukakis proposed moving the facility to South Bay, he also wanted to build a new waste-to-energy facility in the area. Along with Mayor Flynn, who grudgingly supported the new jail, he proposed a series of investments that would have brought heavy industrial uses to the area.[37] None of these other projects were built.

A very controversial proposal in the early 1990s was to build an asphalt batching plant adjacent to the old incinerator. The incentive was Boston's Big Dig, the large-scale downtown construction project. The Big Dig would underground the Central Artery, construct a third harbor tunnel, and build new approaches and bridges. All these improvements required vast amounts of asphalt, but there were few plants inside the greater Boston area, and hot asphalt can only be transported so far and still be useful. The Todesca Company initially proposed to build the plant in Roslindale, but opposition led it to buy a vacant parcel in South Bay, setting off a lengthy battle with residents from South Boston, Roxbury, Dorchester, and the South End.

Todesca and its allies suggested that the area was close enough to the Big Dig yet far enough from residential areas, making it a perfect site for the asphalt plant. Opponents were concerned that the plant's fumes and emissions would impact neighborhoods that were already heavily polluted by the Southeast Expressway and the many bus yards in the Lower Roxbury area. Furthermore, the plant would provide only a few jobs. The community felt that the tradeoff between economic benefits and environmental costs was not worthwhile.

Another force behind the opposition was the idea of environmental justice. The emerging social-political theory stated that everyone had the right to a safe, clean environment. It also highlighted the fact that low-income and minority neighborhoods were often forced to share the burden of development but didn't enjoy the benefits and amenities more upscale communities received.[38] The analytic framework of environmental justice helped energize a number of residents and organizations—including Alternatives for Community and Environment, the Environmental Diversity Forum, and the Massachusetts Toxics Campaign—to fight the proposed siting. Assisted by these allies, residents from the four surrounding communities organized their neighbors to oppose the plant. One important leader was Roxbury's Zakiya Alake, who reached out to others and helped organize Mothers and Children Against the Asphalt Plant, a group that would bring large numbers of residents out to oppose the plant at community meetings.[39] Community outreach workers at the South Boston Health Center also played an important role. Eventually, residents asked the Boston University School of Public Health to conduct an analysis of asthma epidemiology in the communities around the area. Its report called the four neighborhoods a "zone of death" because of their high mortality rates related to asthma and other respiratory disease.[40] This prompted the EPA to become involved and the Boston Health Commission decided to study the proposed plant. Though Todesca accused the opposition of being funded by rival asphalt companies, the residents defeated the project. One side effect of the attention given to the project was that the EPA cited the city for failing to clean up the old incinerator, which led to its demolition and site remediation. Today, the Greater Boston Food Bank has its central facility on the site.

Almost at the same time as the asphalt plant battle was raging, Governor Weld and others proposed building a complex at South Bay that would have included a new convention center and a football stadium. Called the megaplex, it was proposed as a way to keep the New England Patriots football team from moving out of the region and to help maintain Boston as a competitive city for meetings and conventions.[41] Though the governor pushed hard for the facility, it never advanced. Eventually a new convention center was built near the South Boston waterfront and the Patriots stayed in Foxborough, Massachusettes.[42]

Despite its low car-ownership rate, the South End has lacked adequate public transit ever since its trolleys were removed after World War I, replacing them with just two stations barely walkable from the core of the neighborhood. Even the new Orange Line serves the northern slice of the community better than parts farther south. In 2002, the Massachusetts Bay Transit Authority (MBTA) completed the construction of the 2.2-mile Silver Line from downtown to Dudley Square at the cost of $27.3 million—with an addition $19 million spent on roadway improvements on the Washington Street corridor in which it operates. Carrying fifteen thousand riders each day, this Bus Rapid Transit (BRT) line was highly contested throughout its long planning process and was the result of a number of unilateral decisions made by the state authorities responsible for its design, construction, and operation.

Silver line Stop, Washington Street, 2014. The Silver line never fulfilled its promise of completely replacing The elevaTed Train aS an innovaTed bus r apid TransIT line.

12.2 SILVER LINE STOP

Planning for replacement service on Washington Street began in 1975, when the state made an agreement with the federal government to trade highway dollars for mass transportation funding, which allowed the construction of a new Orange Line up to a mile distant from Washington Street.[43] The state took nearly thirty years to create the promised replacement service for the demolished Orange Line.

The challenge was the lack of money. The Southwest Corridor project was over budget with no funds available for Washington Street.[44] Then when planning for a replacement service restarted in the mid-1980s, the state was struggling with financing the Big Dig.[45,46] Despite thirty years of promises of reliable, quality replacement service on Washington Street, the state was unable to find funding for the project. No federal dollars were available for the South End because all such funds had been committed elsewhere.

Community groups passionately argued for better service to replace the slow buses on the street, with most South Enders in favor of light rail with direct connections to the subway. Some merchants were concerned about losing parking spaces, while residents in Chinatown worried about the disruption a portal to the subway would cause there. On the other side of the line, residents in Roxbury became major allies in fighting for light rail, and community groups there and in the South End formed the Washington Street Corridor Coalition, led by Robert Terrell, to advocate for better transit. Despite lawsuits and demonstrations, they failed.[45,47]

The state unilaterally settled on the idea of a BRT, a new form of service that promised the convenience of light rail with the lower cost of buses. Unfortunately, a mixture of bad planning and continuing funding constraints resulted in a bus line that fell far short of BRT operating standards. A well-implemented BRT has dedicated bus lanes, off-board fare payments, at-grade boarding, highly visible branding, and coordinated connections to other transit modes. Except for the branding, the Silver Line, as the Washington Street BRT was called, failed at all of these. By international standards, the line is not considered a BRT at all.[48] Bus lanes are frequently blocked by double-parked cars, boarding is delayed by the buses' complicated fare boxes, and buses must be lowered to accommodate people with disabilities.[49] Even the Silver Line's bus shelters had to be rebuilt; they were the result of a complicated design process that failed to protect riders from the elements.[50] The line is often called the "Silver Lie" because of the broken promise of transit in this mostly carless neighborhood.[51] The line is heavily used, but there are no plans to improve service.

Altogether, the turn of the century saw increased development and rising housing prices. The maturing neighborhood seemed to put the conflicts of the previous forty years behind it. There was substantial new construction and the population increased. For the most part, neighbor-versus-neighbor disputes ebbed, but peace was not permanent.

1. Robertson T. The push and pull of a gentrifying street. *Boston Globe*, 1998 June 22.

2. Campbell R. South End's Atelier 505: Welcome to the neighborhood. *Boston Globe*; 2004 October 3.

3. Doten P. Scaling new heights With modern amenities and a city-sky line view, a new project revitalizes the concept of loft living. *Boston Globe;* 1999.

4. Real Estate. Archdiocese to start building Rollins Square. *Boston Globe*; 2000 November 4.

5. Ebbert S. In South End, revival sidesteps middle class. *Boston Globe*; 2001 October 28.

6. Slack D, McConville C. City's rules let not-so-needy get affordable units. *Boston Globe*; 2005 November 15.

7. Douglas C. The lesson of Crosstown Center and the false promise of a mega-hotel in South Boston. *Boston Business Journal*; 2014 September 16.

8. Bronner E. Gays Leaving City Pace For The Neighborhoods. *Boston Globe*; 1985 September 16.

9. Graham R. Smart, gently barbed look at gay narcissist. *Boston Globe;* 1998 September 11.

10. Rodriguez C. Comfort Zone Census Shows Gay And Lesbian Households Clustered. *Boston Globe;* 2001 June 20.

11. Ghaziani A. *There Goes the Gayborhood?* Princeton, New Jersey: Princeton University Press; 2014.

12. *"Out" in the South End Now Means Moving Out.* 2007. (Accessed February 5, 2012, at http://www.jsons.org/region/out-in-the-southend-now-means-moving-out-1.2503228#.UvJps-7R36HZ.)

13. Grillo T. Overhaul of inner-city units long overdue. *Boston Globe*;1997 March 22.

14. Joppe SL. *Faith, Hope, and Demo Dispo:* Massachusetts Institute of Technology; 1995.

15. Grunwald M. US funds for Hub housing plan in jeopardy. *Boston Globe*; 1995 July 13.

16. Giordano A. Boston project raises concerns group says funds mismanaged. *Boston Globe*; 2000 February 13.

17. Grunwald M. *Boston Globe*; 1995 October 25.

18. Jennings J, Evereteze J, O'Bryant R, Williams R, Kim S, Colon M. *The Demonstration Disposition Program in Boston, Massachusetts, 1994 to 2001: A Program Evaluation.* 2002.

19. Knox R. How to merge remains the issue. *Boston Globe*; 1995 May 18.

20. Editorial. Council Applauded. *Boston Business Journal;* 1995 July 7.

21. Walker A. Panel wants private, nonprofit hospital. *Boston Globe*; 1995 May 18.

22. Knox R. BCH merger faces a troubled prognosis. *Boston Globe*; 1995 May 21.

23. City of Boston. *Boston City Hospital Fact Sheet.* 1995.

24. Boston University. *Facts about Boston University Medical Center Hospital.* 1995.

25. Editorial. Let's move on BCH merger. *Boston Herald*; 1995 June 29.

26. House Officers' Association/CIR. *Merger Briefing Book.* 1996.

27. The Urban Planning Board. *Building a Better Boston.* 1941.

28. Building collapse. Building collapse kills woman. *Boston Globe*, 1957 May 27.

29. Shoham T. *Groundwater Decline and Preservation of Property in Boston.* Massachusetts Institute of Technology; 2006.

30. Dorr ES. The South End sewer system of Boston. *Journal of the Boston Society of Civil Engineers* 1915; 2:355-72.

31. Kenney R. *Undated Letter* to Casazza J. 1976.

CHAPTER 13

The New Millennium: 2000 and Beyond

By 2000, Boston was one of the most prosperous cities in the country. It was a national example of renewed interest in city living that placed it on par with New York, San Francisco, Seattle, and other wealthy, technologically connected regions. With a desirable location and housing stock, the South End's population surged from 22,497 in 1990 to 30,321 in 2000, only to drop to 27,221 in 2010. A third wave of gentrification had caused a population decline as developers recombined units into larger condominiums or even back into single-family row houses, increasing market value but decreasing population size.

While home ownership in the South End had been expensive for decades, the neighborhood continued to house a substantial number of middle-class residents at least until the end of the 1990s when rising prices began to transform the community into one of the most expensive in the country. After the mid-1980s, assessment data became reliable (assessments were very political before that time and their connection to market value could be tenuous). An examination of the history of a few representative units demonstrates the extreme price increases in the last thirty years. The assessment on a one-bedroom condominium on Union Park, for example, went from $110,000 in 1985 to $692,700 in 2013, while a single-family home on West Canton Street was assessed at $172,300 in 1985 and $1,771,700 in 2013.

More modest units also had large increases; a one-bedroom Shawmut Avenue condominium went from $101,600 in 1987 to $366,600 in 2013 while a row house on Wellington Street was assessed at $83,000 in 1985 and $1,106,500 in 2013.[1] Prices per square foot doubled between 1999 and 2005, reaching $591 per square foot.[2] They were $710 in 2013.[3] In that year, an 800-square foot, two-bedroom, floor-through condominium in a row house—a typical unit—would cost $568,000. For such a unit, a household would need more than $100,000 for a down payment and an annual income of at least $227,000 to qualify for a mortgage. That year, the median family income in the United States was $51,939 and in Massachusetts it was $62,963.

There were 13,375 units in the South End in 2014, including 535 single-family residences and 4,480 owner-occupied units, mostly condominiums. There were 5,427 private-market rental units (including rented condominiums), and the neighborhood had 5,468 affordable housing units, representing 28 percent of the total housing stock. While this seems like a high percentage, consider the fact that before renewal, almost all units in the neighborhood were affordable. The affordable stock included 1,536 mostly pre-renewal BHA units and 3,989 privately owned, subsidized units, most built in the 1970s and 1980s as part of the urban renewal project. Most housing built since 1990 has been market-rate condominiums and rentals. Affordable housing production declined, while the number of single-family residences increased; higher income families were moving into the neighborhood at breakneck speeds. The census also reported that the number of occupied units in the core of the neighborhood decreased by about 1,500 between 2000 and 2010. While the census may have miscounted some units, these numbers more likely reflect the effects of developers combining smaller units into larger dwellings to serve more affluent buyers. As of 2015, the neighborhood can be characterized as having a sizable number of affordable units with its condominiums and rentals becoming increasingly unaffordable to all but the wealthiest. As a result, the South End's middle class is disappearing.

The change in South End housing prices is mirrored by its labor market composition. Labor market participation increased up to 1990, when more than 76 percent reported being part of the workforce, but then fell to 45 percent in 2000. Part of this drop reflects the fact that retired people were selling their homes in the suburbs to move back to the city and students in the area were relying on wealthy parents for their condominiums. Another change in the neighborhood's labor force was a reduction in the number of sales and administrative support people who lived there. Changing technologies reduced their number in the economy as a whole. Similarly, the number of service people in the neighborhood fell. The bottom half of the middle class could no longer afford the South End.

Since 2000, the population of the South End has declined by about 10 percent. The white and Asian populations bear the brunt of this fall, while Black and Latino numbers are more stable. The census indicates an influx of white families since 2000. In 1970, there had been 539 white children under the age of five, which dropped to 223 in 2000. But this third wave of gentrification brought increasing numbers of white families to the neighborhood. By 2010, this number had risen to 619, and there was a similar pattern among white children ages five to fourteen. In 1970, there were 809 children in this age range, with a steady decline to 262 in 2000. In 2010, however, there were 398 white, school-aged children. In contrast, there has been no rebound in the number of Black children. In 1970, there were 573 Black children under the age of five. The number decreased to 287 in 2010.

In 1970 there were 1,006 Black children ages five to fourteen, but their numbers declined to 509 in 2010.[4] These rising numbers of white children are particularly interesting in light of the fact that many other large cities have continued to lose white children to the suburbs.

Longtime residents noticed these changes. One complained that "lunch hour at a South End cafe last Friday could have been mistaken for a Gymboree play-group. Strollers surrounded a long table in the window alcove, and more clustered around tables along a wall. Half a dozen young mothers spoon-fed their babies Gerber Organic purees from the nearby Foodie's Urban Market and dabbed globules from chins with name-embroidered towels."[5]

Some residents grew tired of the expensive cost of living and a lifestyle they did not like. For these former residents, "the South End was becoming a dead end. Home was a snug 400-square-foot one-bedroom. Rent: $1,250 a month. Parking? A daily catch-it-if-you-can hunt."[6] The increasing housing costs were creating winners and losers.

To feed its upscale demographic, the neighborhood became a magnet for expensive restaurants.[7] Dining out was becoming an experience, and the South End was now the destination for the best new restaurants. Gone were the days of the cheap diner catering to lodging-house residents.

One well known restaurant in the neighborhood was Hammersley's Bistro, which opened in 1987 in a small space on Tremont Street. It was one of the first restaurants in the entire city, much less the South End, to combine fresh ingredients, adventurous cuisine, expensive wines, and high prices. Gordon Hammersley, who ran the restaurant with his talented wife, Fiona, was a forerunner of the "celebrity chef," one who authors cookbooks, maintains a high media profile, and whose "brand" is as much his personality as it is the quality of food. Reflecting the South End's diversity and commitment to social justice, Hammersley was noted for his work with inner-city youth and participation in charities. His humility kept him working in his kitchen as other celebrity chefs focused on traveling internationally, opening outposts in far-flung tourist centers, and appearing on television.[8] When Hammersley retired and closed his restaurant, there was a rush to experience his roast chicken one last time.

Another high-profile restaurateur is Ken Oringer, whose career began outside the South End with well-received, high-end venues in the Back Bay. In 2005, he moved into the South End with Toro, a tapas restaurant that represented a new cuisine in the neighborhood. Oringer had an international reputation; he worked with Ferran Adria at El Bulli, perhaps the best restaurant of its era and the leader of a new culinary movement known as molecular gastronomy.[9] In what may have been a surprise to the owners of the South End's expensive condominiums, the Boston Globe noted that the site of his new restaurant, near the corner of East Springfield and Washington Streets, was still gritty.[10] Despite the apprehension outsiders had about its location, Toro was very successful. One reviewer noted that "everyone went crazy for tapas, grilled corn slathered in cotija cheese, aioli, lime, and espelette pepper, dates stuffed with blue cheese and almonds and wrapped in ham, head cheese, Kobe sliders, and churros."[11] Within a year, a national magazine named Toro one of the best new restaurants in the country.[12] In 2009, Oringer opened Coppa, which was part of a group of restaurants that included seven different venues.

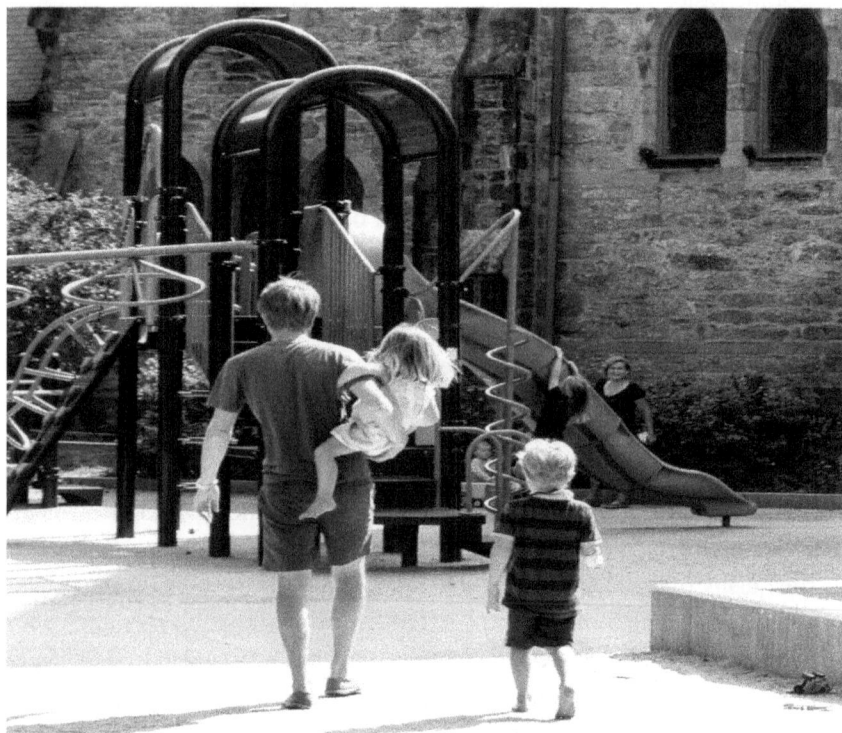

13.1 TITUS SPARROW PARK

The Aquitaine Group, run by three young men, also operated a number of restaurants. Seth Woods, Jeffrey Gates, and Matt Burns had been fascinated with dining and food since they were children.[13] Dining at Aquitaine was a scene. "Every fashionable society has its gathering places where well-dressed clientele go early or late, eat dependably good food, and run into lots of people they know."[14] The new restaurants were also important economic engines and employed many people both directly and indirectly. "Restaurants depend on huge teams to get them going and keep them running—architects and designers, wine dealers and food purveyors, electricians and plumbers, not to mention the staff in the front of the house and the kitchen. If any one element falters, things can fall apart fast."[13]

Perhaps the most famous restaurant owner in the South End was Barbara Lynch, whose tenacity and business sense might make her an heir to the landladies who dominated the neighborhood's economy during its lodging house era. Lynch grew up in the nearby Mary Ellen McCormack projects and came of age during the busing crisis. "The youngest of six, she was born a month after her father, who drove a cab, died of a heart attack at age 32. Much of Lynch's identity comes from growing up poor in South Boston in the 1960s and '70s: very Irish, very loyal, very street-smart."[15] She dropped out of high school (earning a GED years later) and began working in restaurants, slowly rising in responsibility. She never went to culinary school but became a self-taught expert in the kitchen. After working in some of the city's most exclusive restaurants, she launched her own series of venues, including B&G Oysters, The Butcher Shop, and Stir at the corner of Waltham and Tremont Streets. By 2010, her restaurants were valued at more than $15 million. In an industry dominated by men, Lynch was one of the most-recognized female authorities on cooking. When problems with her restaurant forced the closing of her South End outposts in 2024, there was a profound sense of loss among the neighborhood's foodies.

There are restaurants that are offshoots of others outside the neighborhood—such as Stephie's on Tremont, Five Horses Tavern, and The Elephant Walk—and home-grown establishments that have expanded outside the South End, like the Franklin Café. Two venues heavily identified with the neighborhood and indicative of the backgrounds of business owners in the South End are Flour, opened by Joanne Chang, a Harvard graduate with a Masters in Applied Mathematics and Economics, and The South End Buttery, the creation of Richard Gordon, a lawyer who once clerked for the Massachusetts Supreme Judicial Court.

While the food industry thrived, retail development has been more problematic. The small footprints of row houses are not large enough for most types of stores, and the South End faces competition from Back Bay and downtown. Most of its retail consists of small bodegas, service businesses, and a select number of stores and banks serving the neighborhood's moneyed residents. There are florists, athletic wear providers, and upscale bakeries. More difficult to find in the neighborhood are hardware stores, affordable clothing stores, and places to buy household necessities.

Several key new parks have opened in the neighborhood, reflecting the continuing influence of the South End's advocates for open space. The misalignment of the grids of the South End has provided opportunities for the embellishment of two small spaces along Columbus Avenue. Harriet Tubman Square opened in 1999 to honor the woman who did so much to lead others to freedom and who was a frequent visitor to the area. The park was the first public space in the city to honor a Black woman and it features a tenfoot statue designed by Fern Cunningham.[16]

Another square honors the artist Childe Hassam, who lived with his wife, Katherine, at 282 Columbus Avenue (the Hotel Albermarle) from 1884 to 1886. He painted a number of canvases depicting the South End, including one of his most famous, Rainy Day, Boston. The park was renovated in 2014, when a group of neighbors worked tirelessly to raise money for the project.[17]

Though Latinos have been living in Boston in large numbers for more than fifty years, the number of places and institutions reflecting their presence was very limited, and—for the most part—their contributions to the city were unrecognized. In a city that mostly honors its white men, two places stand out: the Jorge Hernandez Cultural Center and the Frieda Garcia Park. The Jorge Hernandez Cultural Center at Villa Victoria was named after the charismatic Executive Director of Inquilinos Boricuas en Accion (IBA). Hernandez led the IBA as it completed its core housing and transitioned into both a provider of social services and an advocate for Hispanics across the state. Sadly, structural problems forced IBA to demolish the building in 2022.

In 2013, Frieda Garcia Park opened on Stanhope Street opposite the Massachusetts Turnpike. It honors the Concord Square resident's lifetime of service to the Latino population of the city. A native of the Dominican Republic, Garcia moved to Boston in the 1960s. In her years of advocacy work, she had been the Executive Director of USES and played important roles at the Solomon Carter Fuller Mental Health Center, La Alianza Hispana, and other organizations.[17] The John Hancock Company funded the park, and its dedication featured a children's choir, local politicians, grateful community members, and a tearful—but always articulate— Garcia. Consistent with her concern for others, the park was designed to be an asset for families in the Back Bay and the South End.[18]

Also in 2013, the city dedicated the Puerto Rican Veterans Memorial at the corner of West Dedham and Washington Streets on a small triangle of land next to the Blackstone School. The first monument to the contributions of Puerto Rican servicemen and women on the mainland United States, it reflected their sacrifices and bravery as well as the fact that the South End was still one of the most important centers for this population.[19]

13.2 PUERTO RICAN VETERANS MEMORIAL

On the southern edge of the South End, the surviving mixture of sturdy, brick industrial buildings and vacant lots stood nearly empty and were severely underutilized for many decades. To the west, blocks closer to the hospitals had warehousing, manufacturing, and wholesaling, but Albany Street was still mostly empty in the early 2000s.[21] Recently, the SOWA arts district which began as a developer's nickname for the area south of Washington Street—came into existence, creating great change in the southeastern corner of the neighborhood.

Artists started moving into the blocks along Harrison Avenue in the 1970s, when high rents pushed them out of downtown. But in 1978, the area was a "dicey neighborhood, filled with empty alleyways and abandoned mill buildings populated by squatters."[22] The buildings between Harrison Avenue and Albany Street, initially renovated by Mario Nicosia and architect Graham Gund, eventually reached a critical mass, and by 2004, more than eight hundred thousand square feet of revitalized space had been created. Nicosia began working in real estate while a student at Northeastern. At 21, he bought his first residential building.[23] By the 1990s, Nicosia was an experienced property manager and developer. As part of the marketing effort for the revived area, he coined the name "SOWA" in 2000.[24] It became a neighborhood of galleries, restaurants, and a very crowded set of open markets in the summer. The retailers coexist with nearby Pine Street Inn, which vowed that it would never relocate from the area.[25]

The development of this arts district complemented the longstanding South End tradition of hosting entertainment and cultural amenities. Galleries began moving into the SOWA area in the mid-1990s from Newbury Street, Boston's traditional location for art, because rents in the SOWA area were about ten dollars per square foot, 10 percent of Newbury Street prices. The renewal of residential blocks between SOWA and the core of the South End also contributed to the area's success.[26]

With the branding of SOWA, the level of activity in the area increased significantly. SOWA became "the central node in the Boston art world" and at times it was difficult to walk on the narrow sidewalks because of the volume of pedestrians. "On a recent evening, the galleries along Harrison Avenue were packed with visitors of all ages who arrived for the monthly First Friday art openings. Plastic cups were filled with wine and sparkling water, the mood convivial. Friends greeted friends with air kisses and hugs, threading their way through crowds that circulated through the white-walled exhibits."[27] It was the place to be.

Nicosia's influence on Boston's art scene was controversial even as he enabled many artists to achieve commercial success. He required formal leases, raised rents, and mandated participation in events such as First Friday, and some saw this as the end of the era of living informally, sharing resources, and partying until dawn. Though many were grateful for the below-market rents, efficient management, and the purposeful recruitment of working artists and galleries, others were resentful of the requirements that came along with these spaces.

Much of the artwork is contemporary and avant-garde, but financial pressures still ensure that the art is targeted toward middle-class tastes; most artwork costs between $500 and $3,000. Interestingly, the artwork on display in the studios is often made elsewhere, usually at or near the artists' homes. For the most part, the artist spaces are empty all week. Artists come in a few hours before events and hang their works just for a brief period of time. Some onsite artists rent out their spaces for events, fulfilling their obligations and providing the opportunity for others to have access to buyers. Many of the studios are commercial rather than working spaces and some artists live as far away as Vermont. However, these artists self-identify as being part of the SOWA arts community, a reflection that the SOWA brand has become well-known outside of Boston.

13.3 SOWA MARKET FOOD TRUCKS

Nicosia also brought in large numbers of consumers with the innovative SOWA Open Market, which debuted in 2004.[28] On Sunday afternoons from May through October, thousands come to buy vegetables and other food-stuffs, peruse crafts and antiques, and eat at the food trucks. As a result of this effort, the area is now one of the most heavily visited parts of the neighborhood, and Nicosia continues to bring innovative programing to the area.

Decade by decade, development reached further into the South End. By 2007, there was enough development pressure on the areas along Harrison Avenue and Albany Street for the city to convene a task force to develop new plans and zoning for these blocks.[29] For the most part, this area lacked row houses; many of the parcels were either warehouses or sat empty. Even though industrial facilities occupied the central blocks and BUMC had dramatically transformed the portion between East Newton Street and Massachusetts Avenue with research facilities, land was underutilized in the corridor. One important outcome of this planning process was the rezoning of the area. The new guidelines allowed buildings as tall as two hundred feet along its southern edge as long as they met certain affordability guidelines. This was not going to be a moderate-density area. Instead, it was an opportunity to knit the South End with South Boston and provide space for residents and businesses.

The new zoning efforts also created an opportunity to rebuild the NYS area, which had been mostly empty or underutilized since it was cleared by renewal in the 1950s. Even in 2010, it was a wasteland of vacant, low-slung industrial buildings and vast parking lots set along barren, wide streets. It was a dead area between the vibrancy of Chinatown and SOWA.

Development was delayed by the slow recovery from the 2007 recession, but over time, almost two thousand units of housing have been built in the area. The area is now vibrant with restaurants, a hotel, a grocery store, and lots of pedestrian traffic. It is far from what it was when it was a mixed use, multi-racial neighborhood in the 1940s, few low income or Black or Latinx people live in these new buildings, but it is a bright spot where once there was nothing but the gloom of a post-urban renewal world.

Development forces have set their sights on the remaining industrial and wholesale businesses between BUMC and SOWA. In 2014, unnamed investors were eyeing the flower market; one bid was reported to be $35 million for the property. Other developers are trying to build housing in the remaining industrial buildings, generating resistance from business owners and creating fears that employment rates might fall. The fate of these proposals are as yet unknown.

One major contributor to the South End's robust economy continues to be the BCA. In 2004, it replaced the National Theater with Stanford Calderwood Pavilion and constructed Atelier 505. Funded by the Calderwood Charitable Trust, the Calderwood Pavilion consists of two main stages and two rehearsal spaces that are often used for performances. Managed by the Huntington Theatre Company, tenants include the Speakeasy Stage Company and more than150 other arts organizations. In its first ten years of operations, nearly 750,000 people have attended more than 4,100 performances.[30] BCA's productions and special events enliven the area, and its ties to artists helped launch the nearby SOWA arts district. The complex's Boston Ballet headquarters and school, galleries, restaurants, and performance spaces help make this one of the more active nodes in the neighborhood.

Other development projects have been unsuccessful. Knitting together the Back Bay and the South End has been a goal of planners since the two neighborhoods were created in the 1800s, but the barriers were daunting. The street networks do not mesh, and the railroad yards, tracks, and highways constructed along the seam between the two areas have proven difficult to bridge. Though the Prudential Center was one early attempt to provide a connection, its initial design was a disappointment. For example, its raised, windswept shopping plaza needed to be rebuilt in the 1990s. The Southwest Corridor Park was more successful. It provided vital greenspace, pedestrian and bike access, and a way to bring people to a neglected edge of the neighborhoods. But from Back Bay Station, where the Massachusetts Turnpike re-emerges from its cover, to South Station, the entry to the South End is an open trench. Healing this wound is a priority for residents in both neighborhoods.

The ill-fated Columbus Center, which was to be built over the Turnpike between Arlington and Clarendon Streets, was an attempt to revitalize this area. The project was first proposed in 1997, when—in a controversial move—the Massachusetts Turnpike Authority gave Winn Companies exclusive development rights in a non-competitive selection process.[31] The complex was to have 1.3 million square feet, two hotels, 451 condominiums, 917 parking spaces, 40,000 square feet of retail space, and a sophisticated recharge system to minimize its impacts on groundwater.[32]

After hundreds of community meetings, the revised project's plan included a thirty-five-story hotel and condominium tower, a fourteen-story apartment building, and a park. For the area between Berkeley and Arlington Streets, they proposed a parking garage surrounded by apartments. This 2002 version of the project had less density and greater connectivity. It was projected to cost $400 million.[33]

Arthur Winn was a respected developer of assisted housing, but he had no experience in building luxury, mixed-used projects, and he had problems advancing the complex. Matters worsened when he was caught up in a scandal involving Diane Wilkerson, the South Ends' state senator. She was taped taking a bribe, part of a sting operation where FBI informants posed as developers interested in building on a lot in Roxbury. Winn was not involved in this scandal, but it was later revealed that he had made substantial contributions to Senator Wilkerson, including $10,000 for her personal debts. Later, Winn and associates were accused of giving inappropriate contributions to a number of politicians.[34] The Winn Company was fined $1.57 million; two of its executives barely escaped serving time in prison.[35]

There were also technical difficulties with the project. It had to bridge eight lanes of highway without slowing daily commutes, and a deck needed to be constructed over the boggy soils of the area. The project was unable to support the cost of infrastructure without increasing its mass and density, but efforts to reduce open space and add height fueled opposition from neighbors. The developers tried to plug the gaps in their budget by securing public subsidies—almost $200 million from various programs— but the unpopularity of the complex made this difficult to acquire.[36]

As it limped toward a collapse in 2010, the total project costs had increased to more than $800 million; the deck alone was slated to cost $200 million. In the end, the state was reduced to begging the financial backer of the project, the California State Pension Fund, to pay to restore the area back to its original state.[37] The Turnpike remains an open trench, though ever so often, ideas emerge to cover the opening with parks or new land uses.

Other projects were also very contentious. In 2008, the battle over a proposed development on Upton Street was reminiscent of arguments from the early 1970s. The crux of the dispute centered on the subjective memory of what the South End had been prior to renewal and a disagreement over whom the neighborhood should accommodate. This all started when the Hope House planned to sell three buildings on Upton Street to purchase a new facility in another neighborhood. Mindful of the difficulties of siting new social services, it sold the buildings to PSI. The homeless shelter planned to renovate the buildings into small apartments for people who no longer needed shelters, staffed by a 24-hour social worker. PSI's proposal did not require any zoning changes or special permits. It represented a continuation of use; there would be no alterations to the facades or building footprints, and the number of people using the facility would not change. It could be built with a simple application for a building permit. Even so, community meetings were held to inform neighbors of PSI's plans.

When PSI met with representatives from the Union Park Neighborhood Association (UPNA), their initial reaction was neutral, and its board declined to support or oppose the project. The staff of the Archdiocese of Boston Urban Planning Office, who were working with PSI to acquire and develop the properties, moved forward with the development process. Thus, PSI believed it would have no problems creating new housing.

As news spread about the development, however, opposition to the project began to grow. At the next meeting of UPNA, all but one of the board members opposed the PSI proposal. The newly elected chair of the group and his colleagues went public with their opposition, using blogs, press releases, online petitions, and appeals to the city to stop PSI from moving forward.

Though the opposing arguments seemed to use neutral language, they were anything but objective. They expressed concern with the lack of parking (though most condominium units in the neighborhood do not have parking and there was little chance that the low-income residents of the building would own cars), the number of residents who would live in the buildings (the number actually would have been lower than when Hope House owned the buildings), the size of the sidewalks (an issue beyond the scope of the project), garbage pickup (a perennial problem throughout the South End), and other similar issues.

Arguments were often based on a memory of the South End as a dangerous place.[38] In an interview, the new UPNA president recalled that the street in 1990 "was pretty seedy, there was lots of crime, petty crime ... I've swept up crack pipes until I was blue in the face, in the alley," he said. "We've cleaned human feces out of our doorways." The president went on to say the street was no longer appropriate for rooming houses.[39] Some feared that the block would revert to its 1988 version if the plan went forward.[40] Many of the protesters were unaware that the neighborhood had expressed almost the exact same concerns twenty years earlier when PSI first moved to the area. Their predecessors had opposed its move into the area using many of the same arguments they were using against expansion.

As the neighborhood association began to publicly oppose the plan, a backlash developed as some neighbors welcomed the project. Both sides reached a compromise; developers would sell one townhouse for market-rate housing and reduce the number of PSI clients in the remaining townhouses. By the time it opened, it had received substantial corporate and area-wide support. There have been no reported problems with the project.

In a homage to the great age of jazz in the South End, Darryl Settles founded the Beantown Jazz Festival in 2002. Settles, an engineer by background, had been operating a restaurant, Bob the Chefs, on Columbus Avenue for over a decade, making it a center of upper-middle-class Black nightlife in the city.[41] Settles said he spontaneously thought of the idea for a jazz festival while hosting a retirement dinner at his restaurant (Mayor Menino was the master of ceremony that night).[42]

Though it took quite some time to acquire city permits and persuade area residents to agree to a festival in front of their homes, within a few years, the festival was attracting more than twenty thousand people to the closed off section of Columbus Avenue between Massachusetts Avenue and Melnea Cass Boulevard. It was also financially successful, donating as much as $10,000 in profits to local charities.[43]

In 2006, the Berklee College of Music took over the festivals' management. With events now stretching for more than a week and attracting more than seventy thousand people, it was too much for Settles, who was busy with the opening of a new fulltime jazz venue and restaurant, the Beehive, at the Boston Center for the Arts.[44] The festival continues to be a major September event in Boston.

While South Enders experience the benefits of their nineteenth century neighborhood every time they walk outside, some of the drawbacks of how the community was built continue to cause problems. The upkeep and maintenance of the neighborhood's private alleys has vexed many South Enders well into the twenty-first century. Below street level and poorly paved, some alleys have badly deteriorated with potholes, poor drainage, and bad lighting.[45] While the percentage of privately owned alleys in the city overall is low, about one-quarter of South Enders own their alleys and are responsible for maintaining the accompanying water and sewer lines. Exasperated owners along some alleys have sought to have the city take them over. On one hand, these alleyways are not up to current design standards, particularly in terms of compliance with the Americans with Disabilities Act and emergency vehicle access, making them a burden. On the other hand, surrendering ownership would have meant giving up coveted private parking spaces and the right to control access. The city was reluctant to take over any alleyway that needed upgrades and balked at potential costs that exceeded $750,000 per alley.[46] Even among abutters, there are conflicts between those who sought to gate off alleys to reduce crime and residents who use them for access.[45] The issue remains unresolved as conditions continue to deteriorate.

The most controversial development proposal in the South End after 2000 was Boston University Medical Center's National Emerging Infectious Diseases Laboratories, usually referred to as the Biolab. Located on Albany Street just to the east of BUMC's other facilities, the building would host specially constructed laboratories that could be used to study the most fearsome of lethal diseases, such as Ebola and smallpox.

The proposal for the facility was developed in the wake of the September 11, 2001 attack in New York City and the subsequent anthrax attacks. There was a perceived need to better understand the infectious disease threats posed by weaponized microbes and emerging pathogens. BUMC successfully submitted a proposal in response to a national competition for new laboratories for this kind of high security research. The region was a natural place to build a major new research facility. Boston University seized upon the opportunity to attract world-class researchers to the area. The potential connections to other Boston-area scientists and the national need for these types of facilities were used as justifications for the Biolab in the South End.[47]

Others were against the lab. Some opposed these facilities in general, believing that they promoted dangerous, unnecessary research and fearing that the Biolab would be used to produce biological weapons. Others were against the lab in this particular location, citing the risk of terrorist attacks, accidents, and the general inappropriateness of a highly secured facility in a crowded urban environment. They argued that thousands could potentially be exposed to pathogens, many of whom were low-income residents or those already in poor health.[48] The facility was constructed and has been in operation for several years. There have been serious biological breaches, but the worst fears of neighbors have not been realized.

More than 160 years after the South End was first developed, the neighborhood had an affluence undreamed of by Bulfinch, Chesbrough, and the many Quincys and Otises who led the city. Residents were both surprised and unsettled by the dramatic increase in the community's fortunes. Some lamented the loss of its more colorful past and diversity, while others were willing to overlook the cost of development as they counted their profits or pondered the present value of their real estate. As 2015 dawned, no one had any idea how long prosperity would continue.

1. City of Boston Assessing Department. *Assessing Records*. 2013.

2. Viser M. Breaching Mass. Ave.: Gentrification that touched the east side of Boston's South End is finally expanding across an imaginary dividing line towards a once neglected neighborhood. *Boston Globe*; 2007 January 14.

3. Steven Cohen Team. *An Open Letter to South End Stakeholders*. 2014.

4. Minnesota Population Center. *National Historical Geographic Information System*. Version 2.0. 2014.

5. Schweitzer S. South End getting (a lot) younger; Influx of babies altering neighborhood's urban edginess. *Boston Globe*; 2008 March 15.

6. Diaz J. The South End Priced-Out Urban Residents Find Grassy Hillside Haven In Diverse Dorchester Enclave. *Boston Globe;* 2002 September 8.

7. Arnett A. Third Time's A Charm In South End. *Boston Globe*; 2005 July 14.

8. First D. Hammersley's lovingly serves a farewell. *Boston Globe*; 2014 August 14.

9. Baskin K. Lynch, Bissonnette win Beard awards. *Boston Globe*; 2014 May 7.

10. Yonan J. Spanish lessons; with his new restaurant, Toro, Ken Oringer brings the flavors - and the fun - of the tapas bar to the South End. *Boston Globe*; 2005 November 9.

11. First D. The tastemakers. *Boston Globe*; 2010 November 7.

12. Beggy C, Shanahan M. Esquire praises 3 local eateries. *Boston Globe*; 2006 October 16.

13. Block B. The big night a summer of sweat gives rise to a new South End restaurant. *Boston Globe*; 2003 October 2.

14. Julian S. Steak frites, blini - it's the lush life. *Boston Globe*; 2000 November 23.

15. English B. The gambler in the kitchen. *Boston Globe*, 2009 December 13.

16. Negri G. Her message cast in bronze In this sculptor's work, the main theme is emancipation. *Boston Globe*, 1999 July 4.

17. Shannon HJ. *Legendary Locals of Boston's South End.* Charleston, South Carolina: Arcadia Publishing; 2014.

18. Abraham Y. The force of a name. *Boston Globe*, 2012 December 2.

19. Lowery W. City unveils monument to Puerto Rican veterans. *Boston Globe*, 2013 November 20.

20. 35 arrested. 35 arrested after violence disrupts Puerto Rican *Boston Globe*, 1972 July 17.

21. Kindleberger R. Developers Tout What They Call Next Hot Spot: Albany Street. *Boston Globe*, 2000 April 14.

22. McQuaid C. The New Art Neighborhood Open Studios Showcases Sowa Gallery Boom Up And Down Harrison Ave., New Galleries Create An Arts Community. *Boston Globe*, 2003 September 12.

23. A man and a neighborhood. This is the story of a man and a neighborhood and ... . *Boston Globe*, 1980 April 5.

24. Wangsness L. Sowa? Eabo? Boston Plays Name Game; In City's Hot Condo Market, Realtors Look For An Edge. *Boston Globe*, 2005 September 5.

25. Laban L. Call it `Mario's Village' -; A developer's devotion to his neighborhood is proving profitable not just for him, but for the South End as well. *Boston Globe*, 2007 June 3.

26. McQuaid C. Galleries Find new South end niche Dealers offer alternative to Newbury Street. *Boston Globe*, 1997 September 21.

27. Regis N. SOWA. *Boston Globe*, 2011 September 25.

28. Moy KW. Today, Sowa's Out In The Open An Outdoor Market Debuts At Parking Lot. *Boston Globe*, 2004 May 23; Sect. 3.

29. Boston Redevelopment Authority. *Harrison Albany Corridor Strategic Plan.* Boston2011.

30. Brown J. A place with room to stretch. *Boston Globe*, 2014 September 28.

31. Ross C. Columbus Center's plug pulled. *Boston Globe*, 2010 March 11.

32. Palmer TC. Columbus Center will make an impact on Boston's skyline *Boston Globe*, 2005 February 21.

33. Palmer TC. South End project revised Columbus Center will be 35 stories with hotel, housing. *Boston Globe*, 2002 November 22.

34. Ross C. Columbus Center a curse - and a cause. *Boston Globe*, 2009 March 29.

35. Casey R. Sentencing in Columbus Center case. *Boston Globe;* 2011 December 9.

36. McMorrow P. The final death of Columbus Center. *Boston Globe*, 2011 November 1.

37. Ross C. Future of Columbus Center site up in air. *Boston Globe*, 2010 March 4.

38. Pazzanese C. Upton St. gives Pine Street cold shoulder. *Boston Globe*, 2008 February 10.

39. Rodriguez L. Nightmare on Upton Street. *South End News*, 2008 March 20.

40. South End Must Protest Pine Street Inn Moving to Upton. *Dwell South End*, 2008. (Accessed June 6, 2013, at http://southend.tumblr. com/post/60984700/south-end-must-protest-pine-street-inn-moving-to-upton.)

41. Ryan SC. Bistro ending its soulful reign. *Boston Globe*, 2007 October 30.

42. Beuttler B. They get the party started; Bob the Chef's owner settles went to great lengths to cook up a local jazz festival. *Boston Globe*, 2004 September 24.

43. Greenlee S. Roxbury/South End fest spotlights top local artists. *Boston Globe*, 2002 September 27.

44. Beuttler B. Berklee to take reins of Beantown Jazz Festival. *Boston Globe*, 2006 May 5.

45. Bayles C. On the surface, not all alleys are treated the same. *Boston Globe*, 2010 November 10.

46. Huffman Z. Private alleys cost more for sewers. *Boston Courant*, 2014 February 28.

47. Editorial. 'Level 4' disease research can be safe, belongs in America's medical capital. *Boston Globe*, 2014 April 13.

48. Smith S. Suit planned to block BU biolab citizen groups raise concerns on safety. *Boston Globe*, 2003 September 20.

Epilogue

Over its **165-year** history, the South End went from a neighbor-hood of great promise to one of poverty and then back to prosperity. It has been home to righteous Yankee families, Irish prizefighters, progressive gay men, fiery Nation of Islam preachers, community activists, and real estate professionals. In a society often fractured along lines of race, class, sexual identity, and religious bigotry, the South End has sheltered nearly all types of people. One can look at the neighborhood's history and dwell on the conflict between whites and Blacks, Protestants and Catholics, rich and poor, or find solace in the coalitions that built Villa Victoria, stopped the redevelopment plans of the 1960s, and created its community gardens. The battles can give us reasons to despair or hope for the future.

Today, the South End is one of the city's most desirable neighborhoods, with a core of restored row houses supplemented by newer buildings that mostly complement its nineteenth-century architecture. The very poor and the extremely wealthy live side by side, even as the percentage of middle-class residents falls. With nearly every storefront occupied, a stroll through the neighborhood reveals prosperity and substance on almost every block, be it the economic excesses of Atelier 505 or the cultural exuberance of Villa Victoria. Evenings in the South End are crowded, restaurants have hours-long waits for tables, and a book reading at the library or a community meeting on a development proposal can fill a room to capacity. The neighborhood looks comfortable and static, though we know that demographic change continues. What could go wrong?

The mercurial changes in the South End's fortunes should give anyone pause when it comes to a discussion of what might happen to the neighbor-hood over the coming decades. Despite the current prosperity of the community, there are serious issues that will have to be addressed in the next few years. The neighborhood isn't at rest.

One tremendous problem is the declining affordability of the neighbor-hood. For the past 150 years, the South End has benefited by being a lower-cost alternative to other neighborhoods in Boston's core. Many of the people and institutions in the community went there because of its cheap real estate, improving the neighborhood as they did so. From amateur theatricals in the 1850s, through the Jazz Age in the 1940s, to the gay neighborhood of the 1980s, the depth of the South End's vibrant quality of life at least partially related to the fact that it was an affordable community. But after three waves of gentrification, the South End is now one of the country's most expensive neighborhoods. The number of people who can afford to live there has vastly narrowed. It is now well beyond the reach of those who can take the risk of trading income for creativity. The South End may no longer be able to shelter artists, musicians, and nonconformists. Will the neighborhood be as good a place to live when only the wealthy can afford it?

Solutions are going to be difficult. Conventional economic theory postulates that housing prices are a function of supply and demand. The way to keep prices in equilibrium with incomes is to build more housing to meet the demand.[1] But the South End has severe constraints on its ability to increase its numbers of units. There is no political will to relax its landmarks restrictions; everyone from the low-income residents of Cathedral to the swells of Union Park are strongly committed to preserving the neighborhood. Demolishing row houses to build new higher-density housing would be a tragedy because the South End is a unique architectural gem. All would lose and future generations would rightly despise us for our destruction of their heritage.

Furthermore, destroying the South End's row houses and apartment buildings to make way for more housing would not necessarily produce low cost housing. The technical difficulties of building larger and higher buildings on small lots of unstable land would require expensive engineering solutions that would make the resulting housing unaffordable, even without the astronomical land acquisition costs. Even though building on the remaining land on the southern and western margins could produce additional housing, there is insufficient acreage to make a dent in the lack of housing supply in the neighborhood.

The high property values strike at one of the central traits that have made the South End special: it's a place that welcomes everyone. As it stands now, it may only be a neighborhood for the wealthy. Worse, many of these very affluent might only be part-time residents, spending weeks and months in their other houses around the world. Not only would these seasonal residents force out those who would live and work here, they would hardly contribute to the neighborhood by their presence only a few days a year. The neighborhood's population might fall, and all residents would suffer.

The South End's five thousand subsidized units are particularly at risk. Many projects were built with subsidies that end when the contracts that connect government funds to individual developments expire, usually after twenty to thirty years. At that point, owners may sell or try to find new subsidies, which will depend on government funding priorities and the politics at that particular moment. If the refinancing programs are not there, this important, vulnerable housing will be lost to the market. Even if funding and assistance were available, some project owners may choose to forgo new contracts to take advantage of high real estate values and sell for the profits. Such decisions would result in the loss of many of the neighborhood's low-income projects, which would create yet another wave of displacement.

Even if subsidies continue, developments will still need new investments to replace aging systems and finishes. Appliances get old, interiors need refurbishing, and roofs fail as rents rarely cover these long-term vital capital investments. The South End's stock of affordable housing could need hundreds of millions of dollars of improvements over the next two to three decades and it is not clear where this money will come from. Losing these units would represent the final breaking of the promises made to the poor of the neighborhood.

Another problem is flooding. The South End barely sits above sea level, a legacy of development decisions that date back to the 1850s. A resulting threat to the neighborhood is global climate change, which may be already causing a rise in sea levels that could once again submerge the South End beneath Boston Harbor, first during storms and periods of extra high tides, and potentially permanently.[2]

If sea levels rise only three to five feet, flooding might occur during high tides, storms, or pumping station failures. If sea levels rise ten feet, something that could very well happen over the next century, the South End would need a new drainage system and a barrier against water from the harbor. The higher the sea level, the more extensive and expensive these barriers will have to be. This infrastructure will have to be integrated with similar barriers around Back Bay, downtown, and other low-lying parts of the city and will take decades to build. Planning and funding these protections will be difficult. With no margin for error, failure would be catastrophic.

Despite future uncertainties, there is a gracefulness and vitality to the neighborhood today that might surprise past residents. Given how closely they worked together, Vida Scudder and Robert Woods must have walked together coming from or going to meetings or events in the neighborhood. What would they think if they strolled around the South End today? Perhaps they would be satisfied that their labors have contributed to the USES's continued dedication to service over one hundred years after the founding of the neighborhood's settlement houses. They would likely approve of the work of Healthcare for the Homeless, the Pine Street Inn, and the many other social service and health care providers in the neighborhood today. Woods might be saddened by the loss of churches to condominium development and appalled that the percentage of single-person households remains high, but Scudder might be happy with the South End's high percentage of same-sex couples and its acceptance of women living independently. Most likely she would be pleased with the role that women played in building Villa Victoria, challenging the South End Bypass, and creating community gardens. She would be proud of the women honored by Frieda Garcia Park and Harriet Tubman Square.

Woods would gasp when told that the building that once housed his offices on Union Park is now assessed at $2.87 million or that million-dollar townhouses line Rollins Square, the site where South End House first began. He might be equally surprised by the throng of people at First Fridays in SOWA or the new apartments rising in the New York Streets area, and he would appreciate the dismantling of the Elevated and approve of the decision to change the name of Dover Street to East Berkeley Street (though he might be puzzled by those wishing to have the name restored to Dover Street).

Both would be impressed by the large crowd of families at the Festival Betances and admire how quickly an audience in the community room at USES can turn on a speaker who dares put down the neighborhood. South Enders, particularly those who lived through the battles of the 1960s, 1970s, and 1980s, have preserved the neighborhood legacy they inherited. The challenge for future generations will be how to continue to protect the South End and keep it special, even if that means working themselves into a level of outrage that will sometimes alarm outsiders. Conflict and caring are as much a part of the neighborhood's heritage as its distinctive architecture. There is no doubt that, no matter what happens, those two elements will always be a part of the South End's DNA.

1. Glaeser E, Gyourko J. The impact of building restrictions on housing affordability. *Economic Policy Review* 2003:31-54

2. Douglas E, Kirshen P, Li V, Watson C, Wormser J. Preparing for the Rising Tide: *The Boston Harbor Association*; 2013.

Postscript

Though there has been economic upturns and downturns, a pandemic, and continuing climate change, the neighborhood is essentially the same as it was since it settled into its post renewal prosperity. It is, perhaps, just a bit older, if not wiser. That said, there are a few items to notte:

In 2024, the South End's housing stock consisted of approximately 5,000 income restricted rental units, a few hundred income restricted condo units, 5,800 owner occupied condominiums, and around 5,000 market rental units. Housing costs are higher than ever with most units selling for at least $1,000 a square foot with luxury developments commanding even higher prices. Rentals are similarly expensive. The number of new income restricted units has been small compared to the total number of new constructed units, 165 income restricted units out of 1300 new units constructed between 2017 and 2021. There have been 263 rental units converted to condominiums over this period.

Many in Boston's queer community believe that the South End is no longer gay, but the limited data we have contradicts this. The number of male-male couples in the neighborhood has increased to 905 in 2020. In contrast to 2010 and 2000 when the number was around 550. There are a number of potential explanations for this disconnect between perceptions and the data. It could be that overall, there are fewer gay men with the loss being among single gays rather than couples. Or it could be that the overall numbers are stable or increasing but that men in couple are less visible, or that this group is older and also not as easily seen. Another potential explanatory factor is that the gay male population has shifted from the core of the South End around Appleton Street to the census tracts on the southern edge of the neighborhood: couples, at least, are more likely to live in the new NYS developments, around Boston Medical Center and other tracts that border the Southeast Expressway. These locations might result in a less visible presence than if they had lived in the middle of the neighborhood. In any case, the South End still is the city's prime neighborhood for gay men.

The rebuilding of Tremont Street was bitterly opposed by some and enthusiastically welcomed by others. When it was reconstructed in the 1980s, it was one of the first streets to be purposely designed for pedestrians at a time when moving cars as rapidly and seamlessly as possible was the priority. But the two travel lanes in each direction proved hazardous and after several deaths of pedestrians trying to cross the street, the city decided to reduce the travel lanes to one in each direction. With already generous sidewalks, the extra space this created was dedicated to bike lanes. While certain segments of the South End, as elsewhere, oppose any and all bike lanes, most people in the community feel the street is much safer now than it was before. There have been no pedestrian deaths to date since they were finished.

Like anyone or anyplace over one hundred and fifty years old, the South End is a bit rickety in places. But the old neighborhood still has a lot of life left in her.

Acknowledgements

There were many people who made this book possible, including the many residents who lived or worked in the South End. Over the years, they educated me in ways not possible at Stanford, Harvard, and Boston University. When I was a young person just arriving in the South End, or later as an older, longtime resident, these people answered my often-naïve questions with kindness, wisdom, and patience. Thank you to Jeanette Boone, Pat Cusick, Jovita Fontanez, Frieda Garcia, Mauricio Gaston, Jorge Hernandez, Barbara Hoffman, Carmelo Iglesias, James Jennings, Betsy Johnson, Michael Kane, Mel and Joyce King, Jose Masso, Myra McAdoo, Nelson Merced, Byron Rushing, Miren Uriarte, Wendell Verrill, and many others.

The research for this book was only possible because of the wonderful research facilities and archives that house important South End papers and resources. I am most grateful for the archives and the dedicated staffs at Yale, the Loeb Library at the Graduate School of Design at Harvard, the Healey Library at the University of Massachusetts Boston, the Snell Library at Northeastern University, the Government Documents Desk at the Boston Public Library, and the Boston Athenaeum. The people and resources at the South End Library, the South End Historical Society, and The History Project were extremely useful, and the many online and digitized materials helped make this book possible must also be mentioned.

There were many individuals at these institutions that warrant mention as well. The South End Library's curators were instrumental in helping me put the pieces together. Thank you to Ann Hershfang, Alison Barnet, Matthew Krug, Judy Watkins, Stacen Goldman and the other people who have contributed to the history collection at the South End Library. Alison was also inspirational and a great colleague through her own writings, and Stacen Goldman, the Executive Director of South End Historical Society, did double duty in finding and making items available.

Special thanks are due to Nancy Pullen for her great photographs and the Library of Congress and the Boston Redevelopment Authority for providing illustrations.

Many friends and family members helped me write this book through emotional support as well as research assistance. Some just expressed a kind interest in my work during times that the project seemed overwhelming.

Therefore, I want to thank and acknowledge Barbara Berg, Brian Gokey, Steve Lopez, Steven Mudgett, and of course, Andrew Sherman.

Index

Grant Manor 175, 176, 222-3
Gray Street 23
Greater Boston Community Builders 161, 207
Greater Boston Food Bank 228
Greeks x, 29
Gregory, Samuel 31-2
Greenwich Park 154-5, 171, 203
Gross, Ida 81
Groton Street 15

H

Hacin, David 217
Hale, Edward Everett 19, 33, 45, 63, 67
Hale House 45, 48, 50, 132
Hammersley, Gordon 235
Hancock, John Company 157, 238
Harrison Avenue 11, 13, 43, 52, 54, 55, 56, 72, 73, 77, 93, 120, 143, 205, 217, 224, 239-41
Harry the Greek's 197
Hass, Gerald 180
Hassam, Childe 238
Harvard University viii, 9, 33, 49, 51, 53, 81, 87, 89, 90, 95, 132, 161, 170, 213, 237
Hayes, Chris 194
Hayes Park 195
Health Care for All 224
Healthcare for the Homeless 209-10
Healy, Alexander Sherwood 76-7
Helms, Edgar 70-1
Hernandez, Jorge 238
Hernandez Cultural Center 665, 238
Hershfang, Ann 187, 190
Hershfang, Herbert 190
Hicks, Louise Day 115, 177-8, 192
Highways vi, 13, 107, 119, 121, 122, 124, 129, 186-8, 189, 202, 228, 229, 254
HIV/AIDS 203-4
Hollis Street Church 63, 91
Holy Cross College 76
Holy Trinity Church 73-4, 135

Holyoke Street 24-5, 78, 88, 151
Home for Little Wanderers 52, 195
Hoover, Jim 197
Hope House 244
Hospitals and health care 9, 27, 30-3, 54, 59, 66, 79, 91, 102, 137, 144, 151, 180, 188, 202, 210, 220, 223-4, 239
Housing vii, xi, xii, 9, 12, 19, 34, 41, 44, 46, 56, 57, 63-4, 73, 81, 86, 87, 98, 99, 101, 108-110, 111, 112-3, 114, 115-120, 122-4, 128, 130, 135-43, 144, 149-55, 167-8, 160-3, 167, 170-9, 181-3, 185, 192, 196-7, 202-3, 205-9, 211, 217-9, 221-3, 230, 232-5, 234, 239, 242, 243, 244-5, 251-2, 254
Housing and Urban Development, U.S. Department of (HUD) 143, 146, 149, 152-3, 158, 163, 174-6, 181-3, 183, 185, 221-3
Howe, General William 6-7
Huntington Avenue 33, 187
Huntington Theatre Company 242
Hynes, John 102, 116, 128, 157

I

Iglesias, Carmelo 160, 166
Inquilinos Boricuas en Accion (IBA) 161
Interfaith – West Concord Development 176
Irish x, 13, 19-20, 40, 50-4, 72, 76, 86, 87, 101-2, 103, 128, 192, 237, 250
Israel, Temple 80
Italians x, 41, 71, 73, 76, 86

J

Jamaica Plain 68, 172, 186, 210, 213
James Street 7
Jazz 113-4, 140, 245, 251
Jennings, James 198
Jews x, 41, 50, 64, 67, 71, 78-80, 86, 102, 162
Johnston, Betsy 211

Z

9 798991 370424